MARGINAL GAINS

The Lewis Henry Morgan Lectures / 1997
Presented at The University of Rochester
Rochester, New York

JANE I. GUYER

MARGINAL GAINS

MONETARY TRANSACTIONS

IN ATLANTIC AFRICA

WITH A FOREWORD BY ANTHONY T. CARTER

THE UNIVERSITY OF CHICAGO PRESS

CHICAGO AND LONDON

Jane I. Guyer is professor of anthropology at Johns Hopkins University. She is the author, most recently, of *An African Niche Economy: Farming to Feed Ibadan* and editor of *Money Matters: Instability, Values, and Social Payments in the Modern History of West African Communities.*

The University of Chicago Press, Chicago 60637
The University of Chicago Press, Ltd., London
© 2004 by The University of Chicago
All rights reserved. Published 2004
Printed in the United States of America
13 12 11 10 09 08 07 06 05 04   5 4 3 2 1

ISBN (cloth): 0-226-31115-5
ISBN (paper): 0-226-31116-3

Library of Congress Cataloging-in-Publication Data

Guyer, Jane I.
    Marginal gains : monetary transactions in Atlantic Africa / Jane I. Guyer ; foreword by Anthony T. Carter.
        p.   cm. — (Lewis Henry Morgan lectures ; 1997)
    Includes bibliographical references and index.
    ISBN 0-226-31115-5 (cloth : alk. paper) — ISBN 0-226-31116-3 (pbk : alk. paper)
    1. Money — Africa, West — History.   2. Africa, West — Economic conditions.   3. Africa, West — Social conditions.   4. Economic anthropology — Africa, West.   I. Title.   II. Series.
HG1370 .G89   2004
332.4'967 — dc22

2003014267

To all my colleagues at the
Program of African Studies
Northwestern University
1994–2001

CONTENTS

FOREWORD

Jane Guyer delivered the Lewis Henry Morgan Lectures on which this book is based at the University of Rochester in March 1997. They were the thirty-fifth in a series offered annually to the public and to students and faculty at the University of Rochester by the Department of Anthropology. Lila Abu-Lughod delivered the thirty-ninth lectures in October 2001. Deborah Gewertz and Frederick Errington presented the fortieth last fall. Elinore Ochs will give the forty-first Morgan Lectures in November 2003.

The lectures honor Lewis Henry Morgan. In addition to playing a signal role in the creation of modern anthropology, Morgan was a prominent Rochester attorney. He never found it necessary to accept a formal academic position, but he was a benefactor of the University of Rochester from its beginning. At the end of his life, he left the University money for a women's college as well as his manuscripts and library.

In recent years the Department of Anthropology has sought out Morgan Lecturers whose work is of interest to a broad range of disciplines in the social sciences and the humanities. We remain firmly situated in anthropology and continue to provide a forum for rich ethnographic description, but we also want to explore the shape of conversations across disciplinary boundaries and the ways in which anthropology may contribute to such conversations.

Marginal Gains is an original and stimulating exercise in economic anthropology, as Richard Wilk puts it, "the part of anthropology that engages in dialogue with the discipline of economics." Drawing on such diverse resources as theories of indexicality in linguistic anthropology, the social construction of value, the practices involved in calculation and commensuration, rank in Melanesia, and performance, Guyer revisits and revivifies the 1970s debates between formalists and substantivists. And, critically, she places debates about economic men and women firmly in the context of contemporary concerns about globalization.

A distinguishing feature of Guyer's work has been her persistent concern with the individual lives behind the numbers produced in quantitative studies. Here she explores the economic lives of Atlantic Africans at the end of the twentieth century. Pulling together her own extensive field research on household budgets, indigenous currencies, taxation, the social organization of market competition in urban food supply, African concepts of wealth-in-people, the recent creation of a system of community banks, and popular money management and financial culture in Cameroon and/or Nigeria plus the considerable historical literature on the region, she asks how Africans make their livings and create wealth in a turbulent global economy.

In *Marginal Gains,* Guyer brings together neoclassical theory in economics and anthropological theories of money, commodities and gifts in the context of Atlantic Africa, the interconnected economies "between the Muslim monetary regimes and bazaar/trading economy of the Sahel and North Africa and the merchant capitalism of the coast." Atlantic Africa has long been open to but on the margins of the global capitalist economy, a position in which it has experienced very considerable economic turbulence. It also is the subject of a rich body of historical and ethnographic studies, to which Guyer has made important contributions. Here she puts the region, its experience, and its literature to work as a powerful catalytic chamber for producing new, empirically based theoretical insights concerning economic transactions and rationality.

Neoclassical economists and economic anthropologists working in the formalist tradition have attempted to make sense of the economies of Atlantic Africa in terms of concepts that were developed in the Euro-American core of the capitalist regime and which rest on the qualitative invariance of money. Economic anthropologists working in the substantive tradition have seen material of this sort as reflecting enduring, culturally specific institutions. Both approaches have left growing and increasingly intolerable areas of residual obscurity.

Guyer argues that economic transactions in Atlantic Africa are best understood neither in terms of the Western logic of capitalism nor as an expression of "local cultural principles" operating in isolation. Rather, they are hybrid institutions that have taken shape at the interface. Economic actors in Atlantic Africa have long sought to produce, perpetuate and profit from a ramifying network of asymmetrical exchanges. "[D]ifference [is] a resource to be cultivated." Diverse and disjunctive currencies and other registers of value, are used to create margins or frontiers across which asymmetries can be enacted and premiums for access charged. The marginal gains from such transactions are in turn invested in more enduring stores of value such as the ranked offices or titles of Ibo secret societies.

The outline of the notion of asymmetrical exchanges comes into view in chapter 2. The argument begins with a discussion of Bohannan's classic paper on Tiv spheres of exchange. Rather than seeing conversions — transactions in which valuables of a lower category are exchanged for or invested in valuables of a higher category — as insulating the Tiv from the corrosive effects of modern monies, Guyer suggests that they are just one instance of a wider class of transactions that index or invoke some sort of difference or frontier across which a marginal gain can be obtained. Chapters 3–5 are concerned with the scales of measurement or value across which Atlantic African economic actors construct potentially profitable difference and the "tropic points" or indexical elements that link one to another. Chapters 6–8 are concerned with the genres of performance that may deployed to bring off asymmetrical transactions. Together, these are what Jean Lave would call the structuring resources of Atlantic African economic rationality. The performance genres are among the informal institutions that give some sense of stability in the stormy seas of the Atlantic African economy.

Marginal Gains is much more than a study of a particular ethnographic region. As Guyer suggests, Atlantic Africa is not the only marginal region of the expanding global monetary economy. Other regions of the world may share some of its dilemmas and are likely to have developed analogous modes of creating marginal wealth. Moreover, the general processes of creating and institutionalizing scales of value and genres of transactions are not unique to the margins of the global economy. The peculiar scales and institutions of the core economies of capitalist theory also are socially and culturally constructed and reconstructed. *Marginal Gains* thus underlines Joseph Stiglitz's recent condemnation, in *Globalization and Its Discontents,* of the International Monetary Fund's "one-size-fits-all approach" to developing economies. Keeping in mind that Nigerian government officials may appear to ordinary Nigerians very much as officials of the IMF and the World Bank appear to the leaders of, for example, Botswana, *Marginal Gains* also sharpens Stiglitz's call for local knowledge and local experts in the design of national economic policies.

Anthony T. Carter, Editor
The Lewis Henry Morgan Lectures

PREFACE

The invitation to deliver the Lewis Henry Morgan Lectures of 1997 was both an honor and a challenge. It was a particular honor because I am a graduate of the Department of Anthropology at the University of Rochester (1972), where I began the work on West African economic and social life that has occupied me ever since. It was a challenge because at the time I was director of the Program of African Studies at Northwestern University and therefore deeply engaged in region-based, rather than discipline-based, debates. The invitation to deliver the Morgan lectures returned me to the discipline, to thinking more broadly about the social scientific challenge posed by modern Africa.

It had been some time since those of us working in Africa had contributed directly to an anthropology of transactions that had been propelled forward by new ethnographic work in Melanesia and new theorizing about commoditization. Having applied some of the Melanesian work to a problem in the study of indigenous currency in Equatorial Africa, I had been invited to contribute a comparative chapter on African currencies to a book by Melanesianists (Akin and Robbins 1999). Their debates about transactions were — on the whole — ethnographically and philosophically richer, more mutually referential, and more clearly indexed to a lineage of classics than were our own in African studies. I found this very stimulating. They did not, however, seem as profoundly answerable to historical and regional scholarship as African studies had become over recent years. There have been important reasons for honing the regional and interdisciplinary work in Africa. Local economies of Atlantic Africa have never fit standard definitions very well: a gift or commodity economy, the tributary mode of production, and so on. The more one plunged into the fine historical work by both African and European scholars, the less comfortable one felt focusing on specific transactions, lifting them out of their historical context to make particular analytical or comparative points. Historical accuracy and sensibility have become fundamental because Africa's place in the global expansion of capitalism is now so thoroughly inserted into the intellectual agenda that neither a knowledge of the voluminous findings nor the suspicion that they are still provisional can be suspended for narrower theoretical purposes. As a result, only very particular parts of the recent African scholarship, including my own, have addressed the general anthropological debate about transactions. And vice versa. Bohannan's spheres-of-exchange model is still the basic text on indigenous African economies.

How, then, to contribute both within and beyond African scholarship? How to address the other disciplinary literatures and enlarge the ethnographic space within Africa, while at the same time making general analytical points? Facing this problem of framing and exposition has taken up the years since I delivered the lectures. By introducing "marginal gains" as a transaction resulting from Africa's long experience with capitalism, I gave a specific focus to the analysis and to the conceptual issues raised in the introduction. All the lectures address one aspect or another of a cultural configuration that emerges from the richness of the different disciplinary traditions within African studies. I learned enough from the stimulating responses in Rochester — from the current faculty, organizer Anthony Carter, Robert Foster, commentators Ali Khan and Paul Stoller, former teachers Stanley Engerman, Grace Harris, and Al Harris — to know that the topic needed a lot more work before the lectures would be publishable. Over several years, the topic seemed to demand constant rethinking, both to push further the implications of the ideas in chapter 2 and also to respond to highly relevant literature published since the lectures were conceptualized in late 1996. In the end, to respond to colleagues' suggestions and to allow the originality of the empirical evidence to speak more loudly in its own voice — as E. P. Thompson (1978) wrote of the ideals of the kind of British empiricism in which I was trained and to which I keep returning — I found I needed to double the number of topics from four to eight. The original lectures are now chapters 2, 7, 8, and 9. Only chapter 2 has remained virtually unchanged. Chapter 9 was cut out altogether and then reinstated. Chapter 8 was totally rewritten. As I worked from one to the other, and from one set of commentaries to another, I decided that the original lecture format fit the material well. The complementarity of the themes is best sustained by the juxtaposition, in sequence, of relatively short and straightforward chapters, without the multitude of allusions, digressions, and footnotes that all these subjects would ideally deserve as full-length journal articles.

Each chapter comes from a different part of my research, mainly from the past fifteen years, but reaching back in places very much farther. Not only did different people help me with that research at the time, but — since my learning has taken zigzag paths — their contributions are all still relevant to the present chapters, and indeed their voices have come back to me as I worked. Given the impossibility of mentioning whole battalions of colleagues and friends, I mention only those most closely contributing to the writing of the chapters themselves.

The work as a whole owes a great debt to colleagues working on one or other of the same issues with whom I have sustained conversations over many years. In particular are all the co-editors and contributors to the three edited and co-edited volumes (Guyer 1995; Stiansen and Guyer 1999; Guyer, Denzer, and Agbaje 2002), the several conference panels, and the special journal issue (*Journal of African History,* vol. 36, 1995) on various aspects of money on which we have worked together over the past ten years. Most of these people's papers have found their way into the text, but the collective inspiration was even greater than its individual parts.

Chapter 1 was discussed in detail with Caroline Bledsoe and Christopher Davis, who insisted on a clearer and bolder statement than I achieved in early drafts. Versions were also presented at the Universities of Michigan and Pennsylvania. Chapter 2 owes a great deal to conversations with colleagues in Equatorial studies: Peter Geschiere, Achille Mbembe, Marie-Claude and Georges Dupré, and many others. Permission to work in the Royal Museum of Equatorial Africa in Tervuren (Belgium) is gratefully acknowledged. The staff were gracious, and the collection was an inspiration. This chapter has been presented at Oxford University and Johns Hopkins University, as well as being the first Morgan Lecture. Chapter 3 owes everything to the enthusiastic participation — verging on co-authorship — of Karin Barber, to the work of Helen Verran, and the ethnography of Mimi Wan. Chapter 4 results from a project carried out in archives in Britain, for which I thank Rhodes House Library, Oxford University, the departmental archive of the Department of Social Anthropology, University of Cambridge, and the Public Records Office. Mariane Ferme and Ursula Jones (widow of G. I. Jones) were particularly helpful in Cambridge. Chapter 5 is based on a field research study for which I had the fine assistance of Olatunji Ojo and advice of LaRay Denzer. This chapter has been presented at University College London. Chapter 6 was first presented as the Distinguished Lecture for the Association of Africanist Anthropology of the American Anthropological Association. I thank all my local colleagues in Western Nigeria for their help with this one, and with the next, chapter 7: William Brieger, Sikiru Ogunjimi, Azeez Adesope. Adigun Agbaje has always proved an encouraging critic on all modern Nigerian issues. Chapter 8 carries many debts: first of all to the Ghana Statistical Service for permission to use the database of the Ghana Living Standards Survey of 1991–92. I am particularly grateful for their willingness to envisage an anthropological approach rather than a statistical one. Then, I owe debts to Markus Goldstein, who mediated this agreement; Chris Udry, for help with data and recommendations for reading at several stages; Shobha Shagle, who did most of the analyses with enormous patience and dedication as I searched for an interpretation; and Caroline Bledsoe, for proposing the idea in the first place, sticking with it through all the logistical problems, and remaining an inspired critic. An expanded version of the section on the domestic cycle was presented in a panel titled "Temporalities of Rationality" organized by Hiro Myazaki at the 2001 American Anthropological Association annual meeting. Chapter 9 would not have been possible without my relationship with the National Association of Community Banks in Nigeria, under the chairmanship of Akin Mabogunje, who has been the most generous and inspiring of mentors over many years of Nigeria research. The students in my first graduate class at Johns Hopkins University have expanded my views of formalization, as have my colleagues on a consultancy for the World Bank. For the conclusion, I owe much, without him knowing, to Souleymane Bachir Diagne, who has given me new hope in the possibilities for rigorous thinking in a postmodern context. From discussions with him and several Francophone friends, I also know that I have not profited sufficiently from the literature in French.

Keith Hart and Gracia Clark read the manuscript with such generous enthusiasm that it gave me the temerity to go further, even when on thin ice. At intermittent moments over five years, Ali Khan has pushed in the same direction: to run as far as possible with the initial idea and then leave the uses and critiques to others. This is what I feel myself to be doing—much later than he advised but, I think, at a higher plateau. Because so few colleagues have taken in the whole scope of the project, those mentioned who have helped so much will doubtless turn into critics—but I hope also users—when they see that some of their own suggestions have still not found their way into the text. This, however, gives me the grounds for absolving them while still appreciating every idea they put forward and reservation they expressed.

Many, many other people have contributed. There are very long-term colleagues without whom nothing could have been done: Karin Barber, Sara Berry, Caroline Bledsoe, Fred Cooper, Christopher Davis, LaRay Denzer, Peter Geschiere, Béatrice Hibou, Eileen Julien, Achille Mbembe, Bill Murphy, John Peel, Pauline Peters, Michael Watts, and many others. The staff of the Melville J. Herskovits Library at Northwestern University worked miracles at finding material. Associate director of the Program of African Studies, Akbar Virmani, ran the program when I was absent for research. Bernard Guyer maintains priceless support for all my efforts.

Field research and archival research over the years have been generously supported by the National Institutes of Mental Health, the National Science Foundation: Cultural Anthropology Section (BNS-6704188), and the Social Science Research Council. I still owe a debt of gratitude to my dissertation adviser at the University of Rochester, the late Robert Merrill, under whose guidance my first fieldwork in Western Nigeria — still represented here — was undertaken.

The best way of acknowledging these vast and varied intellectual and personal debts is to dedicate this book to everyone who worked at, or passed through the door of, the Program of African Studies at Northwestern University while I was director, 1994–2001. I also include here those members of the university administration and the staff of the Ford and John D. and Catherine T. MacArthur Foundations, who made it possible to develop such a stimulating community of scholars. Their concerns have found their way into this book.

PART I

INTRODUCTORY

INTRODUCTION
DIVERSITY, BEWILDERMENT, AND THE
MULTIPLICITY OF AFRICAN MONEY

Since the advent of civilization, the outgrowth of property has been so immense, its
forms so diversified, its uses so expanding and its management so intelligent in the interests of its owners, that it has become, on the part of the people, an unmanageable power.
The human mind stands bewildered in the presence of its own creation.
Lewis Henry Morgan, *Ancient Society*, 1877

DIVERSITY

Our current world is as confusing, over 120 years later, as it was to L. H.
Morgan. The two ends of the spectrum of the current world "market economy"—the "center" of the financial world and its "margins"—could seem
to the historian almost as different from each other today as they were in
Morgan's day, albeit with different critical features. Western currency is
now "hard currency" and "fast money"; it is infinitely convertible, and it
circulates at a rate whereby the equivalent of the entire U.S. money issue
passes through financial monitoring and transaction every day (Passell
1992). Consider the following, by comparison. The Nigerian naira is a
"soft currency," usable to purchase hard currencies only on a limited auction
basis. And within the country, in January 1997, *Newswatch* of Nigeria announced the almost complete monetization of Nigerian business transactions: no checks, no credit cards, no automated accounts, just what they
termed a "cash and carry" culture (Achema 1997) in which—to give their
lead example—a bank transfer of two million naira ($25,000) was medi-
ated in cash, involving the parties carrying it in person and the tellers spending two days counting the bills, because the highest currency denomination
of N50 was then worth about sixty cents. In Nigeria there are thousands of
such transactions, all the time. And this in a commercial economy: one for
which projections suggest that 95 percent of the population will earn their
money incomes in the informal sector by the year 2020 (Bangura 1994)
and that at least 60 percent of the currency, once issued, *never goes back
through the banking system again.* These two economies—that in which the
formal financial institutions monitor the entire money issue every day, and

that in which 60 percent of it is never monitored again in its entire life in circulation — coexist, interrelate, and reconstitute one another. These are two extremes, but other places fall on a continuum between them.

Such variations within the world monetary economy have existed from the beginning of European economic expansion, guided under the same rubrics as simultaneously built national economies and which we now refer to as mercantilism. The coexistence of different institutions of money management and the selective linking and de-linking of currencies from full convertibility are as old as world trade, and were cultivated in specific ways under the mercantilist framework. Indeed, the very idea of comparative advantage rests on the assumption of difference among trading partners: different goods, different values placed on them, and different mediating means of exchange, particularly when Europe was conserving its own currencies within national circuits. What this means for an anthropology of transactions is that there is no essential or archetypical commodity transaction, even though it is useful to construct a fictional ideal type for certain analytical purposes and then debate its characteristics (see Gregory 1982; Gell 1992). Commodity exchange, by sale and purchase, takes on historically and geographically specific characteristics in accordance with experience. Within the West, the rapid circulation of money through the state and banking systems, and the omnipresence of orthodox economic persuasion, means that people's repeated market experience is closely and constantly disciplined. We are brought into line with the institutional structures literally all the time. Elsewhere, as in the Nigerian situation in 1997, the formal disciplines of banking and the state are more intermittent, more patchy, and altogether less ideologically coherent. People's exchanges are no less market oriented or money mediated, because commerce is ubiquitous. They are simply disciplined through popular conventions rather than formal regulation, constructed through market experience rather than articulated models.

It is to the monetary disciplines of Atlantic Africa — between the Muslim monetary regimes and bazaar/trading economy of the Sahel and North Africa and the merchant capitalism of the coast — that I turn in these chapters. Atlantic Africa has been within the West's money economy for at least five centuries, deeply shaped by its demands and its indifferences, by force and neglect, by domination in some domains and refusal to engage in others, by open flows of currency and closed doors to convertibility. Neither autonomous nor subjugated, African economies have been "extroverted" or "open economies" (Cooper 2001; Bayart 1999; Seers 1963; Hopkins 1973), subject to extraction of primary resources, "unequal exchange" (Amin 1976), and rapid changes in conditions over which their populations have had very little control. Yet at the same time, commerce grew and

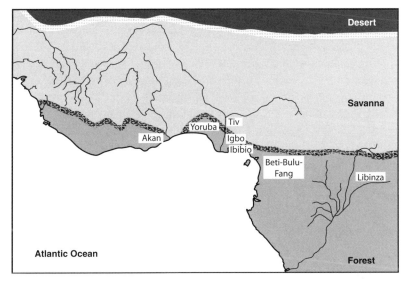

Figure 1.1. Map of Atlantic Africa, showing groups mentioned in the text.

extended its geographical range, on the basis of indigenous transactional conventions, from the beginning of the Atlantic trade onward. New foreign crops were integrated into cultivation cycles and divisions of labor (Guyer 1988; Vansina 1990); metallurgy was refined and expanded (Kriger 1999); marketed products became more diversified (Zeleza 1996); trade diasporas developed, such as that of the Arochukwu in Eastern Nigeria for the slave trade (Dike and Ekejiuba 1990) and that of the Senegalese all along the coast for fishing; and forms of credit developed (Austin 1993). Wider and wider regions were drawn into trade networks, such as the complex interchanges along the Ubangi–Giri–Congo River confluence that I describe in chapter 2. Hogendorn and Johnson suggest that demand for currency goods on a "market for cowries [that] was about as close to world wide as for any other commodity of the sixteenth to eighteenth century and was still extensive in the nineteenth" (1986, 143) was a crucial driver of the steady expansion of the slave trade within Africa (111).

With respect to its money economy, Atlantic Africa has been, in Piot's phrase, "remotely global" (1999) for a very long time. At the same time, internal change has been persistently distinct. It cannot be understood as directly derivative of the interface with Europe, but neither is it understandable in abstraction from the experiences that interface generated. Several recent ethnographers of particular peoples have been making major headway in representing this process, for which Marx's claim remains the most succinct: that people make their own history, albeit not under conditions of their own choosing (Shaw 2002; Ferme 2001; Piot 1999; Geschiere

1997; Barber 2000; Ekeh 1990; Berry 2001). By historicization, these scholars have made real gains in understanding what were once thought to be somehow sui generis components of West African culture: secrecy, witchcraft, kinship, chieftaincy. Some of the most rhetorically powerful recent works have shown how production of items once thought to be iconic of quintessential Africa expanded and changed, perhaps even being invented, in the context of trade. These include fetishes, as a means of securing trust (Pietz 1985, 1987, 1988), religions of "affliction" (Janzen 1982), and art works as commodities for sale (Schildkrout and Keim 1990).

Paradoxically, however, even though the most obvious motive for European presence was economic, less theoretical attention has been devoted by anthropologists to conceptualizing the specifically economic dynamics of this interface. There is an enormous economic history literature, many local studies, and theorization of particular sociopolitical dynamics of resource control, but much less theorization of the growth of economic culture and practice among the population. And yet economic practice was clearly not an ad hoc response to circumstance, nor a direct reflection of the interests of elites, nor a simple extrapolation from existing cultural principles. In some domains of life, the conventions and institutions that were developed in a remotely global context are still deeply plausible enough to have "worked" to organize market economies up until the present, even under conditions of confusion such as the Abacha years in Nigeria. Rapidly expanding urban populations have been fed; consumer imports expanded; apprentices trained; new forms of foreign currency exchange and international contract developed (see Guyer, Denzer, and Agbaje 2002). And all this has been achieved despite enormous obstacles. The form of the money has changed several times (Ekejiuba 1995), European wars and depressions have eliminated markets and reduced the amount of currency in circulation, and, most recently, government and international policies have produced petrol shortages, electricity blackouts, infrastructural degradation, and currency devaluation. In these improbable achievements, generations of scholars have seen flexibility, negotiability, resilience, innovation, and entrepreneurship (Hill 1970; Berry 1989) alongside the dangers of extraction and marginality in the global economy (Castells 1996; Arrighi 2002).

The analytical problem for the study of transactions within Africa is profound because key dynamics originate at the interface. Local constructs emanate from experience and not from modular principles, either as these might be conceptualized in the Western model of a formal sector or as they might derive directly from local cultural principles. If the persistent historical conjuncture must take a key role in explanation, then social theory based on systems—"the market" or the autonomous local society—becomes only of partial use in establishing the persistent elements and relationships by which people individually and collectively create economies. The terms of analysis both for commodities under present-day capitalism, thought of as a system, and for transaction types (modalities) in noncapitalist systems, will be inadequate. How inadequate? This is a practical intellectual question, because the conceptual tools and the accumulated knowledge based on systemic assumptions are so important a resource. A great deal of progress has been made by applying neoclassical economic history, neo-Marxist political economy, and anthropological relativism to the West African experience. The sense remains, however, that only a certain modicum of the reality has been satisfactorily explored with conventional systemic approaches. Contradictions and indeterminacies in the literature abound (for which I give examples later). In the social sciences, some residual noncomprehension is to be expected, debated, and usually tolerated. Tolerance of noncomprehension works on a threshold principle: so far, but no farther. By the 1990s, the state of scholarship and the state of the world showed that the popular economies of West Africa had passed that threshold. General and specialist media alike started using apocalyptic terms: "the hopeless continent" (cover of *The Economist,* Dec. 9–16, 2000); "the systematic logic of the new global economy does not have much of a role for the majority of the African population" (Castells 1996, 135). Analytical assumptions based on foundational invariance, and proceeding by holding variables constant (ceteris paribus), became increasingly implausible. Policy documents came across as casuistry, where only the information that seemed useful for the purposes at hand was, in fact, used (see Castells 1996, 148–50; Hibou 2000). Worse, the methods began to get in the way of understanding. The area of obscurity shadowed the areas apparently illuminated by standard approaches. Let me quote some African scholars on the question.

Economist 'Dotun Phillips (1992) writes of the "nominalization" of the Nigerian economy under pervasive monetization and contradictory official regulation, that is, its retreat from the measurable, the real, and the long term into the named, the performative, and a "tips of the noses" calculative rubric (1992, 4). Historian Achille Mbembe writes of the long lag-time between the instant technologies of global finance and the "structural inertia of African economies" (1996, 2) that encourages speculative advantage, predation, distrust, and ultimately violence. Political scientist Claude Ake points to the "disarticulation" (1981, 43) within colonial and postcolonial economies, where the parts or elements relate to one another incoherently, so that a process begun in one context cannot be picked up in another. Bangura points out the incompatibility between the actual "fragmentation and informality" (1994, 812) of the economy and the hopeful expectation of the emergence of coherent impersonal norms and values on the part of the formal-sector experts charged with managing and directing it. There are other skeptics. They all point out metaphorical, temporal, and geographical disjunctures that are quite at odds with the literature on the free flow and continuous scales of measurement that apply in economic analysis. And the air of gravitas in their commentaries is palpable—gravitas about the situation and about our capacity to make sense of it. Reminiscent of Morgan's "last words" in *Ancient Society* are those of 'Dotun Phillips, making point number 14 of his urgent recommendations to the Chartered Institute of Bankers of Nigeria, "God should be brought into the matter!"[1] Analytical dead ends recapitulate confusions on the ground.

Yet people themselves are employing concepts, practices, and expectations that incontrovertibly "work" in some sense. People appear to be somewhat accustomed to turbulence and policy confusion. Rising levels of what a systems scholar would see as disorder may be familiar, may have landmarks and navigational pathways, to those with long familiarity with this kind of condition. We know from the older ethnography that there are powerful principles of "normalization" to market disorder: in recourse to divination for important decisions, in the view of the market as intrinsically unstable, in the coexistence of contradictory proverbs about money morality (see, e.g., Adebayo 1999). The "overflow" or "residuals," after standard analytical frameworks have been applied, may have a shape of their own, not captured by those frameworks. It is worthwhile at this point to look more closely at some characteristic intellectual limits we have run up against in the past: to illustrate both the strengths and the weaknesses of classic approaches, and in the process to introduce African economic history to readers outside of African studies. Although this history is unique as a whole, many of its conditions have counterparts elsewhere, which should make both the specificity of Africa and the broad intellectual issues accessible and relevant beyond the region.

Chief among these conditions is that key commercial relationships were not, in fact, forged under a generalized "capitalist" influence that can be adequately captured by current general theory. Even at the center, there has been debate about whether mercantilism, or merchant capitalism, can be considered a system of propositions and practices with its own logics (Minchinton 1969) as distinct from a concatenation of policies all geared toward the expediencies of economic nationalism. World systems theory is still persuasive (e.g., Arrighi 2002). But it operates at a very high level of abstraction from the experience of the intermittent turbulence and incoherence its theories predict. Something is created out of that experience,

---

1. After an entirely secular analysis, Morgan closed *Ancient Society* with the idea that social evolution is part of "the plan of the Supreme Intelligence" (1877, 468).

but what? Some of the current "bewilderments" I indicate in the following section stem from the difficulty of grappling with the conceptual contradiction of applying existing systems theories from the center in places that the center has always treated as external to itself and where it has often been the source of disorder.[2] Many of the following incoherent conclusions derive from theoretical application, rather than theoretical innovation, in the analysis of capitalism and indigenous Africa.

BEWILDERMENTS

Capitalism, but What Kind of Productive Investment?

Paul Bohannan's (1955) classic anthropological model of moral spheres of exchange, with monetary transactions kept firmly in their limited place, was early and convincingly critiqued by historians on factual grounds. History shows that people have responded to novelty with more alacrity, struggled for control more fiercely, and attempted varied investment portfolios more imaginatively than Bohannan's original model could possibly encompass, moving regional scholarship back to a market model of price responsiveness (Hopkins 1973). Witness the conclusion of the earliest critique of spheres of exchange in its homeland of Eastern Nigeria, which claims instead "the development of capitalistic commercial methods." Nothing less. Yet, by the author's own assessment, the development of capitalism itself was thwarted by the lack of "suitable opportunities" for investment (Latham 1971, 605). Accumulators invested in slaves, plantations, and luxury but not long-term productive enterprises earning long-term returns. Here the institutional nexus of the commercial interface is critically important. The currency earned by Latham's entrepreneurs in international markets was not convertible and therefore could not be invested in capitalist production or financial markets. So they were capitalist in commercial method but not in the uses of money capital: not different but not the same either. Without a way of disaggregating capitalism—into types or specific institutions— there is a conceptual stalemate here. What, then, should be the terms for understanding the investments that African people have, in fact, made with the money earned in the market?

Investment in People, but What Kind of Accumulation?

There have been subsequent attempts at characterizing the investment side of this conundrum through an emphasis on accumulation of rights in

2. Insofar as economics is a policy science, however, its analytics are aimed at engineering the future, in particular terms and in defined domains, rather than reflecting current practices.

property rather than money capital. Without classes and the state, however, there was no persuasive analytical approach to property regimes. The neo-Marxist response was to keep a substantivist anthropology in the picture to explain local and regional resource control, which was largely framed by an ideology of kinship (see Meillassoux 1978). The next generation of multi-disciplinary scholarship, then, explored "investment in social relations" (Berry 1989) and "wealth-in-people" as a classic African dynamic of investment (Guyer 1995). People put their material resources into demographic and political accumulation and control. While making a great deal of sense in general terms, this left a lot unaccounted for, including the massive fact of the *sale* of people in the era of the Atlantic slave trade, rather than their accumulation. In lived practice, investment "portfolios" with a wealth-in-people model must have been shifting and indeterminate: different types of people, different combinations of people and things. And, in a final complexity, in Equatorial Africa certain things and certain people could be thought of in identical terms (MacGaffey 2000) or maintained in totally separate categories, not only inconvertible but actively hostile (M.-C. Dupré 1995). So the concepts of wealth-in-people and investment in social relations usefully indicate that there have been local architectures to transactional orders, but they do not go far enough to define the on-going implications of one or another form of wealth for distributional dynamics, such as the velocity of circulation of currency and the voraciousness of demand for goods and people of the various kinds available.

Prices, but What Kind of Market Penetration?

Hopkins (1973), Eltis and Jennings (1988), and Law (1992) have picked up the economics argument for price responsiveness in African economies in important ways. It seems incontrovertible now that price is relevant in the analysis of African economies, an assumption that was in doubt before the expansion of African history after 1960. And yet, explanations have limits. Eltis and Jennings suggest three dynamics that are difficult to square either with one another or with other interpretations, without much more historical sociology and cultural analysis. They write, "For most of the 1680–1870 period, Africans were able to buy an increasing amount of imported goods for a given quantity of exports." Yet "European products could not penetrate the African market until the second half of the nineteenth century," in part because elites took most of the imports and in part because "Africans were remarkably self-sufficient" (1988, 942, 957, 955). In what sense then, did price responsiveness work? Hogendorn and Johnson, in contrast, argue that "growth in the scale of monetary transactions was taking place in West Africa during the era of the slave trade," (1986, 146), as shown by the low levels of inflation in cowries, even when very large amounts were being imported. This is quite confusing, unless West Africa's elites were far more efficient at burying money, in the ground or in useless goods, than historical evidence can support. So although the *fact* of price-relevance is no longer contested, its explanatory scope appears to be impossible to state in general terms.

Magic and Realism: Together?

Alongside the economic historian's vision of some kind of calculated price responsiveness, and some version of wealth-in-people as an investment goal, there is a growing literature on money as a different mediator altogether, as a magical good. Money is dangerous, beyond calculation, a destroyer as well as a builder of social ties, aleatory in its origins and effects (Comaroff and Comaroff 1999). It was said that Mobutu had printed evil signs into the paper currency of Zaire, which contaminated people as they handled it. These interpretations stress the fantasies of current "millennial capitalist" (Comaroff and Comaroff 2001) conditions, fantasies regularly recounted in the Nigerian press. The magical conception of money, however, is very old in West Africa and has coexisted with routine numeration since at least the fifteenth century, when the Portuguese started using the term *fetish* in written reports. Pietz writes: "The idea of the fetish originated in a mercantile intercultural space created by ongoing trade relations between cultures so radically different as to be mutually incomprehensible" (1985, 7); "commercial contracts and diplomatic treaties were inevitably put into the language of the fetish (as the vehicle for the creation of new interpersonal obligations)" (1988, 115). Magical or anthropomorphic powers and numerical calculation have never been contradictory understandings of the nexus of ideas around money in Africa, so the analytical purchase on transactional dynamics to be gained by stressing the occult and the public imaginery remains underspecified. Doubtless it is very important for political culture, but how does it permeate daily transactions?

Subaltern, but in Binary Terms?

Political economic theory is also too limited for addressing the sheer multiplicity of forms and meanings that money has taken in African history. Gregory (1996) has taken a large step forward in elaborating a "quality theory of money" that stresses the additional power and value extracted where different currencies are controlled by politically different groups. But he goes too far in contrasting the quality and quantity theories, and has to overstress some historical realities and understress others in order to do so. In consonance with the work of De Cecco (1984), he argues that the gold standard was a politically defined standard that supported the interests of British imperial power: "The money veil that is thrown over commodities, then, is a form of state power that varies from place to place and time to time" (Gregory 1996, 208). Currencies were devalued and replaced, in relation to gold, as it suited the political center. Gregory argues that it was British power that devalued the cowry, not oversupply and inflation. Probably so, but the result was not necessarily achieved through direct action on the nature of the money, that is, by demonetizing it. That would be one possible strategy. But it is not, in fact, historically accurate that the great cowry inflation of West Africa resulted from colonial imposition of state currency. Devaluation set in well before that. Historian Anthony Hopkins summarizes the sequences: "The currency revolution in South-West Nigeria was not a direct result of efforts made by expatriate firms and colonial Government to entangle Africans in the web of a money economy. The European firms clung to cowries and barter as long as possible because they considered that exchange on this basis was more profitable and less competitive than a cash trade. . . . By 1880 the traditional currency system was in decline" (1966, 483), that is, before colonial rule and sixty-eight years before all indigenous currencies were withdrawn from circulation. Even then, in 1948, the government treated different indigenous currencies differentially, for quite contingent reasons having to do with a convergence of post–World War II ideologies of justice, the needs of merchants, and the resale value of metal. Manillas were eventually paid for in state currency at respectable prices, and cowries were not. As well as reflecting differential interests on the European side of the equation, the two currencies implicated different constituencies on the African side. Manillas were more deeply implicated in the male economy of palm oil and "prestige," whereas women worked the smaller-scale commodities that were largely denominated in cowries. Men were compensated, so it was mainly women who suffered the fate indicated by Gregory of having the value of their capital completely wiped out. To follow through Gregory's own argument then, one needs to address the different modalities through which power has been implemented in economic life, in which quality and quantity are *both* important. The "subaltern" part of his title implies too simple a political opposition: two major actors, two currency modes. In fact, we should take his main argument of the politicization of commodity exchange a step further, to envisage that — at least in Atlantic Africa — quantity was *a form of* quality. Number and kind were both scales, among others; none was anchored in a foundational invariant; all were at play. Quantity was a form of power, available for use as a qualitative weapon, as when amounts in circulation were deliberately driven either high or low enough to cross quite-well-understood thresholds of function or conception. Disjunctures and thresholds were treated as resources in practice, even if in theory the West's emerging official and academic doctrines rested on the quality of money as invariant and quantity alone as variable. Although a quantity theory was developing in Europe, monetary multiplicity and other futuristic ideas, like fictional units of account (the "trade ounce" and the "pawn"), were *all* being developed as Western merchant policy and practice in Africa as early as the eighteenth century. In thought and in practice, there was one theory of money and commodity exchange in the metropole and another at the interface.

Negotiable, but in View of What Judgmental Standards?

Sara Berry's (1995) epilogue to our edited collection on money and economic instability in West Africa (Guyer 1995) posed a new, very stimulating problem with respect to disjunctures, fictions, and the condition in which nothing is invariant. She argued that the institutional instability that was induced largely by colonial policy in the twentieth century had rendered indeterminate the qualities themselves that were exchanged in monetary transactions. Far more was "at play" than the indeterminacy of currency multiplicity or market surges and retreats originating from the outside. "Values were shaped by struggles over precedence and jurisdiction, as well as by calibrations of supply and demand," returns to investment in personal allegiances are unstable, and although market information abounds, "there is no consensus on what information means" (Berry 1995, 308–10). Almost all general statements about money stress its reductive potential; witness, for example, Gudeman's recent theoretical work in which he writes that "the alchemy of money, with its power of commensuration, lies in its ability to dissolve distinctions between value schemes or measuring rods" (2001, 15). By contrast, Berry argues that in West Africa, "money payments do not give rise to precise or definitive transactions" (1955, 308).

This seems to me the key insight to pursue with respect to Atlantic Africa's specific history, and one key topic on which that history can speak to value theory more broadly. Mirowski arrives theoretically at the position that arises historically and empirically in an African context: "the insight that value is contingent, hermeneutic, negotiable, and nonnatural" (1991, 706). But having arrived there theoretically, he necessarily asks how to analyze economic life under such conditions: "one must drop anchor at some fixed point . . . after all the actual economic transactors are not paralyzed by nausea"; "a retrofitted social theory of value : . . . should be tethered to the pervasive thought structures in a market economy. . . . value is about conservation principles and invariants" (706). Is it possible to move to that more abstract level from the African case material, or at least make forays that would define the contours of the intellectual challenge? If people inhabit choppy waters, perhaps they do not "anchor at some fixed point" at all. In fact, the literal condition of seasickness is much better corrected by focusing one's eyes on the horizon than by attaching the boat to the ocean floor. Perhaps 3-D vision is a better metaphor for what we are after. The question then becomes: what horizons of value can suggest "conservation principles"—to both actor and analyst—once theory has cut loose from conventional assumptions of stability, trends, and constants? To address this question, and to go one step further than "ambiguity," another level of abstraction from the case material is needed.

INFERENCES

The foregoing examples of intellectual dilemmas all originate in the real and great difficulty of deciding how to proceed on the basis of assumptions about systems and invariants in a historically and culturally different world, over a period when—as Morgan put it—there were rapidly expanding new economic forms. If all the important analytical measures can yield conclusions of "both X and Y," then there may be something wrong with the analytical categories. They are forcing premature classification, assimilating an empirical richness into a theoretical parsimony in which we are more invested than in deeper understanding of other life-worlds. To assume that a life-world can be reduced to another "case" supporting a particular theory stems from an unjustifiable confidence that the parameters are already known and one can bypass the stage of listening, discerning, and imagining. In the end, as Berry argues, either theory or evidence has to give: history "bears out these (neoclassical and Marxist) arguments only in part" (1995, 300).

Here I work outward from the contradictory record about money in historic Africa, rather than backward from an alternative overarching theory, concentrating on issues and case materials that are particularly intriguing. As I studied the records, I focused on historical ethnographic interpretation because it is the most obvious way of "going back to the drawing board." Nevertheless, across time and space, each investigation seemed increasingly to reveal such highly consonant ideas and practices as to suggest to me a distinctive commercial civilization, with both abstractly repetitive and historically emergent characteristics. I draw attention to this conclusion early on, to suggest why applying theories based on European experience to Africa is so acutely awkward. It is an example of, not just "another economic culture," but a monetary culture built up deliberately *to be other,* in relation to European theory and practice. This area of the world has been thrust into modern world history in incontrovertibly powerful and longlasting ways. The slave and tropical commodity trades changed the world, industrial and non-industrial alike. The recalcitrance of European theory in the face of Africa is a construct of the same history, a co-production of Africa and Europe over centuries of economic and political engagement.

Universalist European theory does not easily apply because its coherent models and calculative practices orient to its own frontiers of innovation, taking the institutional frameworks as given. The convoluted history of the western institutions and practices that have created the monetary experience of others is largely erased. Let me give an example before returning to the larger theoretical argument.

Western merchant profit in Africa was heterogeneous in origin although unitary in the final account books. It included components that could be defined in various ways: as seignorage (the margin gained on issuing money); as arbitrage between currency forms (including fictional units such as the trade ounce); as temporal arbitrage over seasons and trade cycles; as cheating and sharp practice; as monopoly advantage, as well as a simple result of equating marginal cost with marginal revenue. It suited merchants who were conserving gold at home to use other goods as currencies for purchases abroad. Cowries from the Maldive Islands appeared as "shells" on the lists of merchants' tradable goods although they served as currency for transactions between Europeans and Africans, and within Africa, for centuries. Brass manillas were manufactured in Birmingham and Nantes and imported into Eastern Nigeria up to the turn of the twentieth century, where they continued in use for the export trade in palm oil until 1948. By buying them in Europe as if they were *goods,* holding them in Africa as *money capital* for security on advances of consumer goods to be repaid in palm oil, and treating manilla transactions as *barter* while Africans used them as *general purpose money* (Ofonagoro 1976; Ekejiuba 1995), the merchants kept the manillas in the *commodity* sector of their own operations, while manipulating them as *money* in Africa. Ironically, large numbers of manillas were later stored in British museums as primitive currencies, only a short distance from where they were first made, in one of the major manufacturing centers of the world.

It is this profound irony—this hall of mirrors of theory and practice, past and present—that makes it so difficult to clarify the contours of an alternative comprehensive view. Nevertheless, a logical consonance does emerge, albeit one that I do not attempt yet to systematize. Certain recurrent ideas and practices within Africa seem uncannily to reflect, or respond to, the political economic practices of mercantilism between the sixteenth and nineteenth centuries: an era that Western theory has largely consigned to the past, along with its theorists. European economic nationalism (Heckscher 1935, 13) created protectionist boundaries, powerful state accumulation, and national treasuries of precious metals. Monetary multiplicity in foreign trade was one way of conserving the national treasure in gold. Policy pursued all opportunities for gain, including warfare. Indeed, it was mercantilist Europe that first postulated the *"love of gain"* (301; emphasis in original) as a primary human motive, an explanation and justification for an "amorality in the choice of means" to economic ends. The slave trade "was one of the gems of trade" (300). European profits were opportunistic, commercial methods were heterogeneous, conditions fluctuated and, wherever possible, European interests were protected and promoted. National interest and an "open economy" policy continued under colonial rule, albeit through different commodities and means of control.

The history and ethnography of currency flows within Africa create a sense of this economic confrontation, comprising both correspondence and resistance, between the conditions created by mercantilism and institutions in Atlantic popular economies. Widespread and varied transactional forms and financial mediations developed which seem to have at their core a certain anticipation of changeability over time and mediation of disjuncture over social and geographical space. There are barriers and thesholds in transactions and multiple currencies on both sides. Even today, and building on a long regional history, foreign exchange trading in the Kano informal financial system works as "localized recycling of currencies for profit" (Hashim and Meagher 1999, 16). The great pervasive difference between Europe and Africa was that African monetary transactions were never continuously governed by *any* of the principles that were institutionally established in capitalist Europe and treated as systemic and invariant in economic theory; that is, the value of money, the irreducible purity of number, and the stability of state legal frameworks for property, contract and credit. The gold standard was several steps removed from most of the continent's own trade, so prices were not anchored, nor profits made calculable, by its stability. Number and calculation were not anchored to formal mathematics and accounting (Bernstein 1996, Porter 1995, Carruthers and Espeland 1991). And ownership, regulation, and struggles in public arenas over regulatory frameworks for ownership and finance were not anchored to states based on the taxation of citizens, property, and commercial dealings. As late as 1990, and in a striking shorthand statement of this contrast, a western banker could claim that Africans were "living in societies that in some very fundamental way are not bankable" (John Reed of Citicorp, quoted in Sampson 1990, 209).

Marketable but not bankable. Commodity economies without formal financial institutions to discipline the money supply and channel it toward capitalist investments. Once the empirical situation deviates far enough from the basic assumptions of a theory based on markets *and* banks (economics), or neither (substantivist anthropology), it is imperative to intellectual artisanship to reposition the elements of theory in the argument. If we abandon generalizing theory for the moment, but still want to keep in view the theoretical and historical linkage between Europe and Africa, by what principles do we proceed? The only possible position is on the borderland, looking in both directions. So instead of an encompassing theory, I work outward from the most characteristic generative element on both sides, namely the expectation of gain: within Africa, across the interface, and all along the transactional chain. Gain is at the center of microanalysis for monetary transactions, while also being the persistent motive behind the macrohistory of European monetary engagement in Africa.

To focus on gains empirically and ethnographically is quite different from assuming them theoretically. Economic theories arrive at gains, or profits, indirectly and end up with a unitary residual that is usually composed of heterogeneous elements. In most theory, profits are a precipitate from application of assumed invariant fundamentals: money, number, law. In neoclassical economics, profits derive from price dynamics. In the Marxist theory of capitalism, profit derives ultimately from legal ownership and other instances of the institutionalization of power. Working in Africa, we face two challenges. First, there is the general problem that theories of profit apply imprecisely to realities, even for the metropole. Joan Robinson (1971) argues that there has never been a really persuasive neoclassical theory of profit. Joseph Schumpeter implied a similar skepticism when he argued that the returns to the entrepreneurial innovation that is key to capitalist growth are ambiguous when viewed through the conventional lens of equilibrium theory: "The gain is attributable to personal exertion. Hence it might be called wages . . . it might also be called a monopoly gain. . . . Essentially it emerges as a *capital* gain" (Swedberg 1991, 415; emphasis in the original).

Then, for application elsewhere, one faces the problem of institutional difference as well. Noting the weakness of profit theory in general and for noncapitalist market economies in particular, Gudeman (2001) returns to Aristotelian categories and to local anthropological understandings based in a logic of community provisioning and artisanal innovation. But in some sense this is a moral rather than an analytical position, supporting Gudeman's plea for "new combinations of community and market" (2001, 163). For analysis of Africa, that aspiration seems distant. Over centuries, the most valuable of African assets have been invasively and inventively monetized for profit—gained in many ways, under changing conditions. The boundaries at which gains could be made shifted, and with them shifted the forms of recognition they received, as being legitimate or illegal, culturally recognized or concealed (see MacGaffey 1991; for cultural recognition see Barnes 1987). Some officially recognized ways of gain-making, such as by seignorage, were implicit in boundary trade before the colonial period. Then they were abrogated by the "metrocentrism" (Hogendorn and Gemery 1982) of colonial state power and international borders. Since 1989, there is an increasing acknowledgement of the power of these and other "disjunctures" (Appadurai 1990, Geschiere and Meyer 1998) in the globalized world.

For Africa, disjuncture is a new version of an old reality. A closer horizon than Gudeman's beckons: simply to reexplore what ideas and practices have been created from historical experience. We do better to address the record directly, focus on instrumental calculation about advantage, describe its disconcerting multiplicity ethnographically, and incorporate the experience of multiplicity into the theory. The production of gainful margins in economies that do not have effective state and bank disciplines cannot be concealed by official definitions that divide and merge phenomena for their own institutional purposes. Without the invariants embedded in western economic theory, the African exchange institutions created with and against western historical practice in Africa produce huge ambiguities when one tries to describe them in terms of those theories. Everything seems changeable, negotiable, redefinable all the time. Ethnography offers an alternative approach. Out of Morgan's "diversity" of the world and "bewilderment" of theory, I want then to distill "the intelligence of interests" that has gain as its goal.

GAINING ANTHROPOLOGICAL GROUND

We have two literatures on value: one cultural and one political and economic in inspiration and method. Gregory in some sense relaunched both new rounds of discussion in his book on gift and commodity published in 1982. Melanesianists were already rethinking "the gift," and a series of new works in the 1980s addressed money and commodity exchange. A particularly signal set of contrasting approaches emerged in the late 1980s. Marilyn Strathern (1988) and Nancy Munn (1986) enormously expanded the imagination about what was implicated in exchange. In different ways, they took a radically questioning stance with respect to every strand of meaning and every configuration of concepts. They made clear that there was no understanding of exchange without putting cultural processes of value definition and performance into a profound exploratory process, taking nothing as given, still less invariant. For example, Strathern (1992) writes of number as a kind of poetics, in a system for which the only really important number is one. Thomas (1991) focuses precisely on objects, their properties, and the encoding of value in exchange, which he sees differing across southern Pacific societies. From this regional literature, Gell (1992) makes the striking suggestion that the alienated exchange of trade was entirely familiar and may even be a logical precondition for "the gift." Following explicitly from the ideas of Munn, Graeber relativizes number in his reanalysis of the gift. Number matters differently in different societies.

Maori heirlooms established unique identities (Graeber 2001, 187), as fixed points in a shifting terrain of social relations, whereas Kwakiutl mythical namings and identities were so varied and "fragmented" that it was the numerical scaling of potlatch gifts that alone made them comparable and indeed ordered in any way at all (216). The nature of relationships between things and people is put into similar question throughout the Melanesian corpus of ethnography (Lederman 1998). The collection by Parry and Bloch, published in 1989, goes some way to bringing cultural analytical methods to the study of money use. This work encourages a kind of analysis that puts transactions into slow motion and lingers on every frame — as Akin and Robbins (1999) summarize, about objects, numbers, scales, the modalities of exchange, relationships.

Although this literature enormously enriches a critical exploration of things and relationships, the authors have worked primarily with the foundational concepts of exchange *systems*. Number and gradations of quality become the next, and logically subordinate, step. Insofar as this limits attention to the judgmental criteria *internal* to scales of value, it is more limited than necessary on the operation of scalar judgments in a field of changing practice and most especially of politically and economically driven change. *More* and *less* may apply to any descriptor: brighter or duller, higher or lower, more or less powerful, heavier and lighter, numerically greater or fewer. Some scalar qualifiers may be simply nominal or classificatory, defining this or that phenomenon as part of a semantic domain. Others will be ordinal, defining cognate things along a standard of "greater or lesser." Some may include interval measurement of some kind, where not only the place in the order but the distance between positions on a scale can be expressed. Only those based on number will be ratio scales allowing infinite calculation of the relationship between any item on the scale and any other. These scales presumably form repertoires in all economies, complete with conventional modes of linking one to the other: quality to object classification, quantity in numbers to money goods. The idea of money necessarily brings number into the scalar repertoire, and thereby "invites" people to modify existing scales for things to be receptive to points of linkage. This process of scale construction is analytically separable from other aspects of "commoditization," such as abstraction, alienation, and appropriation. For economies such as those of Atlantic Africa, which have mediated quantitative currencies for a long time, scale construction is at the heart of the analytical challenge.

Scale construction can link cultural and political economic work. The other seminal work of the 1980s is the Malinowski lecture on money, by Keith Hart (1986). He places money in two different political economic matrices: the state and the market. He insists, then, that money and gain can be quite differentially organized and that money economies are thereby to be studied historically, comparatively, and dynamically. There is a marked difference between the cultural and the political economic literatures at this point, with the striking conceptual sophistication of cultural analysis counterbalanced by an equally striking relegation — or perhaps postponement — of the question of historical dynamics. In a political economic tradition, historical change is at the center of concern. Political economy by itself, on the other hand, contains no strategies anything like as punctiliously ethnographic as the culturalist one, for analyzing how monetary transactions take place within and between the changing matrices of power. Here is where close attention to scales of value, in explicitly dynamic contexts, allows us to draw on both traditions, for a purpose that is also shared by both, namely, to trace out how other orders and disorders have been produced.

The question of order creation is central — in both the cognitive and political senses. The expansion of capitalism has entailed commensuration (Espeland and Stevens 1998) on the one hand and a complex architecture of disjuncture on the other, both emanating in unpredictable ways from the metropole. Standards of commensuration of the ideal modernist type — the metric system, professionalized statistical skills, credit and interest rates on precise criteria, probability calculation for insurance, banks as the custodian and integrator of relevant transactional "memory" (Hart 2000), economic theory on the physical model (Mirowski 1989) — were developed for an enterprise quite different from the achievement of gain through arbitrage, seigniorage, local monopoly control, and many of the points at which gains are made in trade. Within Africa, other cultural and social processes produced their own commensuration and disjuncture — of goods, ethnicity, religion, occupation, and status — resulting in a natural and social geography in which gains could be made at all kinds of thresholds: between kinds of currency, between neighboring groups, between fictional units and real units, between currency and goods, and between one legal-jural regime of enforcement and another.

Recent work in anthropology has drawn repeated attention to disjunctures (Appadurai 1990), the earmarking of monies (Zelizer 1994), and the dissonance of value scales (Ferguson 1992). There are two directions in which the African experience encourages us to take these arguments. First, to encompass multiplicity. Perhaps because of its programmatic nature, much of this literature tends to conceptual binarism. Hart (1986) reviews the theoretical divide in Western monetary theory between the uniformity imposed by states and the flexibility produced by markets. Gregory (1996) refers to dominant and subalternate monies. Cultural analysis by Parry and Bloch (1989), and more recently by a group of Melanesianists (Akin and Robbins 1999), distinguishes between transactions for personal gain and those aimed at social reproduction. Gudeman (2001) writes of the base and the market. Following the historic importance of the work of Lévi-Strauss, binarism implies a generalized, panhuman process. The dynamics of multiplicity in Africa, however, arise out of specific and identifiable historical tensions and ambitions. They belong far more in the domain of "intelligence of interests" than in the fundamentals of mind or culture. The multiplicity, rather than the binarism, that is so evident in the political economic history of Atlantic Africa should reframe our discipline's analytical attention to questions of equivalence, difference, and commensuration as a creation from experience in the world.

Second, the issue of disjuncture and gain invokes the relationship between knowledge and power outside the West. The considerable illumination that has come from studying "struggles over meaning" (e.g., Peters 1984) has shown the practical and political investment in cognitive framing. Study of ritual has defined a domain of deep knowledge from which such meanings arise and are validated (Apter 1992). We have only intermittently linked the two logics to explore how the structure and the implementation of knowledge-framing relate to the validation of recurrent experience. This is not a chicken-and-egg problem of origins and infinite regression but rather one of defining key ethnographic problems in the relationship between knowledge and economic action. In another work (Guyer and Eno Belinga 1995), we suggested that inventive frontiers of knowledge creation in Equatorial Africa were related to competitive and compositional forms of social prominence (as distinct, for example, from hierarchical incorporation and authoritative imposition of the Dumontian kind). The combination of charismatic values and recurrent volatility created a heterogeneous world (comparable to Graeber's [2001] interpretation of the Kwakiutl) for which money was a kind of "receptor" or descriptor (Guyer 1993), giving a basis for ranking on a common scale—at least situationally. Local expertise, in turn, developed and defined the valuation criteria: for things, qualities, people, and indeed anything that could be subjected to judgment. The valuation of self and the world were in simultaneous construction.

I argue in the following chapters that this valuation was on a ranking model, each scale with its own logic and its external linking potentials to other scales. The rank of people is one instance of a wider process, while also providing the means by which the right to interpret and create value judgments was claimed. In this sense, social processes remain central to any analysis. They do figure here, but in the present work I am more concerned with the logical and socio-logical *consequences* of multiple emergent valuation scales: What shape have they had? What logical qualities? What modes of manipulation? And what patterns of economic behavior emerge in aggregate form from people's routine recourse to these modes of reasoning?

The intellectual resources for these explorations are rich: the Melanesian attention to rank (Kelly 1993), the logic of commensuration and calculation (Rotman 1987; Espeland and Stevens 1998; Lave 1988; Verran 2001), the meaning of deixis as referential grounding (Hanks 1990), the social construction of price and value (Mirowski 1991; Ferguson 1992), and the extraordinary new ethnography and social/economic history of Africa, including new work that explores how "pluralistic multiplicity is in fact a historically produced sedimentation of layers of knowledge" (Shaw 2002, 103; see also Ferme 2001; and for a similar position in linguistic anthropology, Hanks 1990). There is a large new ethnographic project prefigured in these studies, and one that only emerged in my own mind as I reordered well-known material into a different shape and a different argument. I leave further speculation about it to the final chapter.

THE LOGICAL SEQUENCE OF THE BOOK

The next chapter, chapter 2, addresses Paul Bohannan's seminal concept of conversion as a specific *asymmetrical* form of transaction, which I argue was a very common Atlantic African exchange, as well as more widely used. Part 2, consisting of chapters 3–5, examines three kinds of value scale at play in monetary transactions, as examples of the nonreductive multiplicity that makes asymmetry possible. Part 3, consisting of chapters 6–8, shows how this repertoire is formed and performed in the practice of transactional life. The final section, part 4 (chaps. 9 and 10), mirrors the introduction by revisiting how conversions (in the African "market") differ from formalities (in the context of the state).

I have used materials that vary by time and place. In part, this reflects the happenstance of my own past research topics. In part, it reflects the fact that the richness of the primary and secondary data dictated my choices; I wanted the history and ethnography to drive the analytical challenges as far as possible. But in part it is by ranging widely in substance that I can juxtapose what I see as cognate analytical themes, thus giving weight to the idea that recurrent themes can indeed be posited for the gainful institutions of Atlantic Africa across time and space. Implicitly then, Atlantic Africa is approached as a single regional system, subjected to similar experiences, and creating the contours of a distinctive commercial civilization. Its commercial civilization is a historical construct, growing up over centuries in dynamic interchange with its two coasts: the Sahel, with its disciplines of Islamic commerce, and the Atlantic, under the expanding logics of merchant capitalism. As such, its characteristics should be seen as potentially shared in part or in whole by others in the expanding monetary economy.

Beyond this list of chapters, I would like to indicate the deeper foundations of my logic in juxtaposing separate analyses that in some sense "add up" to a more general theoretical statement about value and uncertainty. While remaining grounded in the practice of economic life, I do aim toward abstraction and a broader disciplinary intervention, giving an account of certain aspects of collective economic dynamics within a global system. For this topic, the expository style of deriving the problematic in advance from an established framework, and then critiquing its terms and modifying it through empirical application or illustration, is inadequate to the more radical questioning that I find necessary. It would also plunge me into such a morass of legitimate questions about the nature of the archive that I could hardly get to an argument at all. My inclination has been to revert to a kind of empirical "pattern recognition" that builds outward from small insights into an archive that is large and heterogeneous enough to reflect something important about realities on the ground. The larger configurations I build never leave these "realities," but they are self-consciously a construct. In this sense, my ambition and style are modernist, looking for whatever gives persistent shape to a pervasive experience of flux and change, and expressing the argument in ways that make the process of creating the construct transparent to the reader. A modernist approach is most appropriate to the evidence I can mobilize, to the level of my own understanding, and to this stage of analytical thinking about economic phenomena in the non-Western world. Perhaps it is also necessary for clearing the way for going a lot farther than I can here, by other intellectual means.

It is a long time since anthropology has given sustained theoretical attention to the potential suppleness that may be embedded in what has long been branded as empiricism (although see Peel 1978; Jackson 1989). There may be a written philosophical version of what I do here, but if so I am not on firm-enough ground yet to apply it, and the framing would inevitably seem post hoc. There are some very promising new convergences, but their deep exploration properly belongs in another work. I refer in the text to Hanks (1990) on deixis in linguistic practice and Rotman (1987) on deixis in numbers. There is a very close correspondence between my own findings from historical and ethnographic analysis and those of Verran in the philosophy of science applied to Yoruba numbers. Even more striking is my most recent discovery, in the very last days of copyediting, of Eglash's (2002) book titled *African Fractals: Modern Computing and Indigenous Design*. If the convergences that I see here hold up under closer examination, they would suggest a powerful correspondence between the critical features of abstraction that can be identified through a historical and contextual logic and those identifiable through a mathematical logic. I have earlier argued that this should be so: that Atlantic Africa's response to mercantilism must have the qualities of *both* a reaction *and* an autonomous voice because it is based in experience. Experience is both *of* something (an intrusion from the external world) and *in* something (an internalization by reflection). But my grasp of these convergences remains embryonic for the moment, and I have changed nothing in the text in light of my sense of these new frontiers.

Without other footholds, I have for a long time turned to another source of modernist thinking. I hope the following explanation of my exposition does not seem pretentious. It is simply the truest and the most graphic way to represent the order in what may otherwise seem to be a motley collection of disparate interventions. By default and by the accident of personal interest, modern art has offered me an imagery for the search for, and expression of, recurrence in uncertainty. I have long found the work and words of Paul Klee an inspiration. His drawings of dynamically complex and yet geometric landscapes, which bear the traces of their makers' past imaginations toward imminent futures, have expressed precisely my own aspiration for describing African farms. The idea of "cool romantic," with its implication of reaching toward aesthetic (and intellectual) wholes, but by precise — and thereby accountable — analytics rather than leaps of identification, has expressed a process and goal that I found poorly articulated in the concept of objectivity, which anthropology inherited from the sciences. The notion that an artistic or intellectual work can start from elements and yet avoid being essentialist or reductive echoes my own provisional fixing of a conceptual starting point that would be amplified, contextualized, and thereby altered as the work developed. This version of a modernist sensibility, apprehending unforeseen recurrence within confusion and uncertainty, and aiming for an abstract interpretation of that, has been upstaged by postmodernist ideas that dislodge *all* points of certainty — author, master-narrative, and structure — long before its full implications for intellectual practice had been explored.

The sequence in the making of an object, in this tradition, has been expressed beautifully by artist Bridget Riley, writing about the influence of Paul Klee on her own work. She contrasts intellectual and artistic approaches to abstraction: "for the [Abstract] painter the meaning of abstraction lay in the opposite direction from the intellectual effort of abstracting: it is not the end but the beginning. . . . Long before a line is expressive it works in specifically plastic ways, taking direction, dividing up areas, delineating or circumscribing forms, and so on" (Riley 2002, 15). Later she makes another contrast, between mathematical and artistic abstraction: "A geometric form in the picture plane does not work in terms of geometry. . . . the triangle . . . in its mathematical definition is the direct connection between three points not on a straight line. But perceived as a pictorial figure the triangle is charged by the tension between line and point, between a base and a directional thrust" (17).

The three modes of abstraction—linguistic, mathematical, and pictorial—have distinct dynamics. This collection of essays is akin to a set of lines on a page with a shape more like artistic abstraction than discursive argumentation or scientific/causative proof. Discourse and number enter as methods, and should eventually open the subject up further (as I mention in the conclusion), but at this stage they do not determine the connective tissue between the chapters. The introduction defines the contours of the page and spaces the chapters will occupy. Chapter 2 on conversions is the first stroke of a new composition, to which all the others must relate because they were only conceptualized as linkable to each other in light of this first set of ideas. If this "line" is misplaced or misrepresented, all the rest become problematic. The idea of asymmetrical exchange as a fundamental recurrence in African monetary practice defines the field of inquiry. This was the first chapter I wrote, and it remains the least changed. The next three chapters (chaps. 3–5) are like parallel lines, extending the idea of scales and asymmetrical mediations. They represent the form of three different scales of valuation. Chapters 6–8 make intersections by showing how the scales are linked to each other performatively. The final section (chaps. 9 and 10) offers the counterpoint to the conversion chapter by bringing to the foreground a theme that appeared only peripherally there, namely, the fixing of "permanent" points of "equivalence" between scales, as formalities.

Finally, a word on the title. The term *marginal* is multireferential and ambiguous in that it "works" in several conventionally differing theories in different philosophical camps. In microeconomic theory, the margin refers to the "next transaction," to which the rational calculus is decisively applied. Profit is maximized where marginal costs (the cost of producing the next unit) equal marginal returns (the income from the next sale). By using *margin* here, I am endorsing reasoning, purposive behavior, and strategic means–end thinking as appropriate subject matter for anthropology, and even that formalization can be useful, without endorsing any of the overweening claims for a comprehensive marginalist economic theory. "[R]ational behaviour in . . . uncertain times," as Latham (1971, 604) indicates, has to be analyzable in terms that both question and extend the meaning of reasoning as an activity and uncertainty as an experience. In neo-Marxist theory, marginality (or peripherality) has referred to a structural position in a world order in which control of the key resources of the capitalist system is very limited. In this sense, the marginalization of Africa from capital flows is now taken for granted by theorists from all camps. What needs to be brought to the center of concern and analyzed institutionally is the specificity of different margins as constructed orders.

Where *marginality* is used in a vernacular sense, it refers to indefensibly small increments, as in the "gains" that African popular economies have been able to make. Yet the idea of gain is still highly motivating. It appears in popular culture, in the theology of the new "prosperity" churches, and in the criminal arbitrage of business fraud in the formal sector. Atlantic African populations express little of the discouraged passivity attributed to the peasantries of Europe in the past. This persistent possibility of a gainful margin in exchange, what people hope and plan for — that is the analytical problem I concentrate on, leaving for further analysis the determining factors for its size, exploitative or progressive implications, and social organizational concomitants.

2

CONVERSIONS
ASYMMETRICAL TRANSACTIONS
▬

The idea of equivalence has been fundamental to the theory of exchange: the gift and countergift in reciprocal economies, and an equation of commodities through their respective utilities in market economies. Autonomy and equivalence are parsimonious assumptions that allow complex derivations, much as sister exchange offers the basic model of exogamy. Hence the overwhelming emphasis on gift and commodity in the literature, even when the distinction between the two is being brought into question (Appadurai 1986). The historical ethnography of African monetary exchange, by contrast, shows evidence of asymmetry of value, as a permanent and culturally marked feature and not as an ephemeral condition of the first experience of trade (Thomas 1991). African economies were monetized over several centuries, but this feature seems to defy the very "purpose" of money as an unambiguously measured standard of value. Bohannan's concept of conversion provides a key entry point, although—as I suggest later—the Tiv version is not the most dramatic example.

REVISITING TIV SPHERES OF EXCHANGE

All of us in economic anthropology return from time to time to Bohannan's classic article on spheres of exchange among the Tiv, and commemorative lectures encourage a return to the intellectual legacy. To reread it is to be struck again by its combination of theoretical inspiration, conceptual caution, expositional modesty—and historical incompleteness. Bohannan's account is well known and has often been recounted, although not always faithfully. So this is the outline. The Tiv of Central Nigeria define goods as those with an exchange value (*ishe*) that can be bought and sold through a market (*kasoa*), and those goods and services that are only given as gifts. Exchangeable goods fall into three categories that are implicitly hierarchically ranked "on the basis of moral values" (Bohannan 1955, 64), that is, not on the basis of cognitive distinctive features. At the bottom are locally produced food, chickens, goats, household utensils, tools, and any of the raw materials for producing these items. The next higher category consists of cattle, slaves, brass rods, and a locally woven cloth called *tugudu*. The highest sphere consists in rights in people (other than slaves), and particularly women in marriage. Exchanges among items in the same category he terms "conveyances"; they are ordinary transactions, encompassing purchase and sale in the marketplace. They carry no moral or status implication. What Bohannan calls "investment" lies in the rarer opportunity for conversion across the threshold from a lower to a higher category. All men aim to convert up — to invest, in Bohannan's terms — and to avoid converting down.

Bohannan presented this model quite modestly. His was explicitly an ethnographer's systematization of "the Tiv covert ideology" (1955, 61). He openly noted that it was hardly neat. For example, although slaves and brass rods fell into the same category, it was much more acceptable to convert down brass rods than slaves (65). And prestige goods could be converted up into marriages through bridewealth payments; cattle in particular allowed men to avoid the Tiv marriage exchange system altogether and marry wives from neighboring cattle-keeping societies. But he argued that the principles of different spheres were nevertheless basic and persistent.

Subsequent use of the concept of conversion has stressed the barrier effect. In the broader literature — beyond anthropology and the non-Western world, and in relation to invasive commoditization — the Tiv offered a "word-picture" of what was seen as an evolutionarily "early," and therefore humanly basic, moral limitation on what money can easily buy. The multiple currencies, each in its place, ensured the continuing separation of some goods from accumulation or redistribution in socially and morally unacceptable ways. Thus has *spheres of exchange* became a concept in the social scientific toolkit. Figure 2.1 maps the conceptual spheres of exchange as Bohannan described them.

However useful it might be, the transformation of this version of Tiv investment into an ideal-type model of moral barriers sidelines the fine historical studies carried out in the 1970s — noted in the anthropological literature by very few until Gregory's intervention in 1996 — that show the limitations of the picture of the Tiv on which the model is based. Without questioning Bohannan's ethnography at all, one can simply lift off the boundedness of the model and connect each sphere to its regional trading networks, to see not barriers but institutions that facilitated asymmetrical exchanges across value registers. The earliest colonial officers in Tiv country saw the importance of trade very clearly. Advising the government on whether a military presence would be needed, F. H. Ruxton wrote in 1910: "In character the MUNSHI [alternative name for the Tiv] is purely an agriculturalist; he is also a keen trader; he is certainly not a fighting man" (Ruxton 1910). Keen regional trading is an essential element to add, as I schematize in figure 2.2.

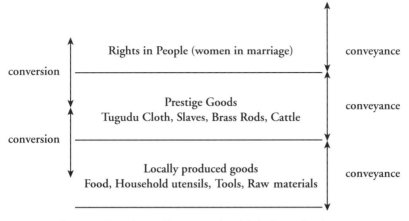

Figure 2.1. Tiv exchange: The structural model of spheres of exchange.

Historian David Dorward mobilized archival and oral sources to show that *tugudu* cloth actually cut across all "ostensible spheres" (1976, 583), being usable for prestige payments as well as — in the form of the separately woven strips that made up entire cloths, or even pieces cut off from strips — for subsistence purchases. *Tugudu* also figured in a marriage system that was much less clearly divided between bridewealth and exchange than Bohannan suggested. A process called *kem,* meaning to acquire little by little, could refer either to installment bridewealth payments or to the offering of material goods as a delay tactic in fulfilling one's exchange commitments, both payable in *tugudu*. Above all, *tugudu* offered an entry into regional trade networks through Hausa demand for peasant cloth; it was traded north along with slaves, ivory, and kola in return for cattle, horses, gowns, dyed cloth, salt, and beads (below, fig. 2.2). Given its multiple uses, one can see why the Tiv historian Akiga could write, "Cotton was the origin of all wealth among the Tiv." An elder stayed at home "spinning unceasingly, till such time as he had enough to start weaving" (quoted in Dorward 1976, 586).

The complementarities of trade with the south were not so neat. Traders bringing European goods, firearms, and gunpowder from the south preferred to be paid in brass rods, which was their own currency (see Latham 1971). It was also nonbreakable or perishable on the difficult overland trip to Ogoja on the Cross River. Cattle and horses were traded south mainly for sacrifice; they would not survive in the tsetse belt as productive or prestige items. Indigenous cloth was less in demand in the south, where clothing styles were less voluminous. Clearly the Tiv needed to get brass rods from elsewhere in the north in order to acquire firearms from the south. Again the trade in *tugudu* cloth to the Hausa could mediate the exchange, because the Hausa were willing to pay for cloth in brass rods, which was not their own main currency. They acquired them through their own trade networks.

So two modifications need to be made to the model as extracted from Bohannan's description: one broadens its geographical range, and the other redefines its key concepts in light of that. Whatever moral spheres might have been as a Tiv mnemonic, the economy at the end of the nineteenth century comprised overlapping geographical circuits at an entrepôt between the Sahel and the Atlantic Ocean. Many of the items in Tiv exchange were vital components of a regional trade that was certainly yet more active and complex than this account can do justice to. The regional view now alters the meaning of conversion because several transactions that look like conveyances within a sphere—cloth to brass rods, brass rods to firearms and cattle, cattle to bridewealth—are better thought of as steps toward conversions, just as Thomas (1991, 78) pointed out with respect to the association between conversions and regional trade in the South Pacific. By passing through the hands of strangers, across spatial boundaries, a conveyance could be turned into a conversion. Cloth is the most striking case. Cloth could be bought through sale of crops or small livestock and sold for cattle to the Hausa, who used it for currency. Brass rods and cattle acquired through sales of cloth currency opened up two different directions of exchange: brass rods opened up the southern routes, and cattle opened the routes into the northern pastoral economies. (As important an item as guns does not figure in Bohannan's scheme at all; this lapse is surely due to the difficulty of reconstructing the full richness of the past, even in the late 1940s.) Conversion involved placing oneself on the right routes, with the right goods. Figure 2.2 adds regional trade to the Tiv map of exchange.

Should the number of spheres then be multiplied from three to many, or should the whole idea be abandoned? The much greater possibility I see here involves two moves. The first is to sever the concept of conversion from a unique reference to spheres of exchange and to "see" it at more junctures in transactional pathways. Tiv currency forms symbolized not a closed transactional model but an open set of directional transactions that work stepwise toward the constitution of stores of value that had greater longevity and security than the currencies themselves. A conversion adds, subtracts, or otherwise transforms the attributes of exchange goods in ways that define the social direction of future transactional possibilities. Conversions are the compasses and landmarks on the navigational pathways of currency circulation. The most striking asymmetry in our case here is simply directional; we know nothing about "real" or symbolic inequalities of value.

This comes to the second move: to shift the focus from a structural view of "spheres of exchange" to the historical constitution of conversions and wealth creation, under turbulent conditions. What Bourdieu refers to as the "social alchemy" of the "endless reconversion of economic capital into symbolic capital" (1977, 195) will appear at more junctures and be more

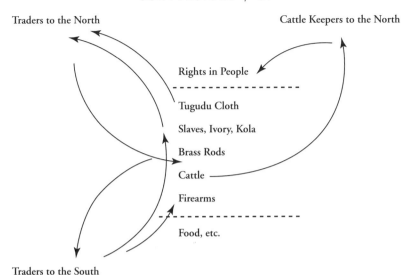

Figure 2.2. Tiv exchange: The historical model of regional trade.

varied than the spheres model implies. The geographical and temporal reach that particular conversions allow will be subject to "endless" reconstitution as currency goods and their circuits change. A picture of "internal" and "external" dynamics of currency before the colonial conquest can now be hazarded, thanks largely to the assiduous historical work of European scholars. So I turn here to the Equatorial sources.

EXTERNALITIES AND LOCAL PROCESSES: THE LIBINZA

I have learned so much from studying the sources on the Ubangi–Congo confluence as it was at the turn of this century, that I turn to them here. They illustrate particularly clearly the stepwise asymmetries of conversions in relation to the Congo River trading system. When I was studying the old currencies of Southern Cameroon, I visited the Royal Museum of Central Africa at Tervuren, in Belgium, which houses the largest collection of Central African currencies in the world. The collection holds over a hundred metal objects, varying in size, shape, and content, all of which have figured at one time or another as currencies in the region. To try to locate the pieces on the map, I matched the items with the acquisition records. Some records were frustrating for an anthropologist because they identified the place of purchase rather than the place of provenance. But among the records was a magnificent list of sixty-eight items that had all been acquired at once in one region, by a colonial officer named Van de Weyer, all accorded a local value in the main currency of the time, the iron *kwa,* and each designated to an ethnic group (see figs. 2.3 and 2.4). A fine historical ethnography by Van Leynseele of one of the groups, the Libinza, offers an interpretation of the otherwise puzzling "message" conveyed by the collection.

First, a comment on the region as a whole. Alison Quiggen wrote that the Congo River basin was characterized by "a jungle of currencies" (1949) of enormous variety and complexity. Some were locally produced, such as the iron *nginza* made by the Yakoma (Samarin 1989, 150), the copper croisettes of Katanga (de Maret 1981), and the varied forms of raphia cloth that were produced in many different societies (Balandier 1968; M.-C. Dupré 1995). Others were introduced from Europe, such as the famous brass wire known as *mitakos,* plate-like neptunes, and idiosyncratic inventions such as de Brazza's geometric tokens and the industrially produced, anchor-shaped *mandjong* that G. Dupré (1995) traces to a single trader stationed in the Congo around 1910. During the second half of the nineteenth century, the pressure from traders trying to penetrate markets with

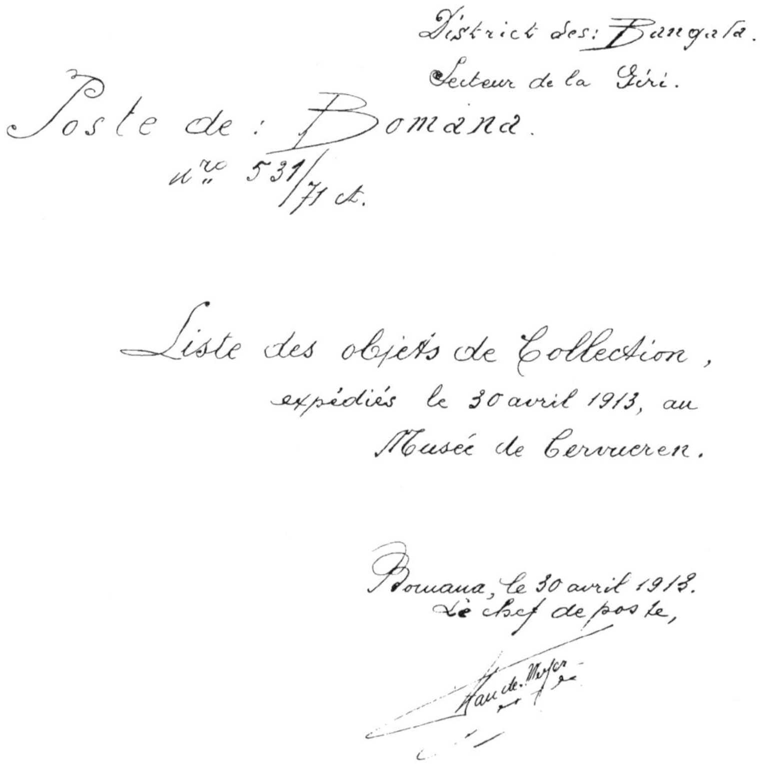

District des: Bangala.

Secteur de la Giri.

Poste de : Bomana.

n^{re} 531/71 ct.

Liste des objets de Collection,

expédiés le 30 avril 1913, au

Musée de Tervueren.

Bomana, le 30 avril 1913.

Le chef de poste,

Figure 2.3. Facepage of the Van de Weyer collection.

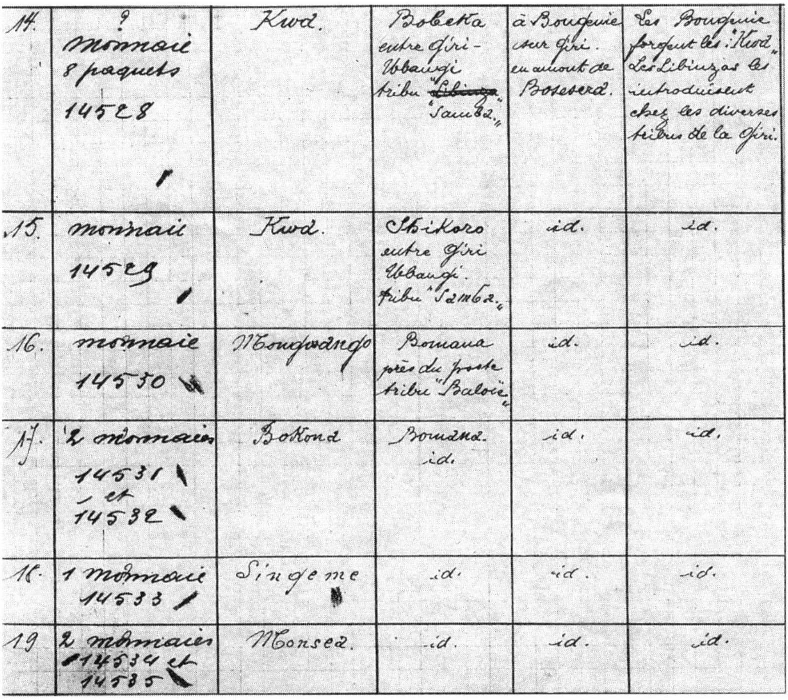

14.	? monnaie 8 paquets 14528	Kwd.	Bobeka entre Giri-Ubangi tribu ~~Libinza~~ "Samba"	à Bouguie sur Giri en amont de Bosesera.	Les Bouguie forgent les "Kwd" Les Libinzas les introduisent chez les diverses tribus de la Giri.
15.	monnaie 14529	Kwd.	Sbikoro entre Giri Ubangi. tribu "Samba"	id.	id.
16.	monnaie 14530	Mongwandgo	Bomana près du poste tribu "Baloie"	id.	id.
17.	2 monnaies 14531 et 14532	Bokond	Bomana. id.	id.	id.
18.	1 monnaie 14533	Singeme	id.	id.	id.
19	2 monnaies 14534 et 14535	Monsea.	id.	id.	id.

Figure 2.4. A page of the Van de Weyer collection.

new currencies was intense, resulting in devaluations and debasement, and money types succeeding one another rapidly over time (Vansina 1973).

The Libinza are just one of several segmentary societies that stood astride the flows of money and goods, just as they stood astride a riverine ecology described as "flooded forests" and "floating savannas" (fig. 2.5). If there is an ideal ecology in which to study money flow, this must surely be it. Because they used the indigenous currency system until 1940, historical ethnography can reconstruct how it worked over time, and not just at one fixed time in an otherwise ahistorical precolonial past. The peoples of the region defy neat ethnic identification; "from one community to another, the socio-cultural changes are gradual, imperceptible" (Van Leynseele 1983, 33). All groups specialize in some good or expertise, and no group is self-sufficient for any major item in their way of life. Peoples who depend on canoes to go anywhere beyond their front doors have to acquire them from the forest; peoples who use iron currencies buy the bloom from smelters beyond their own borders; even specialists in pottery acquire the clay from elsewhere through purchase and transport by canoe.

The Van de Weyer collection, bought in 1913 in and around Bomana, provides a visual and tangible sense of multiplicity and interrelationship.

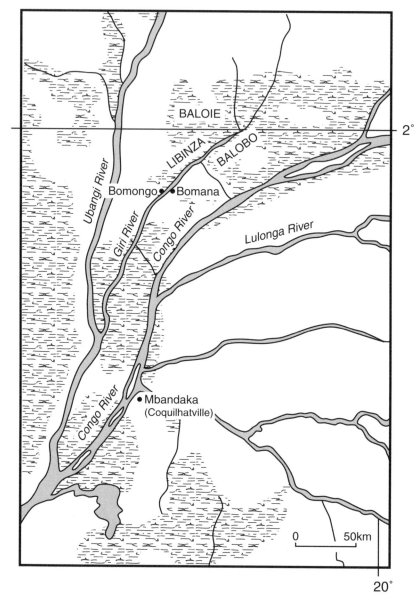

Figure 2.5. Map of the flooded forests and floating savannas
of the Ubangi–Congo confluence.

Table 2.1. Sample from the inventory of the Van de Weyer Collection

Object/ Number	Vernacular	Place found/ Tribe	Use	Value in indigenous money, in francs	Comments
Money 14528	Kwa	Bobeka "Samba"	The Bongenie forge *kwa*: the Libinza introduced them to the diverse Giri tribes	5 c'imes	Melted, forged
Money 14529	Kwa	"Samba"	id.	5 *kwa*, 20 c'imes	Former money, totally disappeared
Money 14530	Mongwango	"Baloie"	id.	30 *kwa*, 2 francs	Disappeared
Money 14531	Bokona	Bomana "Baloie"	id.	20 *kwa*, 1 franc	Money worth 20 *kwa*. Current use, partic. for traffic in wives
Money 14534	Monsea	Bomana "Baloie"	id.	50 *kwa*, 2.5 to 3 francs	Current use for transactions

First a note on the source itself, since it is unusual for an ethnographer to be so fortunate as to find an exactly apposite piece of historical information. Van de Weyer purchased the collection for the museum, noting for every item its nature, name in the local language, locus of purchase and "tribe," place of manufacture, and a series of other comments about use, value in local currency and in Belgian francs, and any further ethnographic notes. The list can be matched by number against the items in the museum collection (for a translation of a small part of this list, see table 2.1).

The sixty-eight items come from seven different groups; twelve are attributed to the Libinza. The collection shows a complexity and variety that far surpasses what we can reconstruct from the Tiv sources. It includes cloth; all manner of tools and weapons; personal items for comfort and elegance such as a headrest, a war bonnet, and a wig; musical instruments; and the raw materials and basic inputs for production—iron ore, a forge bellows, a coffer to put in a canoe. Items identified as money figure prominently: a Libinza brass wire, two Baloie iron machetes (different sizes and with different indigenous names), a Bomana "former money," another Baloie piece named *monsea*, and a slender forklike piece used as money by "diverse groups," named *djendu*, but also identified elsewhere as *kwa*. The collector's note on *kwa* claims "Made in Bongenie. The Libinza introduced them to the diverse groups of the Giri. The iron-ore comes from Bokombe on the Congo River." In fact, according to the list, everything was potentially purchasable with these *kwa*, which exchanged at the rate of twenty to the Belgian franc. Figure 2.6 is a scale drawing of three of the iron curren-

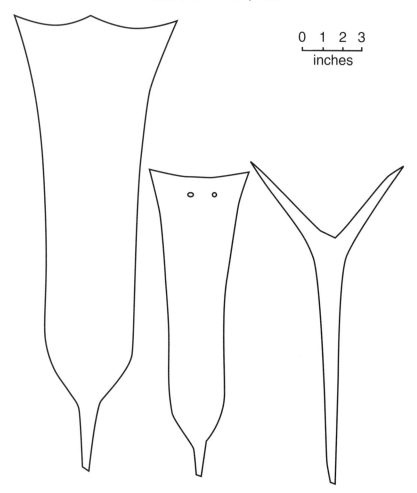

Figure 2.6. Three currency items from the Van de Weyer collection.
(Left to right): monsea, bokana, and kwa.

cies represented in the Van de Weyer collection, and the following list shows a gradient of prices for goods he bought, valued in *kwa*.

ITEM	PRICE IN *KWA*
Cudgel	None given
10 Spear heads	1
Bell	2
"Tool"	3
Trap	5
Raphia cloth	6
Antelope horn	25

Knife	50
Harpoon	80
Brass wire	100
Harpoon	300
Drum	1,000

One looks at the whole list and imagines a vast integrated market system, with a single circulating currency, specialized producers, and trade over quite short distances. But it is unclear, then, what the other monetary pieces were for. They hardly look like denominations, but if they are convertible into *kwa,* what else could they be? The historical view suggests, rather, an intricate multiplicity of currencies, microregions, ecological niches, and "ethnic" groups, linked at their peripheries to form a vast exchange corridor that originates in the Congo River and follows the Ubangi and its tributaries north toward its source. The *kwa* was not the only currency; it was simply the *moneta franca* of a very large region at the time the collection was made. Both the imported and locally manufactured currencies came from the Congo River. They made their way gradually upstream, undergoing physical, social, and symbolic transformations at every stage. Van Leynseele writes, "Every passage from one sphere to another constituted a threshold. . . . The same as for things, ideas and fashions were accepted or rejected, transmitted and diffused" (1983, 78). Even the most minor transaction was an asymmetrical conversion in the sense that it assumed directionality; it referred back to a place, a localized value and a past, and was endowed with a new attribute in the transaction that afforded "candidacy" (to cite Appadurai 1986) for travel along new pathways. The multiple coexisting currencies symbolized, mediated, and were themselves items in the directional orientation of the flow of goods. In every case, either the final money forms or the materials to make them originated from outside Libinza society. All were, in fact, interconvertible through denominational processes, but at any one time, each currency within each group was more or less oriented toward one kind of transaction versus another. In principle, at any one time only one currency in each society mediated social payments—fines, bridewealth, and so on—and others mediated the purchase of utilities such as foodstuffs and productive investments such as canoes. Now we can add the historical dynamic. Each group negotiated its moneys of social payment at one frontier and its purchases of utilities at others. The currency one used for a canoe purchase on one frontier was not the same as the currency one acquired through the sale of fish on another or that was in use "internally" for payments. The kinds of currency involved in each kind of transaction shifted over time as new items were introduced at the Congo end of the corridor. Because of the river trade's capacity to bring endless novelties, the system was probably intrinsically inflationary, with each currency gradually declining in value as the volume in circulation within a payment system grew. Note that these were not destructible moneys, unless they were buried with the dead, so eventually passing them on — by demotion to the purchase of utilities upstream, where novelty value still held — was critically important in safeguarding value.

Historical work is unanimous that the rate of introduction of new currency goods picked up at the end of the nineteenth century, but the basic process of inflation and monetary change was intrinsic all along as a result of the merchants' attempt to find optimal conditions of profit. The "consistent rises in price between the market nearest the input of the good and the market furthest away from it" (Vansina 1973, 296) that are characteristic of asymmetrical exchange were brought under intermittent pressure as new goods were introduced downstream. This resulted in a currency waterfall effect, going in the direction opposite the flow of the river. Van Leynseele writes: "The introduction of a new money, its depreciation, and its replacement by another money is a continual process. Each of these new objects coming from the River and its acquisition permitted considerable profit. . . . Used first of all exclusively as a means of payment, when they depreciated and lost status they continued to be used for current purchases" (1983, 88). A cross-sectional view at a single moment catches a developmental process in a confusing snapshot and misses the intricate architecture made up not of the two or three vertically ranged moral spheres and clear ethnic boundaries of a structural model but of a moving flow across a multiplicity of spatio-hierarchical thresholds, each offering — as long as the system was constantly growing and changing — the possibility of gain.

There were substantial systemic and technological gains as people innovated in items that could cross thresholds. The Libinza expanded the use of iron currencies, which gave them access to dugout canoes from the forest, iron tools, and a variety of foods and livestock, and eventually created the conditions for constructing a canal, about thirty kilometers long, to open up direct access from their home territory on the Giri River to the main stream of the Congo. They continued to produce smoked fish, packed in standard baskets, that was sold into the entire region, and then went into trade as well. They bought ivory, slaves, and livestock from up-country and from the Congo, and textiles, beads, and above all brass goods from Europe. "The Libinza had the monopoly on importation of brass in the middle and upper reaches of the Ngiri" (Van Leynseele 1979b, 125). Without centralized conspicuous consumption to circulate monetary goods, they plunged into a multiplicity of conversions across the ethnic lines of the "almost thirty discrete groups" (Van Leynseele 1979a, 167) of the region, an "immense" and growing population, participating in an intensification of its entire economy. In spite of this pattern of responsive economic growth, the ethnographer insists that this architecture of multiple thresholds and conversions should prevent us from designating even such a pervasively commercialized regional trade as a "market economy" of the uniform-currency, modernist kind (Van Leynseele 1983, 78).

Many of the sources on Equatorial Africa point out that these intra-regional divisions of labor are not simply deducible from ecological comparative advantage. Economic autarky was possible in many environments, but specialization flourished nevertheless. Exchange was not only a way of getting goods and turning a conversion but also a way of validating the broader meaning of value conversions in regional social and political relations. Some of these dynamics are understandable in terms of asymmetries in the power to control demographic reproduction. For example, Georges Dupré writes of the Nzabi, "Each ethnic group in the trade had a field of action that was clearly delimited by barriers of all kinds" (1972, 621). Tsengi iron producers insisted on getting wives for iron and refused to give up women in return (1972, 639), in a way that reminds us of Fardon's expansion on the Tiv ethnography. "Akiga vividly describes the refusal of the Tiv to recognize reciprocity in women with non-Tiv" (Fardon 1984, 9) when they acquired wives from outside. But deeper concepts were also at play. Kriger writes that although "iron seems to have passed through cultural and economic boundaries with ease" (1999, 96), as if by simply "rational" negotiation, in fact iron-working was everywhere associated with the occult, and with cosmic conceptions of the relationship between male and female, order and disorder. The blacksmiths moved iron goods "back and forth between money and commodity operations, serving as currency in closing transactions and as a useful raw material in manufacturing" (Kriger 1999, 96), which suggest to Herbert a "definition of power . . . [that] emphasizes the means by which selected individuals are thought to gain access to and control over people and resources through their mastery over transformative processes" (1993, 3), that is, over conversions.

It was not only calculation and political power that created the spatial geography of exchange but also the ideology of transformation that undergirded it. The capacity to define, institutionalize, take advantage of, technically control, and symbolically represent conversions is at the heart of the extensive regional transaction systems that every autonomous polity built up in the stepwise relations that connected the interior to the changing currency flows of the great trade routes. The pattern of action may partially track what one might predict from functional models based on parsimonious universal assumptions about human behavior: scarcity and demand, returns to risk, or the cost of trust. But the behavior was not generated through those terms of negotiation. Imputing them not only misrepresents the kind of reasoning characteristic of these transactions but it leaves key features unaddressed. Ethnographic skepticism about the adequacy of theoretical models and faithful attention to the evidence serve to open up a new domain of enquiry. In Equatorial Africa one has to take seriously that asymmetry in monetary exchange was understood and expected; it was not masked by a market ideology of equivalence or calculated justifications that reduced the margin to something else (returns to labor, risk, and so on). To the contrary, it was often dramatized.

It is worth turning to one of the most striking ethnographic examples of directional asymmetry in monetary exchange, that of the *bilaba* of the Bulu-Beti-Fang group of Southern Cameroon and Gabon. Georges Balandier attempted to establish the *bilaba* as an exemplar of a "total social phenomenon," like the potlatch or the *kula,* and it certainly would have been considered a vital part of the conceptual repertoire in economic anthropology if it had been described earlier and in greater detail. Without such an ideal type as a model, we in African studies are recurrently confused when we try to apply the repertoire we have from other places. For example, in 1999 Kriger writes tellingly of bridewealth, that it "remains a poorly understood topic in African economic history . . . sometimes described as 'gift giving,' other times . . . to commercial purchase." She goes on to confess that "how distinct or overlapping were the so-called economic spheres of gift and commodity exchange will not be discussed at length here, mainly because precise historical data for the nineteenth century are still so sparse" (1999, 197). A specific case of simultaneous material advantage and symbolic reference, of money and meaning, of autonomy and asymmetry can help to bring into historical and ethnographic focus the otherwise philosophical quality of Equatorial culture that so many ethnographers have referred to in one way or another—the Bantu codefinition of resemblance and difference (M.-C. Dupré 1995, 192; Aniakor 1996).

CONVERSIONS IN A DRAMATIC VOICE: FANG *BILABA*

The full range of West African drama in trade transactions has not yet been defined. Between the "silent trade," which has been partially demystified as hidden brokerage by Moraes Farias (1974) and the "total prestation" I turn to now, there may be a continuum of performative artistic practice. Performance is particularly striking in the Equatorial region. The Fang of Gabon are famous in Europe for their reliquary sculpture. Among their many other originalities was production of iron currency while having "absolutely no commercial tradition" (Alexandre and Binet 1958, 33). *Bilaba* was the institution that moved goods across the natural and social frontiers of the great Equatorial forest. Unlike the Melanesian *kula,* it could not be restudied in full detail as ethnographic sophistication grew and new questions arose, but in its heyday—between the late eighteenth and late nineteenth centuries—bilaba was a major regional institution. As if to exemplify its encompassing nature, ethnographers Philippe Laburthe-Tolra and James Fernandez both describe bilaba under several different headings: as a payment, a "dramatic integration of monetary exchange," and a "trading institution" (Fernandez 1980, 137, 139); as a ritual of competitive consumption that created alliances (Laburthe-Tolra 1981, 224); and as a "transformation of economic inequality [between headmen] into a politico-sexual inequality" (Laburthe-Tolra 1981, 361). Bilaba encompassed all these functions, and much more.

Balandier's (1961) account is the fullest. Competitive exchange was staged between two headmen who were symbolically and geographically differentiated from one another, who offered entirely different goods in the exchange. One side was identified with the north and west, the right hand, the external, the male, and the goods of the import trade; the other was identified with the south and east, the left, the internal, the female, and "traditional goods." The gifts and countergifts competed but were never equivalent in all respects. According to Balandier, "Confronting the partner said to be 'of the exterior,' who brought durable manufactured goods (textiles, guns, ironmongery, etc.) and the iron monies used in the past for matrimonial exchange, was the partner said to be 'of the interior' who brought the products of traditional activities destined for consumption (sheep, chickens, palm kernels, groundnuts etc.) as well as trade goods (ivory, and then cacao in the modern era)" (1961, 28). It is particularly interesting that currency was conceptualized with the goods of the trade, as "exterior" and male, even though, unlike the Tiv brass rods, these did not originate at the coast; they were produced all over the countryside by expert iron smelters and blacksmiths. The distinctions were local and conceptual, and they indexed to the history of the Atlantic trade without being wholly determined by it.

These categories have been adapted to new goods in the twentieth century. Fernandez gives a modern example of a bilaba kind of exchange, from a mortuary ritual. A "sister's son" of the bereaved lineage, taking the male side, contributed a bottle of wine, a sheet and light blanket, a shirt, two cloths, and 335 francs. "And then he gave another seven thousand francs and began to dance bilaba in earnest to the cheers of the crowd" (1980, 140). Another sister's son was only allowed to dance bilaba after he had augmented his gift substantially in response to criticism. The president of the meeting gave each a bottle of wine and a duck in return—a symbolic reference to the country goods of the past. Bilaba required an honorable level of giving; one's gifts had to qualify. Even in this curtailed modern version, bilaba combined pride and humility, giving away and acquiring, antagonism and generosity. It was intrinsically and compulsorily asymmetrical.

Fernandez is worth quoting at length on the social context of bilaba, even though the main institution was defunct by the time he did fieldwork.

> Among Fang, two different clans . . . whose interests were fundamentally opposed, yet linked themselves together systematically so as to find common interest. Self-interest was transmuted into system interest in part by dramatic and often ritualized processes of transformation. The institution of bilaba . . . throws light on the problem. . . . [It] insured continuing exchange of goods and . . . united alien social units in so doing, containing their implicit antagonisms by expressing them in patterned ways. (1980, 138)

Laburthe-Tolra adds that men deemed worthy of leadership were those "able to unite within themselves all these diverse qualities and to sufficiently influence the multitude of independent headmen to orient them towards common purposes" (1981, 362). Through this culture and sociology of competitive precedence among equals, where ranking and autonomy codetermined one another, substantial merchandise was moved from the coast to the hinterland and from the forest to the trading centers. In its historical origin in the expansionary moment of the eighteenth century, and on the coast (at Kribi), and in its asymmetrical symbolism, bilaba exemplifies key features of many African conversionary institutions in the period before colonial rule. So, apart from their intrinsic fascination, these Equatorial economies offer key insights into the operation of thresholds of conversion. First: Bohannan's vertically arranged spheres of exchange are a subtype of a much larger phenomenon, and one that is associated not with ancestral cultural premises but with experience in multiple currency economies in an expanding and inflationary, externally oriented, commercial economy. Second: negotiation on thresholds was profitable, and difference was thereby a resource to be cultivated. Third: thresholds could be socially positioned and validated in different ways as long as there was a disjuncture of some sort; they could consist primarily of status difference, of ethnicity or dialect, of location upstream or downstream, or of ecological niche. In fact, the terms of difference could be partial transformations and indices of each other, always under re-creation and thereby always partially discrepant. With respect to exchange, they appear as barriers but they function as facilitators by setting the terms, that is, the premium to be paid for access. Finally, they were connected to conversions in a European economic practice that all scholars must now surely accept as "unequal exchange" (Amin 1976).

CONVERSIONS IN A EUROPEAN VOICE

Neither the Tiv nor the Libinza dealt directly with Europe, but eventually the European stretch of monetary flows needs incorporating. Europeans created and tended their own barriers to the flow of monies and goods, which were as complex and symbolic as those of bilaba. Two examples offer themselves, one going in each direction: the import into Africa of a batch of outdated guns as currency in the 1880s, and the conversion of Fang funerary statuary acquired in the early years of this century, in Europe, into capital in the strict sense of the term.

Working on a different project I ran across the following incident, written up verbatim in the records of the Discourses and Opinions of Jules Ferry, French president of the Council, minister for public instruction and fine arts, in 1883. Under a law of December 28, 1882, Minister Duclerc opened up a credit account of 1,275,000 francs for Savorgnan de Brazza's mission to the Congo, "to assure the installation, upkeep and supply of stations, upkeep of means of transportation and purchase of diplomatic gifts. In addition, it was understood that a certain quantity of arms, of outdated [hors d'usage] model, would be given to the explorer to dispose of as barter" (Robiquet 1897, 140). The government submitted a law to the Chamber that would allow the Ministry of Finance (Direction des Domaines) to cede for free the following arms to be acquired from the minister of war: 100,000 "armes à percussion et à canon lisse," of diverse models, 20,000 sabers, 1,000 hatchets, powder, gunshot, and so forth. The transaction was voted on and passed without objection.

When the guns were delivered, however, de Brazza did not want to accept them because these were guns *à percussion* and the people of the Congo would consent to accept only guns *à silex*. Silex guns use a flint stone. They were completely phased out in the French army in the 1830s. Percussion arms were their replacement and used a metal-to-metal contact to set off the charge via a new kind of fulminant powder. They were supposedly less likely to misfire. In theory they would be more valuable, but there must have been conditions within Africa to make the older model more desirable (Ken Alder, personal communication): perhaps familiarity; perhaps blacksmiths' capacity to repair them; perhaps availability of gunpowder. At this point "a convention" was reached between the French minister for public instruction and one M. Janssen, an arms dealer of Liège in Belgium, the latter agreeing to buy the 100,000 guns from the French government and give to de Brazza, in exchange, 25,000 guns *à silex* and a certain number of other arms. If the story had stopped there, undoubtedly the scholar would have had to leaf through a haystack of business records to discover the way in which three ministries, a national assembly, several instruments of public finance, and an international convention transformed 1822 model rifles, sixty years later, in line with—as Jules Ferry put it—the banal fact that "all travelers know and all explorers utilize" that "guns . . . constitute the circulating currency in black countries" (Robiquet 1897, 141). Fortunately for scholarship, one deputy challenged the decision, reproaching the government for "mixing with the market, and furthermore, for not addressing the national industry." Ferry had to explain the arms market, with its national specialties, making clear that for the new purchases the government had observed impeccable procedures of asking for samples and prices, and of having them vetted by a specialist. For getting rid of the old guns, they had actually acted most loyally in that the articles in question were otherwise sellable only as scrap on the French market, and M. Janssen was willing to offer a higher price, which made the deal advantageous for the Treasury, via the accounts of the Ministry of Public Education, which mediated the deal. At this point Ferry takes a moment to address the anomaly of his ministry—of public education and fine arts—dealing with arms purchases for Africa; he explains that "the mission of M. de Brazza is peaceful in character, and for that reason the credits were inscribed in the ministry of public instruction and fine arts" (Robiquet 1897, 143).

We have here a window on the commodity and trade conditions in Europe at the same time as the Libinza were moving iron currencies—and probably guns as well—upriver. The unusual complexity of the deal shows clearly how value, meaning, and control are attributed at key conversion points, bringing whole institutional complexes into play. In this case, scrap metal owned by a European public institution was transformed into currency for the segmentary societies of the Congo, via a process that called into action several ministries, the international arms market, conventions of tender and bidding, grades and standards, and an act of the national democratic chamber of deputies. Attributes of value and meaning were both given and taken away—trash to treasure—in several contentious stages.

We lose track of this batch of guns in Africa. If there really had been 25,000 of them, they might have armed a good proportion of the adult male Fang population of the time. If the guns were as poor quality as Inikori (1977) suggests for the arms imported into Africa in the eighteenth century, people would be fortunate to have used them for currency alone. The reader of Laburthe-Tolra's (1977, 1981) ethnography of the Beti can imagine that it is one of de Brazza's guns that figures in a transformed capacity, from anonymity to singularity, as a named component of a bridewealth payment. Wherever they ended up, undoubtedly a series of transformations of value must have moved them into circuits of exchange for which the Libinza perhaps provide a model. On both sides then, there are similarly complex maneuvers, a sequence of negotiable steps and monetary techniques through which conversions are effected.

My second example moves in the other direction, from Africa to Europe: the conversion of a Fang statue into capital. Like most other "primitive art," Fang statuary was acquired for European museums and private collectors mainly in a major rush in the first decades of the twentieth century. The value disparity was radical. While the carving represented value for the European buyers, in the Fang social context the statues guarded the baskets of ancestral bones on which they stood or sat. To the people, the real value was in the bones, not the statues.

The search for authentic African art and artifacts arose out of the colonial project of collecting, studying, classifying, and ultimately also dominating. Two connected innovations in Europe started to raise the value of Fang statuary to a different level than that associated with museum nationalism. Picasso acknowledged the inspiration he had found in the "Negro pieces" (Hunter and Jacobus 1977, 136) in a museum for the conceptualization of *Les demoiselles d'Avignon,* his first major cubist piece, painted in 1907. In fact, he was photographed in his studio with a statue in the background. After the war, investment in the art market picked up, and there developed an extraordinary capitalization of art as an asset, not only for national representation (resulting in theft in World War II) but as personal property, valued, insured, and entering into networks of recording and pricing. The fame of each owner adds to the value of any piece on the market, so that when it comes onto the auction block, its "provenance" of successive owners is an intrinsic part of the description of the piece. Fang statuary was relatively rare as well as carrying the symbolic value of association with the cubist movement. Fernandez and Fernandez have estimated that the total production of quality carvings produced in the two centuries from 1750 to 1950 can only have been about four thousand, of which perhaps fifteen hundred represent the "extant collection of Fang ancestor pieces" (1975, 724). This low number may reflect massive missionary destruction and not just parsimony of production and the happenstance of survival in tropical conditions, but detailed scholarship on the complex interplay of European damage and gain with respect to African art is still ongoing.

The construction of the markets in art, personal fame, and institutional probity as realizable assets means that each symbolic quality adds to the price. Each owner is a threshold, a point at which value scales are commensurated in new ways, of value added or lost. In the case of a "superb Fang Reliquary Figure" sold at Christie's on October 16, 1992, it had been owned by René Mendes-France (possibly a relative of the French president, Pierre Mendes-France), one Morris Pinto, and the British Rail Pension Fund. So stable and high had its value risen that this reliquary's "social life" intersects with the rise and consolidation of a major monetary technique of twentieth-century capitalism — supporting worker loyalty and social peace while putting major investment funds into the capital markets — namely,

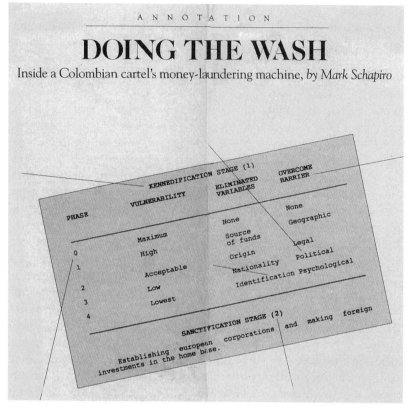

Figure 2.7. Financial pathways in the present: Money laundering.

the pension fund. The final selling price at Christie's was $550,000.[1] Again, like de Brazza's guns, this is a banal case. But it is one for which we can trace out all the steps along the pathway: the shifts in value and the reconfiguration of attributes, most tellingly its attributes as capital in a complex of monetary techniques.

In case it seems a far-fetched argument that Tiv conversions are connected, in their characteristics and in their actual history, to conversions in capitalist economies, let me give a couple of recent examples. Every now and then the newspapers oblige our interests just at the right time. Campaign financing: "D'Amato Converted Donations," reads a *New York Times* article from January 1997, complete with a chart of pathways for "following the money," through "funnels" to "soft money" accounts. Mark Schapiro's chart of bank transactions for money laundering, published in *Harper's*, recapitulates all the components of conversions: phases of a pathway, barriers (or

1. I am indebted to Christraud Geary for the information on this sale.

thresholds), attributes added or subtracted, commensuration nevertheless taking place, and a final destination being achieved (fig. 2.7). Although constructed and expressed in African terms, conversions are part of the repertoire of monetary techniques of capitalism, in particular of merchant and financial capitalism.

CONVERSIONS IN THE ABSTRACT

Bohannan leaves the reader with paradoxes: in their home context, conversions are morally problematic and yet "not only is conversion possible, but it is encouraged" (1959, 498); conversions are made through the use of quantified currencies (cloth and brass rods), and yet "[c]onversion depends on the fact that some items of every sphere could, on certain occasions, be used in exchanges in which the return was *not* considered equivalent (ishe)" (1959, 496–97; see also 1955, 65). Rather than accept these co-existences as paradoxes, I think the historical and ethnographic records are now strong enough for us to make another claim: that nonequivalent exchange, through the use of quantifiable currencies, was a familiar institution in West and Equatorial Africa, to which the spread of currencies may well have profoundly contributed. People gained familiarity with negotiating intervals, performing precedence and exchanging goods and services that were explicitly *not* the match of each other while still measuring value on a monetary scale. Numeration of things and qualities, judgment of relative value, and classification into categories are all at issue. I turn to them in the next three chapters.

PART II

SCALES AND TROPES

The very idea of asymmetry implies the preexistence of measures and of means to bring them together. In Atlantic Africa, neither the measures nor the means of equation were conceptualized, institutionalized, and repeatedly sanctioned by the state and financial institutions. The struggle for control over measures and reductions in the West is central to political economy and political philosophy, as studies of particular moments (e.g., Caffentizis 1989 on John Locke) and of the whole sweep of modernist thinking (e.g., Hart 2001) show. Before analysis can focus on analogous struggles in Atlantic Africa, there is a logical need to describe the measures and mediations themselves, looking at each element separately as a construct.

The possible repertoire of measurement scales that could be relevant to monetary transactions is much larger than I can address with the archive available, and should certainly include the temporality I bring up in the concluding section. The three scales I examine here are numeration, ranking of people, and categorization of commodities by kind and by quality. I use a straightforward concept of scale, or register, although a deeper philosophical analysis might find other scalar principles specific to Africa. Although I work with standard scales — nominal, ordinal, interval, and ratio scales — my invocation of the concept of tropes (linkage points or thresholds) refers to my argument that scales contain the conceptual "hooks" for linkages from one to the other, without reduction to a common denominator. A specific measure can take on one or another form — nominal versus ordinal, interval versus ratio — according to the situation. I start with number: the ratio scale that allows all forms of computation. Its use has been more pervasive in Atlantic African transactions than is usually given credit, because of the striking quality of practices such as "assortment" bargaining and conceptual stabilization in fictional units. Its importance was always implicit in the formalist interpretations of economic history, although it tends to be inferred rather than documented directly. New work on number suggests that numerical scales were not simply incremental, however, but contained tropic points that make them work more like intervals. The distances between two points may be measured, but the entire scale is not calculated on a single axis, in relation to a zero point, thus making its matching to other scales a matter of "fit." My second scale is based on ordinal ranking — of people. Here, the main principle is relative value on a spiritual scale. Again there are tropic points, in this case creating hooks into interval and even ratio scales. In Igbo and Ibibio history, the monetary calculus was complexly but clearly matched against an unusually ratio-like spirituality, through the importance of sacrifice. Finally, all commodification depends on nominal categories. People are transacting "something." One nominal scale quite common in West Africa that may bridge into ordinality is the depiction of things by terms that can invoke their chronology. The other obvious valuational scale that integrates with nominalization in the market is quality.

Chapters 3–5 are examples of scales and tropes, worked up from existing archival and fieldwork evidence.

3

CALCULATION
NUMBER AND ASYMMETRY

In conversions, commodities and money move in their own directions rather than circulating within a circumscribed social field. Tiv could exchange cloth to the northwest but not to the south; cattle moved to the northeast, and brass rods could go either to the northwest or the south; and so on, in probably much more complex and historically shifting patterns than are represented in the published sources. Horses and slaves were in transit from the north to the southeast in the late nineteenth century, as I discuss in the next chapter. The Giri River system was basically an upriver/downriver system, patterned over ecological variation between forest and savanna, but with specialist developments and ethnic distinctions that reduced neatly to neither. These examples modify two simple and tempting reductionisms—that asymmetries are necessarily either a fact of fixed cultural difference or a simple function of fluctuating political power. Directional asymmetry can be expressed in either of these modes, or it can remain culturally and politically neutral. It can be exploited for the pooling of gains in specific geographical and social places (accumulation), or it can encourage boundless terrains of distribution over very large regions. Asymmetry is a translatable quality, a potential, whose realization depends on the definition of *here, there,* and the pathway between them. Conversion does not necessarily presume or promote social inequality, although that is always one possibility. It could be useful to elevate dramatic instances of asymmetrical exchange, such as *bilaba,* to an ideal type for comparative purposes because the asymmetry is symbolically enacted. In African social history, however, conversions belong to a larger and more mundane category of commodity exchanges that involve the regular practice of linking disjunctive value registers. When one scale is not exactly reducible to the terms of another, a margin for gain lies in the negotiation of situational matching. The gain can be either conventionalized or singularized, recognized or concealed, foregrounded or backgrounded, depending on context.

In Atlantic Africa, the most basic condition for realizing these ambiguous (to us) potentials lies in the conceptual separation, the nonreductive quality, of scales of classification and valuation. Every "commensuration"

(Espeland and Stevens 1998) remains open for revisiting, and this potential is in some sense alluded to even when there are accepted conventions for matching one scale of value to another: the numerical scale of amounts, the ordinal scale of quality, the nominal scale of classification. In modernity, number has been made unambiguous and infinitely calculable on a ratio scale by generations of mathematical innovation. Number has also been progressively discovered as one key to the physical world and hence mandated as a universal measure and legally enforced as the common denominator of transactional equivalence. Competing measures and scales that predate number have been restandardized or abolished (Kula 1986). The accommodation of nominal and ordinal scales that are logically, although not necessarily historically, prior to the ratio scale has been more complex. Scalar representations of judgmental concepts — of the goods at issue (quality), of the services they bring (utility, benefit) and the costs their acquisition incurs (risk) — have to be reformulated to be expressed numerically. Some reductions of scalar value to number are historical events, the results of political proclamation. Others are continuously institutionalized by dramatic performances, such as competitions, which in turn ripple out their effects into new scalar formations: for rules of qualification as well as excellence, for judges, for arenas, for training institutions, for materials, for expertise in the materials, and so on. Formal competitions are relentless generators of new scales of value by drawing participants and audience into a scalar logic, a monetary logic, and a mode of binding the two. Gradations are assigned a numerical referent, which affects prize money, stud fees, consultancy fees, access to other resources such as book contracts and foreign markets, and so on. Even when the numerical translation of the ordinal scale is implausible — beauty from 1 to 10? two 5's of beauty as good as one 10? — the capacity of numbers to express other values is now a hegemonic idea in the modern economy, enforced by law and inculcated by competitions and professional organizations. After initial struggles over the terms for each new domain (orchids, aerobics, for example), the equation of qualitative and monetary scales eventually erases the constructions and disjunctures that have been overridden. It is only by a massive discounting of the "tournament of value" that we can retain the notion of the theoretical dominance of supply and demand in "markets" as the main representation of the operations of value in modern economies.

Without this relentless formalization in a money economy, all three of these standards — nominal, ordinal, and interval — remain available in the conceptual repertoire, to be indexed to each other situationally and in nonreductive ways when money is brought into the evaluation process. This has implications for number itself. All relevant measures are potentially at play in a transaction: the nature of the good and its self-presentation (both in nature and in current measurable form); the level of its technical quality; its desirability relative to other goods; and the numerical summary of all this, as a conceptual summation and an actual transaction. People do calculate and mediate exchanges in routine fashions, even with this indeterminacy. They are not "seasick" all the time; conventions and institutions form as the transactional density increases. But generalizations are still better approached as "outcomes" of "routines in micro-worlds" (Verran 2001, 159–62) than as ethnosemantic rules. A number term is at least two kinds of abstraction: a numerical concept and a word in a lexicon. Some number words indicate the movement of counting, the receptacle for carrying, or the purpose of spending. The number scales of Atlantic Africa also include conceptual hooks for linking to measures of other things. Verran has argued on philosophical grounds that whereas number in Western thinking appears "as a dazzling, single purity" (2001, 109), to include African concepts number is better seen as an order of what she terms "clots," in which "an old series of gestures is [still] recognizable" (2001, 11). Her approach opens up the historical and ethnographic library in new ways. A clot is composed of what? Is understood and manipulated how? I suggest that the pursuit of gain is one of the contexts in which the "old series of gestures" was constituted and which marks numerical concepts and practices profoundly. Gain is a challenge: to get, to conceptualize, to justify. Some degree of optative freedom for linking number to object is a resource not just for making material gains but also for representing them in meaningful terms such as number.

Evidence suggests that there developed a pervasive and relatively stable culture of commensuration and calculation over the growth of commoditization in the Atlantic region. I illustrate this argument in two sections. First, I summarize the classic examples from African trade history. Second, following Verran, I look at enactments. In the apparent absence of detailed oral sources or historical records on African commercial calculation in the past, I look at recent sources to explore how numerical and monetary scales are used in practice, giving examples of (a) conventionalized equations, (b) resistance to modernist forms of standardization without rejecting number altogether, and (c) numerical approaches to excess and chance. This is all provisional. A great deal of ethnographic exploration, linguistic elicitation, and philosophical analysis still needs to be done on the linguistics and the mathematics of oral calculation systems. Considering their enormous importance for economic dynamics, it is hard to understand why we Africanists (and I include myself here) have all neglected this subject for so long (although exceptions are cited as I proceed).

NUMERICAL SCALES IN AFRICAN HISTORY

I start from a well-known summary of African counting, in which geographical directionality is clearly crucial:

The cowries were generally counted in groups of five, and then piled into "hundreds." But a "hundred" might be 60, 80 or 100, according to the local convention. Although the Bambara called 8 × 10 cowries *keme*, they also used *keme* to identify the number 10 × 10 when counting objects other than cowries. . . . A more convincing explanation . . . is that the profit is built into the numeration system. . . . An *ackie* [a standard weight of gold valued at 480 cowries] of goods at the coast sold for *soa* [720 cowries], the basic weight of the Asante system, at the first great market to the north as one traveled up the Niger River. At the next market the price was a *gros* [960 cowries], and beyond the Niger bend it was a large *mithqal* [1,200 cowries]. Goods flowed north as gold flowed south and the profits were built into the currency system. (Zaslavsky 1973, 73, based on Johnson 1970)

The same goods were "differently" valued by an equation of terms from the various languages: *ackie* = *soa* = *gros* = *mithqal,* spanning gold values from approximately 0.06 to 0.15 ounces and 480 to 1,200 cowries. The nominal equation could also be expressed as a numerical equation, independent of kinds of goods, places, and transactors. All could be translated into different ethnic-linguistic twelves: the *mithqal* was twelve Muslim hundreds (12 × 100), the *gros* was twelve Bambara hundreds (12 × 80), the *soa* was twelve Mandingo hundreds (12 × 60), and the *ackie* was twelve strings of cowries (12 × 40). The numerical concept of twelve has a constancy that the concept of hundred does not. So it is not just a question of a term from a numerical scale in one language being used as a quasi-nominal term at the interface with another, but of certain key numerical concepts having conventional lability that others did not, across entire regions. Numbers therefore have differential values attached to them and are differentially available for mediating the disjunctures between the value registers on which gain depends. Disjunctures between scales are optatively presentable as offering one margin, or another, or none (i.e., as expressing equivalence), depending on the lexicon applied.

Specific criteria define the points at which scales can be matched. Scale thresholds are one such criterion. In Segu in the Sahel, for goods of 99 cowries one paid 99 cowries; for 100 one paid only 80; for 1,000 one paid 800 (a simple multiple of 100) but for 100,000, only 64,000 (Johnson 1970, 40). This numeration recognizes two thresholds of trade volume, each of the three resulting levels being characterized by a different exchange rate, offering different levels of gain on retail sales. In effect, three kinds of trader are implicitly recognized: the retailer at the bottom, the local wholesaler in the middle, and the interregional dealer at the top. For other purposes, of course, the numerical scale can be conceptualized as continuous. The three-tier system could certainly be a version of practices that honor the Muslim avoidance of profit, *riba*. But it is practiced much more broadly than the Muslim world. Elsewhere, a similar means of incorporating margins depended on creation of conventional collective units of goods in a material summary of numerical form, where the actual composition could deviate in well-understood ways. For example, in Dahomey, close to the coast and non-Muslim, "strung cowries were one cowry short of the nominal 40, the reward to the stringer for the work of piercing and stringing the shells." This equation of one string = "40" = 39 was further manipulated at the palace by the king's stringers, reducing the number per string by three or even six, meaning that one string = "40" = 34, giving the king an extra margin of five without the nominal price of an item in strings changing (Johnson 1970, 45). In both cases, particular numbers mark potential threshold conditions, which in turn index to ordinal status differences.

Alternate ways of using the numerical terms speak volumes about trade relations. Any negotiation along the Asante–Bambara–Niger bend route that started with twelves, hundreds, or strings had already accepted the principle of the margin. On the other hand, any negotiation that started from ones, or introduced any other numerical term, would be throwing the gainfulness of the transaction into implicit question or opening up new spaces for nonconventionalized gain. It is quite likely that such conventions of numeration were also worked out in the trading segmentary societies. Igbo, Ibibio, and Niger Delta peoples have a very long commercial history whose financial concepts have not yet been studied in detail, although there are clues. Sources suggest that there were different monetary conventions along "every river" (Jones 1958, 50). One area is reported to have had a numerical scale entirely devoted to money, distinct from the numbering of other things (Jeffreys 1954). The complexity of Eastern Nigeria monetary systems that I address in chapter 4 is powerful indirect evidence of numerical complexity. Certainly one should look for ways in which numerical thresholds acquired conceptual constancy quite widely within and across trade watersheds. Through the indeterminate match of name and number, equivalence and rank order can coexist. Number can mask or display either quality, never entirely erasing the possibility of knowing and counting in an alternate manner.

In spite of patchy academic attention, one can see principles of conceptual stabilization in many places. A famous description by Baba of Karo, for Hausaland in Northern Nigeria, shows the conceptual linkages in relation to both trade and the state:

> The tax was paid in cowries . . . counted in "mats" . . . containing 20,000 cowries . . . 20,000 cowries was one hundred pennies . . . a dyer paid 2,000 cowries for every dyepit he had. . . . To count cowry shells they spread

them out on the floor. They counted in groups of five; ten groups of five were fifty . . . into groups of two hundred. Ten compounds of two hundred were two thousand . . . when they were arranged in compounds you started to sew up mats. One mat . . . was a man's load. (Smith 1965, 80)

That is, 200 = 1 compound = 1 penny; 2,000 = 10 compounds = tax on 1 dyepit; 20,000 = 10 × 10 compounds = 1 mat = 1 headload. Compounds, dyepit taxes, mats, headloads all index to other scales, some of which may be simply nominal (compounds versus some other grouping, without reference to size at all); some may be ordinal (possibly mats, or dyepits, as judged as bigger or smaller, more or less ornate or well located, rather than by precise measures); a headload may also be ordinal, implicitly by volume or weight, or another kind of load (by donkey?), or some combination with distance to be carried.

One does not see the ramifying set of measurement scales, but the tropic number of 200, where linkage tends to focus, is in plain view. The threshold number of 200 links the Hausa system to the numerical system of the Yoruba, who were major trading partners to the south. Two hundred *(ogún, igba)* refers to an area of 200 heaps on a farm (usually itself called *igba*, or in some places, *adé*) and to a road toll *(igbió: igba-ẹyọ,* that is, 200 cowries), as well as being a key calculation number and an idiom in proverbs. According to one of the first published papers on Yoruba numbers, *igba* derives from the verb *gbá,* to sweep, referring to the practice of counting cowries into fives, and each pile of 5 into groups of 20 until two piles of 100 had been formed, which were swept together into *igba,* 200. The kinetics of counting remains embedded in the numerical concept. Multiples of 200 were very common in trade (Mann 1887, 60). Mann notes that Yoruba numeration contains a large number of basic concepts, and therefore several optional ways of expressing higher values through multiplication, addition, and subtraction. The preferential term for high numbers often employs *igba,* mainly, he argues, because its multiplicands make "fluent words" (1887, 63), poetically pronounceable as a compounded string of terms. Threshold numerical concepts are also used allusively in poetic speech. A Yoruba sack *(àpò* or *òkè,* a headload), originally of 20,000 cowries and later of five shillings, could be lifted out and used allusively, as in "losses in battle are remembered as 'two sacks of ——'" (Johnson 1970, 46).

That such a number might be "accurate" only in a plus–minus fashion was transparent in the kind of conventional margin in Bambara monetary accounting, in poetic approximation, and in allusion to the artisanship of measurement. But it also reflected the fact that, in trade, the base unit was not usually broken once it had been composed. Mann describes numeration in trade proceeding up through the threshold numbers, in fives, tens, and other collective units, thus avoiding "the inconvenience of cumbersome numerals"

(1887, 62). Greater specification was made by subtraction and addition, and only when necessary. "Five" was pragmatically "one": "one five." Numbers were rounded to establish gains and discounts. For example, Johnson writes of cowry inflation: "By the end of the [nineteenth] century, when exchange rates had dropped even lower, 1,000 cowries were valued at 3d in silver; but a penny was worth 300 only" (1970, 46). In the 1990s, a sociologist working with artisans in Ibadan noted that they found small numerical differences and fractions uncomfortable. They "did not display a comprehension of fractions or conversion factors if they needed to name a product slightly larger or smaller than they were used to" (Adam 1995, 132). Calculations that would break down conventional units were avoided in favor of the key procedures of establishing equivalence, marginal gains, and conceptual correspondence by manipulation of threshold numerical concepts.

I ran across a historical case of conceptual correspondence in my work on the iron currencies of Southern Cameroon, in an area less commercialized than Western Nigeria. The Beti number concept of *ntet* for 100 now appears in the dictionary as a homonym of the term for a particular openwork basket. Descriptions of the iron currency pieces of the nineteenth century include allusion to *ntet,* but depict clear variations in numbers in the bundles that were tied up for transaction. By juxtaposing several depictions, one can infer that *ntet* referred to the raphia (basketwork) binding before it referred to the number. A bundle simply happened to contain about a hundred in the currency system of the region when missionaries first defined the meaning of Beti words in translation. On the same principle as the West African transactional process, one can imagine exchanges about *mintet* that did not directly address how many, one by one, were contained in each bundle. This is very similar to the recent practice in Zaire of transacting a debased paper currency in bundles *(briques)* that were never untied. In a longer-term historical context, this apparently pragmatic response to inflation was made through the medium of an old practice from the regional trading repertoire.

So the prominence of either ratio or interval concepts of numeration in the matching of value scales appears to have varied by place and time. At one extreme end is the use of numbers as an almost entirely ordinal scale. In the Kabre economy of Togo, as Piot describes it, "Quantities . . . make no difference . . . thirty yams is the same as fifty, 1,100 CFA is the same as 750, and so on," through what Piot refers to as a "tropic logic" (1999, 65). A trope is a turning point, a punctuation, which is exactly how some numerical concepts worked to peg nominal and ordinal scales to each other, and back again to a ratio scale. His insight deserves to be taken much further, into its active use in transactional calculation. For example, in Eastern Nigeria, the word *nnu* — meaning 200 in the cowry system and 400 in the decimal system used for other things, including people (Jeffreys 1954) — probably allowed a particular tropic logic across value scales of the kind Piot suggests.

This nexus of asymmetrical transactional possibilities was deeply institutionalized. In some instances people resisted reduction or simplification of numerical scales when faced with Western efforts to enforce commensuration on a single numerical scale. For example, the Niger Expedition of 1841 tried unsuccessfully to introduce a new volumetric measure for larger numbers of cowries to avoid the "very tedious affair" of stringing them in hundreds and grouping the strings into tens. Measurement by volume was tried in several other places but never became established. Johnson suggests that "it offered altogether too much scope for ingenious dishonesty" (1970, 44). One might rephrase this: measurement in new and potentially heterogeneous units, such as volumetrics rather than conventionalized stepwise additions and multiplications, would have changed the tropic points, along with their associated accepted principles of threshold and margin in exchange. This, in turn, would have altered the ways in which adjustments in the equation of value scales could be made, and especially perhaps for transactions completed over a time lag, such as bridewealth. Where economic conditions could shift unpredictably, more rather than fewer tropic points allows greater room for recomposition of the material transaction without changing the nominal agreement. A colonial officer in Eastern Nigeria in the 1930s wrote that

> it was common some years ago in the Native Court for refund of dowry to be 5 pounds in manillas at six manillas to the shilling, and no litigant would be satisfied if any reviewing officer attempted to render this either as "six hundred manillas" or as "five pounds." The phrase used in the claim has some treasured significance which still escapes me but which is plain enough to the parties. (Grey 1951, 63)

Two numerical thresholds is better than one because the base unit can be redefined without the total amount being altered; five pounds is still five pounds, even if the manilla falls to eight or ten to the shilling. A later colonial officer pointed out the gains to be made by this: "the people prefer all payment of dowry by manillas since they hope of its fluctuation to make more than the face amount. Till today manillas have no fixed value in Ibibio land" (Offiong 1949).

Thresholds or tropes in numeration were like thresholds in the geography of distribution: points where disjunctive values could be linked — transformed, mutually translated — in ways that could produce gain. One continuous, incremental, uniform, relentlessly incremental scale is not only difficult to calculate and retain in one's head (where most of these numerical systems *were* retained), but it would be ruthlessly unreceptive to aspirations and exigencies to dramatize or mask the links across the different scales of judgment that make up value repertoires. In accounting, one needs the balance to be (or to appear to be) explicit and precise, neither dramatized nor masked. Exigencies or ambitions to which tropic logic lent itself could include collective adjustment to turbulent economic circumstances as well as exploitation of ignorant and powerless individual buyers or sellers. Both processes employed the same transactional frameworks.

To emphasize the deep-rooted nature of these practices, one can look not only at their long history and their widespread distribution but also at their consonance with much broader ideas of the nature of the market. In Yoruba views, money profit is a much less aleatory quality of the market than the conditions of one's presence in it. According to Belasco, "the Yoruba anticipate its disorder because the indigenous view is that the market, in contrast to its Western antithesis, is characterized by a natural tendency towards disequilibrium. . . . Uncertainty among the Yoruba is not fixed on the unpredictability of profit in a market enterprise, but rather it is concerned with the possibility of existential reversals" (1980, 26, 32). People operate in a fundamentally "unpredictable, fluctuating and competitive world of individual self-creation" (Barber 1995, 217), where money is a primary means of achievement, "the indispensable one" as Adebayo (1999) puts it. In a recent time of economic turbulence, Adam notes of Ibadan artisans that "challenges were considered quirks of personal fate or bad luck, and most masters attributed their success to divine intervention or their trust in God" (1995, 138). The comparatively small asymmetries produced by the pegging of numerical to ordinal and nominal scales, *as institutions,* would remove much of the uncertainty about gain *within each transaction.* The great risks then lie in the domain of other imponderables of life: the availability of goods; the peace of the caravan route; the politics of tolls and taxes; the weather; and all the human factors of strength, weakness, and social recognition that affect supply, demand, and personal success. For these, people needed divination.

I cannot leave number and price without describing one further pervasive and well-known practice that affects the "real price" of a good within routine transactions. The "real" amount of goods for a given price can be altered. One method is by varying the measure, from heaped to leveled (see Wan 2001). Another is through the "dash"—*èèní* in Yoruba—which is an ancillary payment, given after the basic equation has been agreed on (with its implicit or explicit margins). It can be an extra portion or a higher pile on the last measuring container. Another version of the same general idea is the addition or subtraction of qualitative elements. None of these is included in the negotiated price for the item itself. The principle of adding qualitatively new elements to the transaction, separately conceived from the central price, is amenable both to rapacity and generosity, revision up or revision down of the "actual" margin given and received.

Ardener describes an Igbo festival in 1950: "When the funeral drummers arrived they asked for sixpence *Nhwe oku* ('Something for being called'), and some gifts for *Ihiwe ala nkwa* ('Setting up the dance drums'). When the hornblower, and his assistant who interpreted the things he blew, were invited, they would not come until they had received three shillings for the *Eke aka* ('clapping hands')" (1950, 1). And so on through four other nominal payments, until the fee was set at three pounds, for which they were given eighteen shillings. Ardener continues, "Even when the price is fixed finally, the host is not free from depredations," all of which had to do with how much of the payments gradually squeezed out of the celebrant were allowed to count against the agreed price. Panicky as a reader or analyst may feel in the face of such apparently indeterminate predations into the pocketbook beyond the agreed price, they do follow some clear principles: nominal definitions of the kind of occasion, the kind of drumming required, and the sorts of gifts that match the two as the performance unfolds; ordinal definitions of the status of the deceased and the celebrant, and of the relative importance of various ritual components; and a ratio scale of money that might, nevertheless, also be designated in units that lend themselves to conceptual as well as numerical application. The schema gives the drummers pressure points at which to make extra money, but it also allows the payer considerable leeway about which precise points to accept, which to exploit for his or her own ends, and which to reject.

This set of scales does not constitute a cognitive map. It is a repertoire, the elements pegged to each other in performance. If flexibility is to be retained, there cannot be lockstep mutual entailment or automatic derivation of one from the other, and there is no external authority, political or mystical, to impose it. So I turn now to enactment, using some modern sources to illustrate calculation across scales, the room for gainful maneuver, and the limits of admissible advantage.

ENACTMENTS OF VALUE MATCHING

To some degree, the cases speak for themselves. So I give examples of equation, transgression, and excess across scales, as close as possible to the original source and with minimal commentary.

Equations

ARTICULATED LORRY

Oyin Adejobi's play *Articulated Lorry* is from the Yoruba-language popular theater repertoire of one of the most successful traveling performance groups of the pre-television era in Nigeria. In the following quotation, a landlord is calculating the income from renting out a house with sixteen rooms at 10 naira per room per month, for three years. He starts out in English (in italics), working on an imaginary calculator, and then moves to Yoruba concepts of bags and pounds, using additive and subtractive logics.

> Landlord: It comes to *five thousand seven hundred and sixty.* Or if we calculate it according to the number of bags, *one thousand,* it's five bags. *Two thousand,* two bags, ha, ten. *Three thousand,* fifteen bags. *Four thousand,* twenty bags. *Five thousand,* twenty-five bags. The *seven hundred and sixty* on top of that, makes it thirty bags, less forty pounds [Ọgbọ̀n àpọ̀, ó dín ogójì pọ́n-ùn]. (Adejobi 1981)

Note first that the root concept remains 200: 1 bag = 200, in this formulation. In Abraham's *Dictionary of Modern Yoruba* (1958), one bag referred to a hundred pounds sterling, which is far more than the cowry value of a bag in the nineteenth century. At some historical point, the numerical equivalents must have been adjusted from the 20,000 cowries or five shillings mentioned by Johnson, suggesting that established terms can adjust to change as they are brought forward into new monetary eras. The value of one pound at two naira derives from the exchange rate when naira first replaced the pound in 1973. Although the value of the naira to the English pound now hovers around 150, the tropic moment is enshrined in the conceptual scale, and market traders still observe the stabilized old equations. Thus the current Yoruba numerical concepts for naira refer back to the cowry and colonial and postcolonial pound systems, with threshold values that index to historical events, in a piling up of allusion.

The resulting number in the play follows Mann's principle: it is easily pronounceable, and conceptually diminishes the use of number radicals from three (5, 7, 6) to two (30, 40) by adding types of unit (bags and pounds) rather than zeros. If one were working orally, with a limited type of numerical manipulation (no percentages or fractions), there is no doubt that the Yoruba concept is more conducive than Western numbers to long sequences of calculations that could easily be reviewed and recapitulated by any party to the transaction.

Another point: according to Barber's annotation, the Yoruba translation of the number is inaccurate; it should be minus forty, that is, minus *twenty pounds.* We don't know why the landlord "gets it wrong": just a mistake? a dramatic point for the audience to discover for themselves? or perhaps the accommodation of an understood margin on a large number, a kind of discount, once one moves into Yoruba numeration?

RUNNING AFTER RICHES

Okediji, in his play *Running after Riches,* describes a group of gambling addicts calculating how much they stand to win on the football pools, at 200 to 1 (note the allusion to the base 200).

Kola: . . . What's the total?

Tunde: Two thousand four. Twenty-four hundred when you spell it out. And each naira will win two hundred. In all we're going to win. . . .

Kola: [in English] "Four hundred and eighty thousand naira." How do you say that in Yoruba?

Tunde: Twenty thousand naira times twenty-four! That's what we'll win.

Kola: We're going to really hit the jackpot this time. We'll be rich, we'll be absolutely loaded! I'm now a money-bags! (Okediji 1999, 146)

Numbers are translated into the old cowry equivalence with "bags" (20,000) and then linked to the common Western Nigerian idiom for excessively wealthy people as "moneybags." On my first introduction to Western Nigeria in 1968, a senior woman trader asked me whether I "counted my money in bags" (which I completely misunderstood at the time). In the contemporary press and cartoons, *moneybags* also indexes to political corruption. Hence the translation from English to Yoruba links to scales of moral judgment about other domains of life, even when the number equivalence is the same.

IBADAN MARKET WOMEN

Anthropologist Mimi Wan worked with the women sellers in the urban food supply system in Ibadan. Characteristically they worked in more than one commodity, with each commodity's money kept and calculated separately; each has its own "purse":

> Funds for each food item are stored in a particular part of a trader woman's "money belt." Specially designed underwear and money belts, or igbanu, represent the foundations of a trader's accounting system. The back zippered portion of an igbanu stores all the profits from the sale of gari [cassava flour], the side-zippered pocket of the same belt holds all the money from on-going maize sales, while the front slot of the belt holds transport money. When the goods of a particular investment are completely sold, a trader takes out the money from the appropriate part of her belt or other storage garment and calculates her profit or loss. (Wan 2001, 236)

The equation *gari* = *back* indexes particular gains and their expectation to particular routines of movement, corresponding closely to the composite of routine practice of nominal/numerical translations that Verran (2001) refers to as "clots."

Transgressions
ILÉ OF YAMS

To break into the conventions by reasserting the ratio scale in infinite increments of one is a breach of practice and therefore incurs costs. Karin

Barber (personal communication) gives the following example from her own early bargaining in the market. A trader had an *ilé* of yams (usually three, but in this case one large and one small), which she was selling for seven shillings. When K. asked how much the small one would be, she answered two shillings, to which K. replied, "In that case I'll take the large one for five shillings." The trader was offended. If she really wanted to break the *ilé* in that way, the large one would be six shillings. At a stretch, one might see this in Western terms as the premium on buying in bulk; the margin of one shilling is the cost to the seller of having to find another customer for the small yam. Most Western premiums on bulk, however, set in at higher aggregations than this, such as a cigarette package of twenty broken down into singles, where the costs of finding additional customers may be high. In Yoruba marketing, time spent selling is not quantified, either implicitly or explicitly. Rather, the complete conversation gave the impression that K. as a buyer had simply transgressed the principles of price chunking and must be, as she put it, "punished." When the seller finally gave in, it was in exasperation at the irretrievable illogicality of white people, not at an incontrovertible numerical logic.

"CHEATING"

An ignorant or careless buyer who does not follow the conventional manipulations and correspondences of value registers is considered to deserve any price disadvantage he or she suffers. No one is held to an absolute standard. Belasco quotes the saying, "If you don't cheat a fool, where will you find a wise man to cheat?" (1980, 21). Adam concurs that during children's training in trade, "successful cheating was rewarded" (1995, 140). A girl sent to the market to sell oranges in set amounts at a set price can only make a personal margin by reporting one stolen or by putting too few into a customer's bag. She then conceals her gain, reporting only the standard expectation of item–price correspondence and keeping the rest. Even if her deception is punished, it does not involve restitution and is generally thought to augur well for future market "savviness" (Adam 1995).

THE MALICIOUS AND THE FOOLISH

A popular play shows how a worker loses part of her wages through allowing herself to be deceived, without the daily wage being explicitly renegotiated. The example also shows how units are broken out of larger amounts:

> Labourer: When we finished the job, he took the money for us twelve women, and he split us into groups of four. And he gave each group twenty naira. And I was the one he gave the money to [in my group]. I said I haven't got any change [for the twenty-naira note]. Then I picked up a bowl and went to the river to rinse off my hands and feet. Well, when I got back,

it was five naira your husband ought to have given me, but he'd only left four naira for me! . . .

    Tafa [employer]: . . . lazy bitch. She can't work. . . . When it's a question of money she's full of energy. When it's a question of work she'll say she's going for a pee. (Barber and Ogundijo 1994, 535)

The intensity of work was not part of the original bargain about the daily wage (although piecework does exist in the repertoire of employment), so Tafa is just trying a ruse. The laborer eventually gives up, hurling a threat as she departs, and Tafa makes the extra one naira of gain. Later in the conversation he tells his wife that he has a certain amount left from the contract, "after I'd taken out the money for the labourers. I rigged it as much as I could, as you saw just now" (Barber and Ogundijo 1994, 538–39).

Other sources imply that the "fault" here, if there is one, would be judged to lie with the laborer who didn't stick to her guns. She just accepted what might also have been understood as a small premium taken by the one who broke bulk.

Chance and Excess

The play of chance falls outside of the calculative nexus. Here the unpredictable and the occult are linked, characteristically, to an idiom of enumeration that is poetically excessive. Money as excess does not invalidate money as number and value, as Adebayo (1999) emphasizes in his detailed interpretation of Yoruba "contradictory" ideas about money. Money is both calculative and excessive, and morality plays can be built on the struggle and the complementarity between the two.

Okediji's play *Running after Riches* is a savagely biting attack on the modern belief in chance. His football-pool addicts and aspiring "money-bags" are lavish quoters of the Bible as well as voluble citers of Yoruba proverbs, and his swindlers are sanctimonious cult leaders across the entire religious spectrum, from Christianity to Islam and traditional religion. All are searching for answers to how to make money, how to justify it, and how to use it without working for it. The only solidly decisive person in the whole play is the wife of the central character, who "earned money with the sweat of my brow" and manages to hold onto some of it as the contents of the house disappear around her and she herself takes leave, pouring scorn all the way. "Your television, your radio, your wristwatch—you bought them all with the sweat of your brow before your brain was cut off from its fuel supply" (Okediji 1999, 31). And so on. All the numbers are excessive; none indexes to the prices of goods.

In Adejobi's play *Articulated Lorry,* the main characters are a lazy man who is ambitious for money without work; his lifelong friend, who is wealthy (as he claims in the beginning and we find out later to be true) through work; the wife of the former, who embodies a desperate effort to get her husband to bring in money, in any way; and a man of the cult, who is supposed to come up with a talisman for opening up an endless flow of money, after the supplicant has passed suitable ordeals. Here are excerpts from their initial discussion:

> Wife: So please, I'm asking you — the way you found, the trick you used to make your career prosper . . . It's not a question of working, sir. . . . We just don't have enough money. . . .
> Friend: [W]hatever small amount of money you've got on you, you'll throw it away on useless things, like playing the pools.
> Wife: Why shouldn't he play the pools — you use money to fetch money! When he hasn't had a chance. . . .
> Friend: You think maybe there's a kind of medicine for money . . .
> Wife: Exactly!
> Friend: [A]re you saying that a house builder can't make any money from it? (Adejobi 1981)

Phoney ordeals and humiliating failures follow. The play is a homily on work and trade in the old style, where one makes marginal gains as distinct from using money to fetch money.

Spectacular gains preexist the monetary chaos of the petro-naira era. Excessive monetary wealth can be alluded to in numerical terms. But here the words indicate excess, by their sheer repetition, as in the praise poem quoted by Barber (1995, 219):

> He has 420 china plates
> He has 440 tin ones
> Old-fashioned plates made of clay total 2,000
> . . . Ogunmola has 400 slaves
> . . . "I suppose there are 400 chiefs who serve me"
> "Each of them brings 500 bags of cowries"

Most of the numerical terms are benchmark terms, tropic thresholds, rather than accurate counts. In 1887 Adolphus Mann wrote that Yoruba "can boast of a greater number of radical names of numerals" than other "nations" (60). Here they are used precisely to boast; by juxtaposition and poetic rhythmic structures and (doubtless) conceptual allusions, they evoke a world of ramifying excess rather than reporting accurately on an inventory of goods.

Finally, it is interesting that very large numbers allude in some way to exteriority as well as excess. In one of Adejobi's plays, the gamblers first refer to their winnings in English. In the famous work of Sonny Labou Tansi, fantastic numbers and hyperbolic sequences of numbers, expressed in French, are used to parody the claims of the ruler: the Guide "has 362 illustrious ancestors . . . will father two thousand little Jeans . . . celebrates 228 holidays . . . [creating] a Brechtian refusal of the 'reality' depicted" (Julien 1992, 133). Laburthe-Tolra (1981, 249) remarks that the old Beti word for 10,000 (or perhaps 1,000) refers to something beyond common sense: *akuda*, from *akud*, meaning folly. In context, then, an otherwise exact numerical term can refer beyond itself to another domain altogether. Whereas the numbers of routine trade mask a gain that can be unmasked at will, by referring back to a referent scale of value, some large numbers are rendered opaque, placed in the realm of chance, and can become sinister. One powerful correspondence is between excess money and blood. Falola argues that the manufacture of money by sacrifice is very old: "a whole routine of such magic did develop; the most extreme was ritual murder to make money" (1995, 166). One imagined origin was the use of children's blood in medicines that caused money to "shower down" (Barber 1982, 439). This kind of money magic has been reincarnated in new forms in the 1990s (see Enwerem 2002). One could certainly ask whether there is any commensuration here at all: for example, how much blood and of what status or sex or age of child for how much money, acquired in what installments, and over what time period. The degree to which "magical" gains have ever been negotiated as marginal gains might indeed be describable in these terms. To investigate this question through scalar and numerical analysis could show the sense in which economies were occult, where and how their scales of measurement and correspondence were routine, or link the boundless edges and the bizarre intervals of the numerical scale to the embodied powers of the spiritual world.

CONCLUSION

Number as an exact scale seems to have stood *within* the repertoire of scalar values and not at its point of culmination (or reduction). At each end of the repertoire are enduring propositions: the nature of "things" in nominalized schemes on the one hand and the nature of power on the other. In between, each scale acquired its own elaborated logic in which history and experience played a contingent and changeable constitutive role. Numbers linked the scales for monetary transactional purposes. But any number, and especially a tropic number, retained its potential referents across the registers, to words, things, bodily kinetic and spiritual powers. Neither fetishism nor abstract number dominates the scalar repertoire, whose historical tendency has been toward elaboration rather than reduction. The maintenance of parallel scales in monetary valuation provides what Rotman (1987) terms "deixis": the capacity of number to be indexical of something, to refer to "anteriority" or to a diachrony that recounts its achievement of value and meaning. Context in deictic linguistics is addressed by Hanks (1990). The erasure of deixis in modernist monetary practice has generally involved powerful political intervention and legal institutionalization. In the absence of formal-sector disciplines, Atlantic Africa has retained and even expanded the deictic quality of its monetary numeration by proliferating scalar criteria. One of these is the ranking of persons, to which I turn next.

4

RANK
PEOPLE AND MONEY
■

The numerical monetary scale can be pegged to any other scale of "things": objects, skills, personal qualities, services, and so on, as far as the cultural imagination can go. Economic analysis rests on the assumption that the relative value of these things on a money scale is actually *generated* in the diffuse supply-and-demand conditions of competitive markets, that ordinal ranking of goods is malleable and responsive to changes in money price. Cultural and sociological analyses, on the other hand, such as Sahlins's (1976) intervention against a materialist understanding of practical reason and Bourdieu's (1984) argument on distinction, claim that value scales are autonomous and preexisting, because they derive from a conservatively tenacious valuation of persons in the social hierarchy and to fundamental ideas in cosmology and ideology. Only with a cultural imperative of "trust in numbers" (Porter 1995) are those other orders overridden. Even then, and even when demand for goods responds to price, Bourdieu argues that there are underlying criteria based on social class that persistently order the world. In his view, the outward signs of symbolic value are fundamentally arbitrary; it is class power that defines the standards. Tiv spheres of exchange are often invoked as a classic noncapitalist example of the sociopolitical definition of the ranking of things in accordance with preset value hierarchies.

There have been important critiques and additions to the social structural aspect of Bohannan's argument (Piot 1999; Akin and Robbins 1999), identifying the limitation of indexing objects to only one scale, the social hierarchy. There are other relevant and crosscutting scales of social valuation, they argue, such as the social distance of partners to transactions and the modality of the exchange (sharing, credit, trade, and so forth). These critics rightly point out that *multiple* registers are at play. But they do still imply a logical priority to moral/cultural schema, to which the circulation of money is adapted. The experience of Atlantic Africa in general, and Eastern Nigeria in particular, suggests that the quantitative register became more important than this disciplinary credo implies. Money wealth was culturally marked and referred to as a benchmark, not in the simple reproduction of established social statuses but in the expansive formation of a more complex social ranking, within and beside social or conceptual "classes," than preexisted the trade. The focus on class analogs, such as free/slave or elder/junior/women, has drawn attention away from the evidence for florescent social ranking *among* those of free status, which grew up in tandem with and dependent on monetary expansion. Inevitably the historical accounts focus on flamboyant leaders and extreme deprivations. But in between, most of the social orders of Atlantic Africa offered intricate criteria of stepwise status recognition, where money was converted into position at regular quantified intervals. Nowhere was rank more elaborated as a primary social principle than in the otherwise designated "segmentary" societies of Eastern Nigeria. The Igbo and Ibibio peoples developed a particularly formalized and monetized scale of ranking in the late nineteenth and early twentieth centuries, even without imposition and validation from a central political hierarchy. The intervals in ordinal rank were quantified in money and associated with competitive acquisitiveness. And yet they were so deeply spiritually meaningful and religiously sanctioned that continual conversions upward were intensely motivating to personal accumulation of monetary wealth, as evidenced in an unusually highly developed system of saving. The biblical religious calculus with respect to the equation of wealth with value is indirect. One version inverts the entire scale, making it easier for a camel to pass through the eye of a needle than a rich man to attain heaven. The other reduces the absolute scale of wealth to a logic of proportionality, to make the gift of the widow's mite equivalent to a much larger donation by a rich person. The Igbo equation of monetary wealth and spiritual worth, by contrast, was direct, which I argue is largely the result of the centrality of sacrifice. This configuration helps to make sense of some of the confusions and residuals in the literature to which I alluded in chapter 1: that ordinary people saved money, even where the most obvious gains were from keeping the flow moving; that people were sold and sacrificed, even in a "wealth-in-people" context; that it was precisely those peoples, such as the Igbo, who had been most successful in trade who insisted until well into the twentieth century on using what, by then, was referred to as "primitive money"; and that neither class nor market analysis alone can do justice to the crucial importance of religion in anchoring and motivating the pooling and spending of money, particularly for sacrifice. The concepts of conspicuous consumption, or destruction for prestige, miss the point. We are far better with the literal and metaphorical meanings implied by sacrifice.

Igbo and expatriate scholars alike have suggested that a coherent set of economic practices was forged in Eastern Nigeria, even in the absence of formalized central power to set it in place. G. I. Jones wrote that while "every river"— of which there are hundreds—"had its own mode of reckoning" (1958, 51),

> the economic organization of the Ibo is more complete and extensive than their social and political. One can with some degree of accuracy describe the village group as the highest coherent political grouping and the lineage as the highest unit capable of effective executive action. But one can equally correctly insist that the whole of the eastern provinces excluding the Cameroons that is roughly the Niger and Cross River hinterland forms a single integrated whole. (Jones Papers, box B1)

Ekejiuba writes, "It is thus feasible to conclude that a monetary system and policy existed in Eastern Nigeria prior to British colonial rule. There were accepted standards of payment for commodities, as well as for social services, across currency zones" (1995, 138). Ofonagoro (1976) argues that there were general principles of reckoning. Certainly in some key regional markets, where many traders met, there were appointed mediators who insisted on standards of commercial practice. For example, Dike writes that the Niger Delta states set the terms of market engagements in the hinterland, including severe penalties for breach of monetary conventions: "Should a trader refuse to accept a particular kind of manilla agreed upon as local currency, he was sacrificed to the market juju, unless able to find a substitute" (Dike 1956, 42–43). The ranking of the people, and the ways in which this was linked to quantitative scales of money, lies at the heart of this sense of regional coherence.

To digress for a moment on rank: Less attention has been devoted to the comparative sociology and economics of the incremental ranking of people in Africa than this important topic deserves. Precedence accorded to age, gender, or primacy in a particular location tends to naturalize what is a much more elaborate construction. One traditional Yoruba mode of ranking, according to Bascom, corresponded to the wealth-in-people model. A man of wealth in this "pecuniary society . . . may have even greater economic resources [than the man rich in money], but they are not liquid, so he may have to sell a chicken, a goat or, in former times, a slave in the case of minor emergency" (Bascom 1951, 491). Wealth lay in followers, alliances, the breadth and prominence of one's social networks, all of which had to be cultivated by spending money. So status for the wealthy derived from the capacity to deal with needs, which derived from claims on goods, which in turn derived from money. Money was a medium for a relational life rather than a goal as a store of wealth: "To be part of Yoruba humanity, it is necessary to take part in this cycle, which is mediated by money"; "Money is a river: if it flows up to you it will flow away again" (Barber 1995, 208, 217). By contrast, in a florescently monetized era, the rich man's status depended directly on money. Spending was not necessarily elicited by "emergency." Both the scale of needs and the scale of wealth-in-people disappear, and one is left with desires and cash. The logic becomes conspicuous consumption — competitive display of wealth rather than its circulation. Barber (1995) has argued that the "rich man" configuration rose to prominence in nineteenth-century Yorubaland and that it corresponds to a process suggested to be more general in Equatorial Africa (Guyer 1993), namely, the search to exceed the constraints of known scales of value and enter into the domain of singularity.

Igbo and Ibibio ranking seems to me to contrast with both principles. Money was neither primarily a means toward relationality nor a support for singularity. Money was put to all purposes, most prominently the development of a continuous principle for ordinal scales of human value that even played with the concept of quantified intervals. Ranking was comprehensive and puritanical in its discipline (although not in its aesthetics, which were expansively dramatic at every step). There was much less emphasis on undisciplined charisma at the top than in some other systems of wealth. There was no exemption from the struggle at the bottom (for those of free status). And there were many intervening steps all the way up, with little in the way of alternative status hierarchies to aspire to. The most original feature of the Igbo rank order was quantified intervals, which I might argue was made possible by the conceptual terminal points at each end. Ritual slave status held fixed the bottom end, while ancestral status pegged the top. Both were absolute statuses, but both were also just a "step" away from the ranking of the living and the free, as I illustrate later. Just as zero makes ratio scales thinkable, the absolute terminal anchoring of ranked scales makes possible — beyond ordinality — the contemplation of intervals.

I look first at the monetization of the Igbo/Ibibio economy in manillas, which were its most widespread and important commercial and ritual currency; then at the expansion of ranking; and finally at the impression created among scholars that there were systemic dynamics, in particular a connection between a high rate of saving and stability in the value of manilla currency over wide regions and quite long periods of time.

IGBO MONEY

Manillas were only one of several currencies that circulated in Eastern Nigeria, but they are among the oldest, as shown by archeological finds at Igbo Ukwu that date from the ninth century (Shaw 1970). Manillas were the most prominent currency import from Europe during the Atlantic slave trade, in which the Niger Delta states, the Cross River polities, and inland peoples were all engaged — as traders and as victims — for at least two hundred years. Among the many currencies, manillas circulated the most widely. And finally, only manillas were redeemed for colonial currency at near value when they were demonetized in 1948. Because manillas were redeemed, they are the only indigenous currency for which estimates of the quantities in circulation can be hazarded. The common *okpoho* manilla was copper, bronze, or brass, weighing about three ounces, and, for much of the late nineteenth and early twentieth century, worth about three pence in British currency. The growth of the slave trade was linked to the growth of the British brass industry in the eighteenth century. Most of the manillas were made in either Birmingham or Nantes (France). Herbert's "very conservative" (1984, 182) estimate of quantities of copper and brass ending up in Africa up to the late nineteenth century is 50,000 tons, and if one included Dutch imports, the actual amounts might reach as much as twice this. The quantities were clearly massive. This amount would be equivalent to several hundred million *okpoho* manillas, spread over the entire West African and Equatorial regions — as neptunes, *mitakos,* wires, rods, and a variety of other shapes. Herbert infers that "[t]he huge quantities of copper and brass from Europe and the Near East that flowed into sub-Saharan Africa over the centuries grew to be integral to all aspects of African life, complementing and eventually competing with copper produced indigenously" (1984, 302).

The only accurate count of the manillas in use in any defined region comes from the colonial administrative action to rescind them in Eastern Nigeria. In 1902 manilla imports were forbidden, and in 1948 they were entirely withdrawn from circulation by the British colonial government, which paid the holders at the rate of eighty to the pound sterling, or four to the shilling, which was probably not far from their current exchange rate.[1] More than thirty-two million (32,350,096) manillas were withdrawn in the main manilla region (the Calabar Provinces), from a population of one and a half million people (census of 1953). The amount collected represents some unknown but probably quite large fraction of the amounts people actually held. Each person was allowed to retain up to two hundred manillas for funerals and other celebrations. Amogu reports that "[s]ome people could not be persuaded to give up all the manillas they had and a handsome number can still be found in the area" (1952, 139). If we go with thirty-three million, and an adult active population of 400,000, the total stock amounted to around ninety per person, or twenty-two shillings' worth. Of course, the distribution would be skewed. The withdrawal campaign made special provision for "individual holders of large quantities of manillas (in

1. The United Africa Company (1949) reports prices in Opobo of between 103 and 108 to the pound from 1943 to 1947, or 5 to the shilling. Ardener (1950, 5) reports that the rate was 6 to the shilling for some payments and 12 for others.

excess of 18,000)" (Turner 1950, 11), because 18,000 was the full capacity of a lorry (30 bags of 1 cwt each). The value of a lorry load in colonial cash would be £222. The highest level of holdings I have come across in the archives on Eastern Nigeria was about three times this amount. The budget of the king of Opobo (one of the coastal trading states) from 1945 gives the cash and manilla alternatives for running a state banquet: 48,000 manillas or £600 at the going rate of the time (Jones Papers, box A5). All these amounts—from the low of 90 to the high of 48,000 as individual holdings, and to the total of 33 million for the population—are very large amounts relative to purchasing power in market goods.

The Eastern Nigerian economy of the nineteenth century was highly monetized. Many sources attest to the rich variety of products, the large catchment areas of the markets, and the crowds of buyers and sellers. Isichei quotes from a source on Port Harcourt in 1896: "At Obegu . . . an extremely large and important market is held every four days, people coming from immense distances to it. [Some articles are] brought by the Aroh people, who come from the far interior. Some thousands of people attend this market every time. Its trade is drawn from the far interior" (1978, 211). Ekejiuba writes of Bende in 1896 that it was the emporium of the hinterland, attracting 20,000 to 30,000 people to every fair, from as far as Onitsha, Ibi, Bonny, and Calabar, under the market regulations of the Aro (1972, 20). Establishment of a new market was a major occasion. When the market was moved from Bende to Uzuakoli, the Uzuakoli town chiefs gave the Aro council "2,800 brass rods, a cow, a ram, goat [special breed called Azuzu], a cock, 4 stone jars of gin, sixteen yams and 4 kola nuts. Each of the Aro chiefs was given a slave while other members of the Aro council severally got presents ranging from 100–150 manillas and a bottle of gin." Sacrifices added to the cost (Ekejiuba 1972, 23). As for imports, Dike writes of "the endless flow of novelties that descended on them from the treasure houses of Europe" (1956, 112).

As for currency use, Latham's argument against Bohannan rested on an insistence that currencies on the Cross River could be used for anything, from imported "novelties" to local provisions to rank. Copper rods "were the ordinary everyday medium of exchange. They were freely obtainable in the market in exchange for other goods. . . . both provisions and status-conferring offices could be bought" (Latham 1971, 601). There were, however, understood currency zones. The peoples of the great trading systems of the Niger and Cross River Deltas imported goods that they only used once as currencies: to purchase goods from the north. For example, and to anticipate the description of titles, at the pinnacle of ceremonial sacrifice in the nineteenth century was the horse (Talbot [1926] 1969, 775) imported from the north, via intermediary groups such as the Tiv. A horse sold for four to six slaves (Ekejiuba 1972, 21) or their equivalent in the currencies that the sellers were demanding. In the late nineteenth century, the people of the Cross River basin, while not using cowries as currency themselves, were re-exporting them north to the Adamawa against slaves and livestock (Lovejoy 1974, 575). Within the area, some significant quantity of both local and nonlocal currency income was converted into rank.

IGBO RANKING

The cardinal features of Igbo ranking are its multiple steps and — in addition to free status — money as the sole criterion of access. The level of ranking corresponded exactly to the level of money spent to achieve it. "The Ibo has developed, to an extraordinary degree, a system of what is called 'making the title,' by which . . . a certain rank is attained on the payment of a fixed donation" (Talbot [1926] 1969, 771). "The love of riches is very great; it is a result of offices and dignity being sold. Everybody hoards up in order to be able to buy them some day, or to reach a higher grade; for on passing from one rank to another they must every time pay a fresh tribute" (Henderson 1972, 256, quoting Burdo in 1880). The total value in pounds sterling of going up to the top of the hierarchy was enormous. It would have been far beyond the reach of an ordinary wageworker of the time in Britain. Talbot reported that the Ekkpe Club "cost £200–300 to go through all the grades" ([1926] 1969, 784). And this was clearly accessible to anyone and affordable by many, because, Latham notes, "it was possible to save rods from everyday transactions with which to buy offices in the secret society" (1971, 601). Of course, affordability was not easily reached. Titles were a major incentive to economic effort, and those efforts could include deep cuts into a man's assets. Talbot reports in 1923 that "To raise the sums necessary for entering this [Egbo] cult, aspirants sometimes reduce themselves to penury and even sell wives and children into slavery" ([1923] 1967, 171). One aspirant sold his daughter: "they fixed the sum at twelve hundred manillas" (172).

The steps were numerous and the qualifications intricate. Asaba in the nineteenth century had five hundred Eze titles (Isichei 1973, 58). In Talbot's experience of the early decades of this century, the first step into the Egbo cult required 900 manillas (about £6), 15 pots of palm wine, 20 fowls, 20 sticks of dried fish, 23 seed yams, and 23 cooking yams ([1923] 1967, 172). The Ozo title system of Nri was "organized as a series of eight stages or grades, each marked by various ritual acts and by the payment of fees to those persons who had already made the grade." The first stage, made by all able-bodied men, cost "a few pounds." At the fifth stage, fees in the 1930s were about £240 (Jones 1958, 44). Accession to higher levels of the Ibibio Ekong society could, in the past, have involved human sacrifice (Talbot [1923] 1967, 179). Oracular demand for sacrifice and/or body parts continued in some places into the first half of this century (Mayne 1946; George 1935). As mentioned, horses imported from the north — via mediators such as the Tiv — became the most expensive sacrificial choice by the late nineteenth century. The bottom end of the hierarchy was also elaborated. There were various temporary arrangements. The criminal investigations into the Leopard Society in the late 1940s in the Ibibio region noted that the Idiong society had a kind of temporary right for nonmembers to have access to their divination services for "a few corns, a yam and one to five manillas" (Mayne 1947, 9). At Ibibio harvest celebrations, "For two hundred manillas [a man] might, though an outsider, enter the Ekkpon shed and drink with members of the society" (Talbot [1923] 1967, 189).

The sources concur that ranking became more elaborate during the nineteenth century — by adding grades, by raising the price, and by expanding the number of societies in which the members were graded into levels (Isichei 1973, 57). With expanding wealth, "[m]ore people in the community were able to obtain titles and they formed themselves into associations to regulate the taking of these local titles"; "[t]he Ekpe and related societies of the Cross River developed higher grades or orders within the society which carried heavy entrance fees" (Jones 1956, 36). Another development was the elaboration of titles relevant to different domains — to internal and external political and ritual fields; "[t]he Ndiama titles are graded into greater and lesser titles, the lesser titles are recognized within the village but not outside it" (Jones 1956, 38–39). New divisions of labor also developed; Jones notes that in the Offot clan, there were seven highest-level judicial chiefs, each with special duties (35).

This ordinal scale of rank and the ratio scale of number (applied to money) approach one another in the explicit negotiation of intervals. Jones writes that title ceremonies "performed the important function of imposing a means test on aspirants for political leadership. . . . [High titleholders have to be] able to provide a succession of expensive feasts and fees and other awards for the elders of the group" (1956, 34). The funds were counted: in Onitsha, there is a "closely accounted redistribution of the wealth that a candidate has managed to mobilize" (Henderson 1972, 254). The demands of promotion — indeed the monetary demands of any accession to power — were increased as the process itself unfolded. In Onitsha, "the titled men of the group concerned assess the candidate's ceremonial efforts; these efforts are invariably found to be wanting, and additional fees are levied. The levies made on the candidate are so repetitious that observers in the nineteenth century reasonably interpreted title-taking as a kind of purchase"(255). The standard payments were never enough, and people themselves sometimes outdid them on their own initiative, to be sure that the rise to a new level had been well and truly achieved. According to Henderson, "no formal limits are set on the amount of ghostly money that may be requested" from *ozo* men of the new candidate's patrilineage (255); "the process of 'attaining ozo' entails continual tests and transformations of a man's relations with his ancestors and with the spirits of his patrilineage," each test entailing haggling over the cost (252). Money — counted, in numerical amounts — is at issue at every step, even though it may be referred to symbolically as "ghostly money," and those same numbers might be imbued with symbolic as well as numerical meanings. Of number and symbolism, Green wrote in 1947 that "ritual, formalized patterns of behaviour regulate innumerable situations, and have certain common elements running through many of them. Of these, the use of definite numbers, and particularly the sacred number four and its multiples, is specially marked" (1947, 249). As discussed in the last chapter, tropic numbers were both literally numerical and symbolic, and could function in either discourse.

I have come across no detailed discussion of the links between money, ranking, and the florescence of plastic and performative arts that continues to be an aesthetic inspiration up to the present. Clearly display was important, and certain items were required. At the funeral or the consecration of an important man in the past, the deceased club members performed, slaves might be sacrificed, and the "dead man's wealth was brought into the central court of the compound, and there displayed under guard" (Talbot [1923] 1967, 147). A giant manilla, "worth the value of a cow," might be needed. What is striking in the sources, however, is the low profile of symbolic explanations of the items for display. The indexing of this or that item to a scheme of referents for sources of power and meaning is not explored in detail anywhere. It is hard to know whether the market prices were so impressive as to outshine all other perceptions. But I doubt it. Igbo and Ibibio spectacles of masked performance must have been thrilling. But in the Western sources, items are systematically related to their market price. Is this a deficiency? Perhaps so, especially because many of the early sources in English were written by missionaries. The emphasis on monetary wealth, however, does seem to pervade discussions of spiritual life. Talbot relates, supposedly verbatim:

> Sad, indeed, from a poor man's point of view is the state of affairs in the spirit world. This is situated neither in the sky nor beneath the earth; but side by side with the abodes of living men, from whom, however, the dead are separated by a fence, impassable to mortals. . . . Abassi asks: "What gifts have you brought?" and the rich ghost answers "I bring cows, sheep, goats and fowls. Cloths also and manillas in plenty have I, together with many pots great and small." To this Abassi replies "Welcome to my king-

dom," while to the poor he says "Go forth to the place of the poor and those of no account." ([1923] 1967, 140–41)

Onitsha candidates for ritual promotion "carry money for the ghosts," and during the ceremony they chant "he has money, he has money [literally cowries]" (Henderson 1972, 254, 260). The ghosts listen. The money is blessed. Numerical accounting, in market prices and equivalences, is clearly a readily accessible and legitimate standard in people's minds for the value of persons and their performances in ritual contexts. What makes this plausible, however, is not an abstract faith in numbers or secular acquisitiveness but a pervasively spiritual standard of worth, relative to the ancestral world.

RELIGION AND THE RISE OF COMMERCIALISM

At the end of the nineteenth century, Mary Kingsley made the perceptive comment that "it is to that occult influence that I trace the general ill-success of the educated native of the Delta . . . unless he returns to the pagan gods of his forefathers, and until he does so many channels of prosperity are completely closed to him" (quoted in Jones 1956, 164). Even with Christian conversion and colonial rule, the price of Igbo religious observance was very slow to change. Consultation with oracles was expensive and essential; "[m]any tall, fine pots . . . are ranged round the shrine. . . . Manillas used to lie there also in great heaps" (Talbot [1923] 1967, 39). The Aro oracle most closely associated with the slave trade, the Ibinukpabi, was destroyed by the British in 1917, but people continued to consult it long afterward. Dike and Ekejiuba suggest that "if economic gains were the primary or main motive, oracles which to this day operate in parts of eastern Nigeria would have long disappeared" (1990, 140). Oracles guided the timing and pathway of people's careers, including success in business and spiritual advancement.

The source that comes closest to detailed description of the spiritual scale of worth to which money was matched is Ejizu, writing of the meaning of *ofo,* the personal "staff of office" to whose ownership all men aspired. The simplest *ofo* is a staff of a particular wood, a modest object of no intrinsic rarity or expense. Its transformation into "an object of communication with the divine" (Ejizu 1986, 164) required payment of a fee (73) and consecration by the custodians of that line of *ofo,* with the highest grades requiring "expensive gifts" (75). There are both grades and types: "a multitude of ofo types" (54), and "higher grades of ofo, professional and institutional ofo" (75). The *ofo* system is a "vital instrument for the classification of persons, for the differentiation of roles" (144).

Socially, *ofo* was used to lend authority to any occasion. It "empower[ed] their performers, for social and moral control" (Ejizu 1986, 144). One could swear on it or by it. To hold it in one's hand gives gravity and spiritual meaning, implicating both the holder and others present. At base, that power comes from the personal connection of the holder to the spiritual world. Possession grants access to the spirits (124). The staff is a personal object, used to ask guidance from the spirits and to mediate prayer. So high is its spiritual value, so explicit its monetary basis, and so profoundly identified with the person that *ofo* can be used as security on a personal money loan (27). The linkage to the monetary scale is clear, firmly founded, and recursive; one can move back and forth in more than one way without recourse to other standards and mediating classifications. Again, there are symbolically marked numbers: "the number 'four' and its multiples have the symbolic meaning of fulness" (75). But there is no indication that a symbolic four is different from a numerical four.

This ease of translation from one scale to the other rests in part on a concept of the composite person; one component carries the capacity for spiritual divinity, which can be separately represented in material or kinetic form. "The personal god possessed some aspects that were ancestrally conditioned; other parts of it were nonancestral. It was also a unity greater than the sum of its parts . . . a potentially divine self who had to work out his own destiny on the economic base of his own household and gardens" (Henderson 1972, 505, 508). Proximity of one's most valued self to the ancestors was courted in dance and ritual. In dance one could literally cross over the thin line between this world and the spiritual world. People cultivated the capacity to be almost there, in a world that was side by side with this one. Title objects were stored in rafters, close to the ancestral shrine, along with all the important items that "extol the force of individual status and achievement" (Aniakor 1996, 226). In many mundane and celebratory contexts, the placement of things and the use of space referred to spiritual proximities.

Assimilation of this use of wealth to standard categories, such as "prestige economy" or "conspicuous consumption," would be limiting. Not everything of value seems to be displayed conspicuously, for general contemplation anyway. The prestige is secondary to the spiritual trajectory. The conversions have an inner as well as an outer or utilitarian material referent. The steps up the ladder of conversion of money into spiritual power are a realization of the inner self of the free person on the way to ancestorhood and life in the ghost world, just a veil away from the land of the living. By comparison with the fluctuating availability of the means for getting there, the course itself is true and certain. The money gained — through whatever mediating sales in a general purpose and often multiple-currency monetary economy — was as close as one could come to accuracy of value on the spiritual "gold standard." The value of the spirits, and one's own spiritual potential along a scalar progress, was anchored at each end. At the bottom was ritual slavery, which disqualified a person from making sacrifice to any supernatural agencies (Harris 1942, 49). At the top was an optimal continuing life in the hereafter, complete with worldly wealth.

I speculate here, but at least I can suggest an argument. The Igbo monetization of religious rank has quite different economic implications from the drive for singularity in other segmentary societies. The logic of religious rank is not one of redistribution, or of charismatic performative conspicuous consumption and destruction, or of accumulation of wealth in people. All these may exist as secondary themes. But the striking implication of an economics of rank, by contrast with a consumption logic of spending and maintaining monetary flow, is that rank encouraged an unusual level of saving in currency. This in turn would slow down, but not block, the circulation of money (see Meillassoux 1977, 170). It was eventually converted into another value, and much of it returned to transactional use, but in the meantime, "[t]he creation of large treasuries of currencies had in itself the effect of drawing currencies out of circulation and of stabilizing their value" (Muller 1982, 21). The most striking difference between the Igbo/Ibibio peoples and others lies in the broad social generality and the cultural cultivation of saving in money, linked, I have argued, to quantified religious aspirations.

IGBO SAVINGS

In addressing the recurrent intellectual problem of "the absence of hyperinflation during a period of huge money imports in West Africa in the era of the Atlantic slave trade" (Hogendorn and Johnson 1986, 146), Webb (1982) suggested long ago that saving or hoarding might be part of the answer to relative stability in value over quite long periods. It is worth remembering that money supply was uncontrolled:

> The wide fluctuations in English exports of copper and brass to Africa year by year through the eighteenth century would disappear if we took only decennial averages or a single total for the entire century, and yet each fluctuation tells us something about the societies in questions (or if we were able to decipher them fully): about production, demand, profitability, communications, conflict, human fallibility. (Herbert 1984, 180)

Webb is equally cautious about all assumptions of equilibrium dynamics: "the sheer variety of moneys, the varying rates of consumption, the vagaries of their supply, and the greater degree of flexibility in currency substitution obviously compromise these assumptions" (1982, 463).

One can never be definitive on these points, but the circumstantial evidence is quite strong that in Eastern Nigeria manillas were both relatively stable in value and relatively widely saved—two conditions that reinforce each other and that derive, I argue, from a very-long-term interaction of religious and commercial value. Insiders and outsiders alike note the relatively narrow range of variation, and the apparent self-correction, in the manilla's value at the interface with Europe and within Africa. "Unlike the iron bar and the cowrie the value of the manilla was enhanced during the nineteenth century, particularly in relation to the iron bar" (Jones 1958, 52). In 1856 a manilla cost 3d.; in 1873, it was 6d.; in the early twentieth century, it fell to between 2d. and 3d. (52); and in 1948 manillas were redeemed for 3d. Several summaries infer stability (Leonard 1998, 3; Ekejiuba 1995, 138).

The evidence for saving, of all currencies, is yet more persuasive than is the evidence for stability in value. Missionary George Basden wrote of the area he knew best, around Onitsha,

> the tendency to hoard . . . is as strong as ever. . . . I have been in some treasure houses where the store of cowries has reminded me of heaps of newly threshed corn. . . . It is a commonly accepted theory that money is hoarded, and this is indeed a fact. . . . money—either in cowries or silver coins—is banked extensively, native fashion. I have seen hundreds of pounds of silver and immense stores of cowries in a man's possession. Then how is it banked? Some say it is buried; if so, how and where? These questions I leave others to answer; it would not be cricket to reveal what one has learned in confidence. It was a matter of years before I was let into the secret, and then I made the discovery more by accident than design. (1921, 199, 200)

Basden's observation is reiterated in many sources. For the very rich, there was special architecture. "The famous architecture of one Chief Mbonu of Ndikelionwu referred to as the "maze" [Ogbaburuburu] was, like many others with similarly impressive architecture, designed to protect the cowry/manilla storehouses from being invaded or damaged" (Ekejiuba 1995, 139; see also Dike 1956, 163; Isichei 1973, 53). Smaller householders often had storerooms rather than treasure houses: "Several Aro and Delta State compounds also stored brass rods and manillas in special rooms, both in the main communities and in their settlement market centers" (Ekejiuba 1995, 146). As Basden says, storage was secret, on principle. It was surely known, but it was so deeply institutionalized that "[g]enerally people used bamboo doors for their houses even though the rooms might contain large amounts of money" (Isichei 1978, 90). Some was carefully buried, with oil as a preservative. When manillas were retired by the colonial state in 1948, "[m]any dug pits and broke casks where manillas had been stored as savings" (Amogu 1952, 139). In other cases, money was stored in shrines, with the threat of spiritual damage in case of theft (Nnamdi Elleh, personal communication). So without central political control of money wealth, there were nevertheless prominent and widespread practices of saving.

Under the economic and political conditions of Eastern Nigeria, stabilization of a currency value is so surprising that Nigerian scholars have even suggested that there was a kind of "policy" (Ekejiuba 1995, 138), a "genius . . . in their extraordinary powers of adaptability" (Dike 1956, 45). There certainly were centers of distribution such as Brass (Grey 1951, 53) and centers of commercial storage, such as the Ibibio "money magnets" who have "plenty . . . in store" and sell out when the prices rises (Offiong 1949). There were also specialists in recognizing counterfeits, a few of which turned up in the redemption campaign in 1948. Members of the Aro trade diaspora developed trade practices that were both imposed on and offered to their hosts, including the *nsibiri* writing used by members of the *ekpe* secret society and which crossed the Atlantic into the artistic and religious practices of the New World (Isichei 1978, 137). It is hard to imagine, however, that a few centers of specialist monetary skills could account entirely for the United Africa Company (UAC) finding that "the velocity of circulation of manillas was relatively stable" (1949, 47). In some sense, this retention of value was recognized when the manilla was withdrawn. The official UAC article on the campaign explains:

> One of the reasons why the African clung to the manilla was that its value tended to rise. If we could bring about a fall in the value of the manilla we could perhaps eliminate it. But this would be absolutely unacceptable: it would be equivalent to robbing the African peasant of the value of the manillas he holds, and would cause grave social unrest. (UAC 1949, 53)

It is significant that when manillas were redeemed, the majority of holders preferred to take shillings rather than the lower denominations of colonial currency that they were also offered (UAC 1949, 55). The government report summarizes the account: 308,991 shillings given out, and just over 50,000 of the four other denominations (6d., 3d., pennies, halfpennies) (Turner 1950, 11). The upward aspiration toward bigger things in life could hardly be more dramatically expressed. By contrast, the total loss remarked by Ofonagoro (1976), Hogendorn and Johnson (1986), and Gregory (1996) applied to cowries and other currencies whose performance had not resisted the onslaught of turbulence and manipulation that particularly marked the latter half of the nineteenth century: "Stocks of . . . cowries hoarded by being buried in the ground, a testimony to centuries of accumulation, have since been abandoned in their mute graves" (Ofonagoro 1976). They were more likely to have been placed there by a woman than a man, a trader such as Madame Naomi in the 1930s, who, "when her cowries reach too much . . . she digs a pit, a deep pit, and into it her cowries are poured. When this pit is full, she seals it and digs another and another" (Leith-Ross 1972, 94).

CONCLUSION

The gender dimension to ranking, religion, and savings remains a question and a puzzle because the sources are thin. The one point I make here is that all money valuation must implicate the social order. Until the originality of history can be explored, we cannot assume that we know what forms of that order make a difference to monetary dynamics, by virtue of both the internal ordering structure and external points of anchoring to the monetary scale. For Igbo and Ibibio economy, the intricacy, the formality, and the sheer imperative power of the ranking of persons were outstanding features, and they were central to economic life in "a pecuniary world" (Bascom 1951). The ranking structure may have differed in other societies in Atlantic Africa, but the fact of a ranked view of the social world as distinct from a class view or a simple age-seniority view, seems widespread. Lloyd writes of urban Yoruba in the mid-twentieth century that they see "society as a ladder up which individuals have risen to various degrees of success," by self-employment and self-improvement, through "entrepreneurship and individual achievement" (1974, 225–26).

This is as far as I want to take an argument here for the economic structuring power of competitive ranking. Does it affect consumption as well as saving? It is simply worth prefiguring my Ghana national household budget survey analysis. The aggregated result of individual economic practice in a ranking system may not correspond at all to the classic patterning by social class. Lloyd observes that even though there may be wide variation between rich and poor, "the Yoruba well fit Marx's classic description of the French peasantry as undifferentiated potatoes in a sack" (1974, 226). Chayanov (1966) and Western economists put the life cycle into the analytical tool kit for peasants and wage/salary earners alike, which reduced this sense of formlessness considerably. But the historical Igbo case shows that we have to go a very great deal further to understand how original economic patterns in savings and investment become visible in a new light through looking at competitive ranking in a money economy.

5

QUALITY
COMMODITIES AND PRICE

Application of numbers in transactions presumes other scales to which transactors peg them. There are types of goods, on a nominal scale, and within each type there are different qualities, on an ordinal scale. Neither of these orderings by themselves makes quality ranking directly amenable to numerical calculation. Another measure has to be added that explains and justifies the quality intervals. This, too, will tend to be numerical, by specific criteria: how long something lasts, how many times it will perform a task, how strong it is, and so on. In modern bureaucratized economies, nominal and ordinal scales are generally accepted as being established outside the price-setting market, by formal institutions such as expert panels, trade associations, and competitions. Goods reach the shelf via an intricate fine mesh of regulations in a degree of detail that probably completely escapes the ordinary consumer. There is a "moral economy" here that is also an expression of political struggle for the market (Busch 1995; Busch and Tanaka 1996). Is a two-piece woman's outfit, in which the pieces are made of different cloth, a "suit" or a "skirt" and a "jacket" with respect to trade within the European Community? Is 55 percent cocoa butter enough to classify a bar of confectionary as "chocolate"? The problem is particularly striking when the commodity at issue is intangible, such as intellectual property. But the challenge of turning a good "into something else with its own independent value" in order to make it "socially transactable" (Strathern 1999, 161) arises across the board. After classification, interval scales of quality are defined and attached to the goods: How much meat has to be in various grades of sausages, and how long can fresh food items remain on the shelf before sales?

Because there is no meaningful "zero" point with respect to quality, the pegging of quality to price necessarily involves criteria of judgment and expertise, as well as political pressure. That "this item" is better than "that item" has to be translated into "how much better," if not to set price (as in an administered price system) then to make price differentials meaningful and amenable to budgeting by consumers. Consumers in formalized economies are encouraged to see these quality scales as *emerging from* supply and demand, for which price (on a ratio scale) is the outcome. This price comes to stand plausibly for all the other scales, even if we have to be reminded of the expertise that supports them ("80 percent of doctors interviewed advised . . ."). For many mundane purchases, above all in a fairly stable economy, people can ask themselves whether they want the five-dollar hamburger or the ninety-nine-cent hamburger, with the quality difference of "worth" understood to be acceptably encapsulated in the price differential. In economics this follows by definition, since demand reflects utility.

The accuracy and usefulness of this reductionist approach to the analysis of demand has been open to new question in recent consumer economics (see, e.g., Mason 1998). A fortiori, in economies in which standards, measures, and their reductive commensuration with one another have not been institutionally enforced or culturally validated, the means of bridging the ordinal with the ratio scale, through intervals, remains open. Relative "worth" in a nonformalized price system is not just a chaos of "price response" behavior. It cannot be; no one would know how to judge the goods. Not only "value for money" would be up for grabs but so would product safety, as well as consumer standards of desirability on far more symbolic grounds. Criteria must be created and validated outside the formal sector, and it is to these other scales that I now turn.

Although the historical sources bear indirect witness to product classification, we do not have enough on what Mary Douglas has referred to as "the private conflicts being resolved in public fora" (1986, 49) through which novelty is legitimated. Working on Atlantic African economies, one hardly has to insist on one version or another of a constructivist theoretical argument because large domains of the commercial economy were literally historically constructed on the border between Africa and the West. What is more difficult is to identify and analyze the process of emergence itself. The kind of numeration I have discussed already facilitates conventional equations, which could be seen as invariant "custom," as expressed in the idea of "the customary price" (see Sundstrom 1974, 73, on "triangular exchanges"). Bohannan's concept of spheres of exchange picks up on this aspect of stabilization — as custom. Such institutions may well have worked to stabilize random fluctuations, and certainly people may have invoked them to defend tradition. They were not, however, fixed or inimical to novelty. How can one focus empirically on the creation of the other scales, besides numerical measurement, as they emerge and are matched with each other?

The reception of imports into African markets offers one possibility. Imports have a very long, varied, and shifting history, which continues in new surges since the opening up of the global market (on central Africa, see Hansen 2000). Throughout its trading history, Atlantic Africa seems to have relied heavily on experts to judge the quality of goods. As de Brazza's experience with guns exemplifies, African consumers were discriminating in their choices (see also Steiner 1985). Doubtless some rubbish was also floated into the trade networks by opportunists and idiosyncratic adventurers. Colonial control — at least in anglophone Africa — changed this. Colonial governments promoted the interests of larger corporations, which could be relied on logistically and politically, as against a multiplicity of potentially fly-by-night enterprises. So for most of its colonial and immediate postcolonial history, Nigeria imported predominantly through the large companies that worked in partnership with government. As a result, for most of that period imported goods were expensive but of similar standardized quality to the same goods sold in the metropolitan countries. For just a brief moment, when the Nigerian currency was "overvalued" in the late 1970s and early 1980s, international standardized quality and Nigerian affordability coincided — with each other and with Nigerian self-valuation. The price of new cars, tractors, textiles, and other high-end goods fell within the reach of quite ordinary people. Even a dependable small-scale commercial farmer in the food supply hinterland of a major city could buy a new vehicle in installments from a dealer. People now refer to this moment as "when Nigeria was Nigeria," when their collective judgment of their own worth was implicitly endorsed by the international market.

The decline of postcolonial states' capacities and the surge in the entrepreneurship of traders in the popular economy have shifted the whole process of product definition and quality standards back again into the popular domain. From 1986 to 1996, the currency (the naira) devalued against the dollar from parity to eighty, in a series of lurches. Consumer prices responded, lurching upward over the entire ten years: one week, toothpaste, the next macaroni, and the next, local foodstuffs. The price of new vehicles, and even a new tire for an old vehicle, quickly rose beyond middle-class salaries because wages and salaries were controlled. The 1989 riots against structural adjustment marked a moment of desperation before a new set of accommodating forces set in. In the 1990s, a flood of low-quality goods from all over the world poured into consumer markets. By the mid-1990s, with the currency deeply devalued and the collaborative relationship between the military state and major economic actors deeply corrupt, the value registers seemed in profound disarray. An impoverished population was presented with a new consumer situation: totally new goods; goods from new producers and places; goods in a variety of qualities and prices they had never seen before; secondhand (and third- and fourth-hand) goods; goods labeled in Chinese, Russian, and other languages that even a widely traveled population might have no expertise to decipher; old goods in new packages; and harmless counterfeits, ineffective copies, and dangerous substitutes. People have been poisoned by tainted oil, burned by adulterated kerosene, and sent into kidney failure by fake or contaminated injections. The opportunity for outright fraud is great, and danger can never be out of the consumer's mind. At the same time, goods with defined and understood qualities are moved through a pricing mechanism that delivers them to customers and makes gains for sellers, under conditions in which formally standardized goods are simply unattainably expensive.

QUALITY CONTROL: WHAT IS A FAKE?

Classification/Product Definition

In Yoruba cultural process, nominalization carries deeply significant implications. Novelty is embraced, not necessarily by adopting the foreign word for the new good or by assimilating something new to an existing classification but by inventing a completely new term that may indicate the history of its arrival on the scene, or the circumstances or person associated with its origin. Rather than developing intricate taxonomic structures, Yoruba culture is particularly brilliant at designating and manipulating names for things (and people, and all other phenomena) that are encapsulated narratives. Names make possible what cognitive anthropologists call "chunking," that is "to package together previously formed structures and treat them as if they were single objects" (D'Andrade 1990, 77). I have noted how the tropic points, or pegs, on the numerical scale can be allusive across value registers, even invoking history and morality when placed in particular discursive contexts. Very many Yoruba words are polysemic, and there is a constant inventive play on new configurations. A term for frozen fish *(okú Èkó)* means literally "corpses from Lagos"; financial crime is referred to as 419, a reference to the clause in the penal code on advance-fee fraud; a fifty-naira note is a *muri*, after President Muritala Muhammed, because his face is on it; a very bright kind of cloth is referred to as NEPA (the Nigerian Electric Power Authority, which fails so often that this cloth can serve as a substitute to provide light); a Datsun pickup is a *jálukere*, "let's all descend into the potholes," indicating exactly the rural nature of the market for the vehicle and the state of the roads when it was introduced. Being an educated consumer in a Yoruba market requires knowing a large vocabulary of terms, being able to identify the specific attributes that are "chunked" together, and staying aware of fast-moving changes that mix and match the attributes of goods. A seller can always try to gain the premium on novelty by inventing a new term for the good she puts up for sale. But rather than allowing an unlimited expansion of the nominal process, the Nigerian market of the 1980s and 1990s adopted a set of qualifiers.

Attribution of Quality

In a volatile mass market, the consumers know nothing of the producers, and both products and prices change quickly. Beyond stretching nominalization toward its outer limits, the greatest innovation in this situation has been the introduction of a series of qualifying terms added to the name of the good, each of which has an expected price effect. This benchmarks the purchase. In Western Nigeria, two great crosscutting categories have been invented to describe goods. Each can then be combined with a profusion of other qualifiers, many of them specific to each commodity. The basic structure is two dichotomous categories: *original* versus *fake* and *new* (*tútù* or "fresh," or *tuntun,* "new," in Yoruba) versus *tokúnbọ̀*.

To take *new/tokúnbọ̀* first: New (*tútù*) is not a new concept, nor one applied only to goods in the market. It has a very broad meaning, as does the word *new* in English. People can talk of a new wife or boyfriend as well as a new car. When used for goods, as a contrast with *tokúnbọ̀* and pronounced in English, it probably now refers only to imports.[1] *Tokúnbọ̀* is unique to the structural adjustment era and can be defined approximately but inaccurately (as I explain later in the chapter) as "secondhand." The word *tokúnbọ̀* itself is a personal name, a diminutive of Adetokúnbọ̀, which means literally "a crown [*adé*] returns [*bọ̀*] from overseas [*ti òkun*]." It is given to a child conceived or born away from home, generally (for Nigerians) in Europe. It was explained to me that designating secondhand imports as *tokúnbọ̀* probably started with cars around 1986, in the first stages of devaluation. The name indicated that this commodity had already lived a previous life abroad. It had then, and has to some degree retained, a wry allusion to a personal honorific. As prices rose in the mid-1980s, and people could not afford new things as they once had, they dignified secondhand goods with an honorific. The term is still applied exclusively to secondhand imports, and not secondhand goods in general. Even secondhand parts from articles that were originally imported as new and have already served in Nigeria — such as spare parts of tractors — are not referred to as *tokúnbọ̀* but as *àlòkù,* a Yoruba term for "used things." People will correct one's usage if the wrong term is used.

Original and *fake* may well be older than the structural adjustment program era, but the expansion of their use is certainly related to the conditions associated with that era. They are terms that apply across the board to both new and used goods, local and imported. As the Asian market expanded, as the range of *tokúnbọ̀* goods broadened from cars and engines to everything else, including dated pharmaceuticals and used medical equipment, and as the government took less and less interest in quality regulation, this distinction has set into the market vocabulary. Because it is more

---

1. Although I'm not entirely sure of that. Made in Nigeria goods tend to have their own names that take semantic precedence over newness and perhaps are not conceptualized as amenable to trade on a secondhand market at all.

complex than *tokúnbò* and *new,* I look at the distinction in more detail later in the chapter. Suffice it here to summarize that every imported product can be bought in one of four categories: new/original, new/fake, *tokúnò/* original, and *tokúnbò*/fake. This provides a nominal grid for descriptive purposes. A consumer can always go back to that and make independent judgments of quality between them on personal grounds. The institutions of the market, however, rank the four.

Grading

The terms *original/fake* give structure to product grading by benchmarking quality and price to an ideal at the top of the quality scale. Each product has its own benchmark in a brand and/or a country of origin; *original* refers to this benchmark. It resembles top brand-name recognition in that it encapsulates a perception and an experience of quality: of the time the good lasts, the way it works, the replaceability of parts, dependability and longevity in the market, desirability, and so on. Another definition given to me was "goods that can be traced to the inventor are also termed original." When versions of a trademarked good come from different countries, only a very restricted number will be designated as "original," and this designation is commodity specific. In 1997, Phillips electronics marked "Made in Holland" were more likely to be judged original that Phillips made elsewhere.[2] But not everything from Holland is original. Neither is everything from England or the United States necessarily original, at least not to the highest standard (*gidi gidi,* really real). The United States is best in rice but "struggled for no. 2 in textiles." In tailoring and other artisanship, London used to be the pinnacle of originality; as my student research assistant 'Tunji Ojo wrote: "As a small boy growing up in the 70s, there were drivers, tailors and seamstresses, native doctors, bicycle repairers, wrist watch repairers, goldsmiths etc. whose advertisements were incomplete without a phrase 'trained in London' or 'London trained' written boldly on their cards or signposts." Over time, however, a country's preeminence can be lost and gained, according to the judgment of discerning Nigerian expertise. In cars, the Yoruba word *japan* is synonymous with original. In the 1970s, Datsun dominated the Nigerian market in rural transport because its pickup truck so perfectly matched the need: small and tough enough to manage any road conditions, with two rows of seats for passengers as well as storage space big enough for a large number of sacks or baskets, and with an indestructible radio. Designation as original may refer in part to the operation of formal standardization in the countries of origin and to international criteria of excellence. But it surely also indexes to predictable quality and ser-

2. The rise of China as a source of so many consumer goods may change this.

vice, as established by experience with a product in the Nigerian market and constantly verified by Nigerian practice.

The term *original,* then, designates a restricted category of high-status commodities, the top of the quality scale for each product. *Fake* refers globally to all the rest, and therefore contains the potential for further internal differentiations. The term does not mean fake in the sense of a product aimed to deceive. Neither is it the same as our *imitation* (or genteel euphemisms such as *faux*), where close resemblance is aimed for but without any intent to deceive, as with pearls, furs, or art prints. The scale of *fake* works along the lines of a leader/follower model. The first, the leader, the exemplar, the name given, the benchmark, defines the standard. *Fake* bears the implication of a pale copy, a derivative, a lower standard, but not necessarily that the commodity is fraudulent, much less that it does not work at all. The products of some countries are — by definition — fakes, at least for the moment, until experience suggests a shift. Here are the manufacturing countries associated with *fake* according to my research assistant: Belgium, Taiwan, Brazil, Malaysia, Thailand, India, Holland, and Africa. Nigeria has its own manufacturing sector, especially in automobile spare parts. These all fall into the "fake" category, or can be referred to alternatively as "Igbo-made" (referring to the ethnicity of the producers) or "Aba-made" (referring to the major industrial town for automobile spare parts). On the status scale, Igbo-made falls at the bottom of the fakes, at least within Nigeria. A colleague tells me that elsewhere in West Africa, Nigerian-made commodities fall higher up the scale.

One major justification for the difference between original and fake is implicitly quantitative: that fakes won't last as long as the original, that they won't produce as much output, that they won't give — to use a common Nigerian-English word —"satisfaction." Let me quote from 'Tunji Ojo's diary, on soap powder:

> Omo washing detergent for many years was the leading detergent, followed by Surf. Omo is blue and Surf is white and green. Other brands soon came with other colours but the people do describe all blue detergents as Omo and white and green as Surf. . . . At the retailers' table [where bulk has been broken into small non-identified plastic bags] the terms "fake" and "original" converge, except for the experienced buyer. But as soon as you wash and you don't get enough satisfaction as with Omo detergent produced by Lever Brothers, then the original and fake terminologies come in. Original meaning the one that gives the best satisfaction.

Satisfaction corresponds to a Yoruba word, a verb, *to,* meaning "to be enough." It refers to completion rather than a measurable amount, that is, to a concept of wholes that surpass the parts; Helen Verran (2001) has elucidated this concept in Yoruba quantification. That standard, and the comparison with the performance of a fake, can yield an interval scale that, in turn, can justify the price differential. How many loaves can a sack of this flour make versus that flour? How big a pile of clothes can this versus that detergent wash? How long will this brand of spare parts last, and what stress can it support, versus that one? Judgments can only work to structure pricing if expertise is brought to bear on the problem. For example, one often-used measure with respect to many manufactured goods is time: how long will it last? Experts can predict this quite accurately: "What of electric light bulbs? I doubt it you would use any for two months again" (Ojo, quoting a consumer).

The combination of nominal and quantified characteristics means that a fake may be preferable to an original under certain conditions. An honest and friendly seller will ask you outright: Do you want original or fake? The buyer may well decide for a fake. For example, a cash-strapped tractor owner who has to make repairs toward the end of the season may decide to accept his mechanic's advice and buy a fake spare part, so he (and the tractor) keep working for a short while longer. At the beginning of the plowing season, he might try to stretch his budget or take a loan in order to buy an original.

A newspaper cartoon illustrates the reasoning with elegance and precision. Titled "General Knowledge," the sequence of three pictures follows a conversation between a seller of automobile spare parts and the owner of a *tokúnbọ̀* car during one of the periods of increased police surveillance for breaches of the road safety code.

> Customer: D'you have piston and rings? I want to refurbish my smoking *tokúnbọ̀* car, before those road marshals impound it.
> Seller: Yes, *oga* [boss]. Original is N3,000, while fake is N1,000.
> Customer: I see. Can the fake last three months?
> Seller: Well, yes, *oga,* but the original will last at least two years. I strongly recommend it.
> Customer: Anyway, give me the fake. I'm sure their *shakara* [bluffing] won't go beyond two months.
> Seller: (Getting the goods.) You're right, *oga.*
> (Obe Ess, *The Guardian,* April 30, 1996, 16)

I could not wish for a better example of the consumer calculus, complete with its repertoire of scales, here extended to include a quantified expression of civic experience with the law. The consumer combines a measure of the commodity with a measure of the demand it has to satisfy and comes up with a binary standard of success: either it will save his car from impoundment or it will not. Having rehearsed the logic with the seller, it is strongly implied that the latter will be accountable for the "satisfaction" his product affords. These equations can never be exact or completely dependable, but people are clearly working with a quantified "general knowledge" of some complexity. The cartoon may exaggerate the relative prices this reasoning produces, but not by much, as the following exploration of price scales suggests.

Scales

These large-category distinctions are combined to produce price scales; "new original," "new fake," "original *tokúnbò*," and "fake *tokúnbò*" can be ordered. A single price scale is made out of a mint condition name-brand product, a new lower-standard product, a secondhand import of a name-brand product, and a secondhand import of a lower-standard product. I tried tabulating the price scales that emerge from these definitional processes. With not much expectation of illumination, given the complexity and turbulence of the market, I elicited notional prices for original, fake, and secondhand (in this case *àlòkù*) tractor parts, from expert dealers. Ojo collected prices for automobile parts and hair relaxers. To my surprise there were patterns in the ratios of prices across the products. Of course, one would need to test them out on a whole variety of other products; perhaps the correspondence is an artifact. It is interesting, nonetheless, since none of my discussions had prepared me for the price comparability of new fakes and original *tokúnbò*s, or their solid position at about two-thirds the price of new originals. The fakes with additional disabling features fall to half or a third of the price of the new original (table 5.1).

These are very unlikely to be the "actual" prices for any specific transac-

Table 5.1. Nigerian Price Ratios, as Elicited from Expert Operators, Ibadan, 1997 and 1998

COMMODITY			
1. Fuel injector pump for a tractor (1997)			
Original	New fake	*Àlòkù* (used; in this case not *tokúnbò*)	
100	70	55	
2. Toyota Corolla spare parts (1998)			
	New original	Original *tokúnbò*	New fake	Fake *tokúnbò*
Radiator	100	60	66	33
Gearbox	100	66	66	50
Carburator	100	60	80	50
3. Hair relaxers			
Imported (mean of 4 brands)		Local fake (mean of 15 brands)	
100		31	

tion, conditioned as these are by all the calculative flexibilities already discussed. What I take them to represent is an expert's rule of thumb, that—if stable over time—might yield a concept of right or fair price, that everyone can rely on to some degree. They may be the modern equivalent of the tropic number: a guide to orders of magnitude, possible thresholds of relative value where price and quality can be pegged to each other, and the dimensions of the marginal gains can be judged in a very uncertain economic world, all anchored by the benchmark of the "new original." Even with this kind of guideline, judgment is complex and knowledge is at a premium. The seller has to know the benchmark and be able to judge the interval deviations from it. Quality control has always been a critical, but underplayed, function of the well-known institution of the "customer" relationship (Trager 1981). A good seller has to know the full range of qualities for the commodities she deals in and be able to give reliable recommendations to her regular customers. In their focus on credit, economic sociologists (e.g., Granovetter 1993) have overemphasized the monetary side of trust and not recognized the critically important element of trust in quality. Someone has to know how long an Igbo-made spark plug is supposed to last and therefore how much it should usually cost relative to one made in Brazil. Textiles are another example. Unless a consumer buys regularly from her own trader, she should never buy after dusk or in a dark corner; she should always fray the edges of the fabric to see the nature of the weave; if possible, she should burn a thread to see how it melts or flares; and so on. Access to a helper who can provide sound advice on the product and its properties, or preferably accompany the buyer to the market, is a valuable resource to be cultivated.

Fraud

The ultimate danger is not fakes, where the damage from ignorance is usually within the limits of the accepted value scale; it is outright fraud. As Adam (1995) and Belasco (1980) both pointed out, cheating by the seller is not necessarily regarded as reprehensible. Looking at the issue analytically, it seems clear that this kind of "traditional" acceptable cheating deals only with the secondary qualifying and ordinal scales, and is therefore self-limiting: the buyer gets less, pays more than they "should," but by a conventional margin. Fraud, by contrast, breeches criteria for the primary naming of the commodity. The goods turn out not to be what the seller said they were; they only resemble the real thing. During the market scramble of the 1990s, the most common method of fraud was by "recycling" labels, bottles, and boxes by packing original containers with fraudulent goods. Original containers commanded their own market (see Sridar et al. 2002). There was a period when Eagle flour bags were stolen much more regularly than the flour itself because the bags could be used over and over again to validate a substandard product. *Tòkúnbọ̀* clothes are raked over to find name-brand labels, and empty bottles with intact labels and corks command a price. Returned to the market by the recycling industry, gin bottles contain water and a television cabinet may contain rocks. One of our colleagues saw gelatin capsules for medication being laboriously filled with cassava flour. Commodities became chaotic pastiches of counterfeit boxes made in China, instructions in Arabic, bottles recycled from Western or Nigerian goods, filled with contents that defied all identification. That "original" brands actually *were* now Made in China added enormously to the classification and valuation challenge.

Further notes by Ojo are illuminating:

> Look at that iron. I saw it at Ogunpa and I liked it. Very light. Phillips, you know. I was given its container and on it — look at it here — "Made in China." So not Igbo-made. The boy even gave me his business card. The iron never worked for two months, and when I took it back to the seller he simply blamed me for not regulating the voltage. N1,500 gone.

That fraud occurs in certain commodity markets, however, draws attention to the fact that there do exist regular frameworks for product definition and "quality control," over a remarkably wide array of commodities in spite of minimal regulatory attention from the formal sector.

Central Places

Speculations remain. I feel convinced of these ordering processes. But where do they come from? New cognitive categories and price-stabilizing concepts are created. Rather than imagine that they emerge by anonymous cultural processes, I suggest that there are market leaders, places where the expertise is localized, where new names are launched and product quality assessed. Here I am extrapolating from my previous work on "wealth-in-knowledge" and building from a few clues from field research. Certainly West African populations index judgment: to benchmark qualities, tropic numbers, specific locations and — I believe — concentrations of expertise. Ojo described how certain markets are thought to embody the right price/quality nexus: "The Agodi Gate Motor Park market is the leading 2nd hand vehicle spare parts market in Ibadan, just like the Daleke market in Lagos. . . . So the spirit is to know which market sells what and of what quality." Una Okonkwo, an economist from Eastern Nigeria, also suggested to me that there are particularly powerful nodes in distributive systems, or particularly powerful operators, who anchor market conditions and create key conceptual innovations. For example, she thought that Onitsha was a great center in the imported cosmetics market for the whole country. Consumers learn to read the indicators in their own local markets, but the system as a whole is regional, referring to central places in new geographies of a market power that goes far beyond material control: to sources of goods and to conceptual control over the terms of market operation and criteria of consumer valuation. Here the analysis would move in new directions, to link the creation of commodity categories and registers, modes of calculation and projection of gains, to the social organization of market expertise and market control. It would demand new research to do justice to this critically important nexus in which cultural and practical knowledge meet market control.

CONCLUSION

A plausible market regime depends as much on nominal and ordinal processes as it does on the numerical expression of price. They are all logically necessary, socially organized, and culturally represented. The view I have pursued in these three chapters of part 2 is of a dynamic market in Atlantic Africa. It is intrinsically linked to the interface with the Western world's merchant capitalism and economic nationalism, yet because of the relative absence of formal-sector imposition of standard commensuration, scales of value have been constructed and the disjunctures between them both cultivated and bridged. The ways in which these were mediated had material consequences: for the facility of trade and the domestication of an economy of marginal gains, for the velocity of circulation of money and consumer access and safety. The nonreductive nature of the repertoire of value scales, in the absence of formal insistence on reduction, means that people have worked back and forth across them. Each one has been a product of local emergent processes, in which reasoning is intrinsic to performance and social action. Gains large and small can be built into the linking of one scale to another. In the context of expanding industrial capitalism, Europe's gains have been vast, as the resources acquired in Africa were revalued according to its own modes of reductive rationality expressed in formal accounting of profit on capital. This revaluation was intrinsic to trade, as I illustrated in one small example in chapter 2 on conversions. My main concern, rather, has been to show how ordinary gains on monetary transactions have been framed within Africa: by maintenance of repertoires, linkage of scales, elaboration of criteria for the valuation of people, and orientation to expansive frontiers.

Recent scholarship in the humanities, especially on Yoruba creativity, has been an inspiration and a guide. The ethnography and history of the market I have summarized here corresponds closely to aesthetic and philosophical themes studied from text and performance. The cultivation of multiplicity and the protection of alternatives are recurring themes. Barber writes of

Yoruba oral literature that "[i]n the Yoruba case . . . the proliferation of al-ternative perspectives, the holding open of possibilities, the deferral of final ideological resolution, is itself a dominant value" (1991, 13). Historian Adebayo (1999) describes the coexistence of contradictions and disso-nances in the morality of money. And in her detailed philosophical analysis of Yoruba numbering, Verran writes that colonial officers and Ibadan citi-zens "invented routine actions [about numbering] that linked them up in contingent ways" (2001, 98). Monetary numbering "encodes the patterns made in the process of material ordering" (199), and in "modes of present-ing" (70), that is, in performance. She insists that the numbering embedded in any transaction is a "punctuation point," a temporary "clot" generated by and dissolving back into "a set of routine and repetitive practices" that are never erased. Multiplicity and contingency are pervasive. The routine marginal gains of life are produced on these disjunctures between scales, through performative skill at successfully bringing them together.

This exploration can be satisfying for cultural anthropologists. And yet for economic or social anthropological analysis, the approach must do more. It must necessarily link the frameworks of cultural and social construction to people's actions and to the outcomes of their actions. From conditions to purposes; from number as a cultural scale to number as a tool in eco-nomic and social practice. We need to return, with greater nuance, to ra-tionality. Rational economic thinking has come to be equated with the quantitative logic of choice among alternative allocations of scarce means. How then to explore and depict the "intelligence of interest" (to quote Morgan again) in the Atlantic African context? According to Adam's care-ful ethnography of Yoruba artisans, they prevent paralysis of indecision precisely by *avoiding* "rationality" in this recent Western sense. She was par-ticularly struck with the lack of accounting logic in artisans' business plan-ning, even though they are so savvy about margins in individual transac-tions. They rarely summarize the past in calculative terms; they do not keep account books, even when they are literate and know how to do so; and they do not plan in precise terms. "Costing is seldom based on calculation, as the term is understood in Europe. Most small scale entrepreneurs do not plan in advance and they do not assess their total costs" (Adam 1995, 78). They are finely focused on intricacy in transactions while almost completely "neglecting" to make any integrated calculation of the business as a whole.

Adam argues against a cultural explanation, in favor of a historical and situational one. Rational projective calculation would even be detrimental, she argues: a waste of time, intelligence, and nervous energy, under the conditions in which these producers and traders find themselves.

There is no regularity in their obligations, no organized system imposed and maintained by the regular arrival of accounts due for services: bills from public utilities are not sent on a monthly or any other regular basis and the amounts to be paid often seemed equally arbitrary. Thus it was common to hear of small businesses with only a light bulb or very few electrical instruments suddenly being billed for several years of industrial consumption. . . . Expenses of this type are in their nature utterly unpredictable. No rational plan could altogether prepare for such events and none of the small-scale tradesmen/women even attempted to develop such strategies. (Adam 1995, 78)

Unpredictability and a nonexistent, or intermittently incoherent, Western formal sector are the conditions under which the varied commercial cultures of Atlantic Africa developed and expanded. Its economic practices today are still consonant with those realities.

Does this mean, then, that there is no way of addressing purposive economic action in the small-scale popular economy, except perhaps as short-term "coping"? If people cannot reasonably be "rational," in the very narrow sense this concept has acquired, can their actual reasoning and its results be understood at all in purposive terms? I turn to facets of this question in part 3, shifting the emphasis from the construction of scales and the logic of gain to the way these are used in practice: as always, in the popular economy of the vast numbers of small operators.

PART III

PERFORMANCES
AND REPERTOIRES

In historic Atlantic Africa, the terms for mediating value scales have not been comprehensively imposed by the authority of the state, financial institutions, or religious officials (as in Muslim economies). The nature of currencies, the status implications of goods, the quality of commodities, and even the numerical systems at play become even more complicated to study than they were in life if we apply methods that derive from assumptions of natural or official certainty. Everything becomes "complex" when anchored to those standards. I like Mirowski's (1991) imagery of preventing seasickness in choppy waters: better to focus on the horizon than weight oneself down to a single spot or a pure measure. There are three implications that I follow out in this section.

First, transactions become performances when more than several variables (or scales) are at issue. Western market organization is finely structured, practically and ideologically, to place price at the center in each transaction. Everything else is ideally decided in advance, so that there is a single point at which supply and demand intersect through the implicit bargaining embodied in market forces. The concealment of the regulatory mesh on which the market depends is the key defining feature of Marx's concept of commodity fetishism. In African transactions, more than the social relations of production is at stake. Scales of various kinds, tropic points, and numeration conventions may all, or severally, enter into negotiation. The scales, like perspective, eventually meet somewhere, but there is considerable leeway about exactly where that point is in each case. A conversionary transaction can be made more or less "equivalent," according to the context in which it takes place. The fact that there is leeway offers the opportunity, and even the need, for charismatic resolutions — new ways of bringing the scales together in novel situations, or enactments of one or another established configuration that are perfectly attuned to a specific context. Mundane charisma is exceptionally important. People are entrepreneurs, in the literal sense of "bringing together" the valuation repertoire, much of the time. The equation of Schumpeter's (capitalist) entrepreneurship with Weber's concept of (nonrational) charisma is not the paradox in Africa that it has seemed in Western theory (see Swedberg 1991, 1999). Chapter 6 describes such a charismatic performance in the kind of mundane crisis situation that I am suggesting characterizes, and to some extent explains, Atlantic African economic experience.

Second, important conversionary transactions — that is, transactions that transform ephemeral income into more enduring assets — become institutions in the sense that names are fixed on them (such as *bilaba*) and their components become conventionalized. The view from experience should suggest that stabilization is both highly desired and very problematic. Standard economic theory produces another contradiction here, beyond those I addressed in chapter 1. The macrotheory of "small open economies" predicts recurrent instability, whereas the theory of institutions is predicated on incremental growth. By the macrotheory, it would be hard to predict any kind of practices as producing enough confidence in enduring conditions to take on the aura of stability. A variety of logics converge in my own suggestion here (chap. 7). Like scales, transactional institutions do not form mutually entailed systems but rather relatively open repertoires. New institutions can be added, without necessarily eliminating the precedents, especially where official interdiction is rare. People preserve the repertoire, rather than "rationalizing" it unto a system, Weberian style. This, too, involves performative reinterpretation of the elements that compose transactional institutions. The evidence suggests that this expansion and contraction of the compositional elements of an institution may follow a finely tuned sense of *priority* and *proportion,* qualities that I rediscover in chapter 8.

Finally, the conventional concepts of profit margins as destined to "investment," of personal income margins to "savings," and the purchase of goods to "consumption" derive from the logic of formal banking. "Savings" and "investment" become capital through loan institutions, as distinct from money devoted to "consumption," which continues in circulation as currency. Without these financial technologies, there is no clear basis on which to classify either people's spending patterns or their assets. The purchase of "consumption" items may offer a return in the future, exactly as Bohannan argued by calling conversions "investment" and as many examples in the previous chapters illustrate. In a competitive social-ranking system such as that in Eastern Nigeria, "distinction" is not only expressive but instrumental. A radical methodological alternative to classifying almost everything as consumption, with the residual seen as savings and investment, would be to think of almost everything as an investment, a performative conversion, a devotion of present income to the hope of future gains. In chapter 8 I try out this idea on a national budget study, again addressing a conundrum that has remained difficult to address for decades.

6

VOLATILITY
A PERFORMANCE IN MODERN NIGERIA

With respect to any particular transaction, the institutions that have been built up over long-term experience with volatility and with marginality to the formal sector presume a certain indeterminacy *other than the final price*. The relevant scales and the tropic concepts that link them are at play, as well as the final amount that the calculus produces. Before trying to place these varied results into existing analytical categories — as a discount for personal ties or a premium on trustworthiness — it is worth looking at transactions as they unfold, as performances. In many contexts, reaching an agreement about the matching of value scales has been not just a performance in the anthropological sense but a full-fledged drama. *Bilaba* was a performance in all the most obvious senses of the term. It was dramatically competitive; roles were improvised upon; goods were displayed; the audience participated vociferously; personal charisma was paraded. The outcome was not only a price but the restatement of all the relevant scales of value: for goods, people, currencies, numbers, directions, ethnic communities, kinship relations, and so on. Even in small and routine contexts, scripts were played out and played with, as in the elaborate episode of dissimulation, described by Adam (1995, 83), to establish a high price for a particular customer at a garage mechanic's workshop. Multiple discussions and decisions may be required to establish what exactly is at stake in any particular instance, as Berry (2001) has emphasized. The resolution then places this particular configuration of recognitions, terms, and novelties within the ongoing market repertoire. In more or less subtle ways, it may set precedents of inclusion or exclusion, in comparable manner to the way in which Moore (1986) suggests that sequences of legal adjudications may gradually make certain claims inadmissible.

The concept of performance can apply to all transactional institutions. But particularly dangerous or exigent moments dramatize the techniques of resolution and suggest how a particular intervention may configure the terms in new ways. It is only logical to my overall argument that I take a response to crisis circumstances as my signal example. By *crisis* I mean simply a situation so difficult to bridge that violence was an imminent possibility at all stages. The incident I analyze here hinged on a classic condition of Atlantic African trade, namely, a sudden and incomprehensible shortage of a widely demanded good. Shortage is a different phenomenon from complete penury. It means that some of the good is accessible, but the place, the time, the terms, the amounts, and the identity of the brokers are all at issue. The classic market solution is to allow the price to rise. The managed solution is rationing. Neither solution may be socially tenable. Price rises for highly desired goods breed a rising hatred of brokers and eventually conflict over control. There are many historical examples of inland populations trying to oust the coastal middlemen and cut their monopoly advantage by force of arms. Rationing, on the other hand, is very difficult to manage because the potential loopholes can be so numerous. It was from daily experience that the architect of Britain's food rationing system in World War I referred to it as a work of "toiling ingenuity" (Beveridge 1928).

The fuel shortages in Nigeria during the Abacha regime (1993–98) were the most severe in the history of that oil-producing country. Whenever and wherever some petrol became available, or a rumor about availability arose, the crowd that gathered was anxious, angry, and exhausted even before distribution began. And distribution was largely left in the hands of the station owner, hindered rather than helped by the arm of the law.

The following vignette shows a resolution that depended entirely on the sophisticated manipulation of scales and equivalences. I am not going so far as to claim that either particular conversionary institutions or their use in crises is necessarily "successful" in buffering the effects of volatility or in redistributing resources justly. In fact, I have pointed out that the conversion dynamic can be a wedge for differentiation, even under the rubric of conceptual stabilization. But when people "act," as Mirowski (1991) put it, in conditions of radical indeterminacy, there are some actions that play the registers in ways that maintain the market and diffuse the danger of outright violence. Multiplied thousands of times, such mediations may account for the sheer continuity of commercial life under conditions of unpredictability probably as serious as any since the great cowry inflation of the previous century.

PETROL IN NIGERIA

The national economy of Nigeria was astonishingly badly — venally, corruptly, incompetently — managed during the 1990s, and yet life within the popular economy was not lived on the brink of disaster (see Guyer, Denzer, and Agbaje 2002). There were protests but no major riots over food prices and availability. The standard of living was severely eroded, but there was no mass outright starvation. Vehicles of spectacular decrepitude still ferried goods from place to place. This was not because the so-called informal sector was either independent of the state and the formal sector, or was in some generic way "resilient," but because the economy and society through which livelihoods are made and assets are created was intensely active. Life and livelihood were at stake in the skills brought to the performative arena, as one must imagine they had also been during earlier centuries of commercial life.

Why look at petrol in particular as a window into much more general processes? Because petrol is now the lifeblood of an economy in which a myriad of dispersed small producers do business with a myriad of dispersed small consumers. Petrol is almost the analog of imported currencies in the past; commercial life is impossible without it. Everyone needs a tank of petrol: for a motorbike to get to farm or to work; for a taxi for mobility from town to country; for a truck to move produce to market. Every shortage created a collective crisis. As managed by the Abacha government, the petrol price created thousands of turbulent situations a day, and at every petrol station across the country. The potential for chaos, and therefore the importance of the popular transactional institutions, cannot be overexaggerated.

This is the background. In March of 1997, a new phase of shortages began to set in, adding to a situation that had been intermittently threatening for several years. In hindsight, it seems that officials of the government at the time had compiled several different opportunities for rentier gains into one encompassing scheme. All four Nigerian refineries had been allowed to fall into disrepair. Several years' worth of allotted funds for their upkeep had disappeared. The necessary imports from South America then offered several other thresholds for gain by officials, using the power of formalization (customs, licenses, allotments, currency arbitrage, and so on, of which more in chap. 9). A lid was kept on the official price, which allowed a favored sector in the "black market" to work several kinds of profit of its own, while making the government look as if it were a friend of the people. The official price of eleven naira per liter (about twelve cents at the time) immediately came under pressure whenever shortages threatened. There was no information about when the pinch would be felt, what its causes were, how serious or long lasting it might be, whether it would be nationwide or whether favored regions would be spared, and so on. As supplies ebbed and flowed, people tried to guess the causes and second-guess the rumors about which tanker was driving where. Official silence dragged on for weeks. Rumors became more elaborate, or perhaps more accurate. It was said that the Nigerian elite had acquired direct ownership rights in the Venezuelan oil that was intermittently being imported to fill the gap, adding yet another reason to suspect that there was no end in sight. Eventually, after several weeks of desperate difficulty, the military head of state stepped in to promise, as a personal gesture, to import enough petrol to service the nation's needs within forty-eight hours, thus forcing the population into a position of personal, if highly skeptical, dependence on his patronage.

Some catastrophes occurred during those almost-dry weeks. Perishable products destined for the urban markets perished. Severe accidents resulted when people tried storing petroleum products in their houses and doing amateur mixing at home. Petrol was sometimes mixed with kerosene, causing danger to both the machines and the people. Car motors were ruined. On at least one reported occasion, a frantic customer threw a match into the crowd pressing around a petrol pump, causing an explosion and loss of life. Sick people failed to get to hospital in time. Students trekked to their research sites. But, as far as one could tell from being there and reading the press, the kind of measured distribution of the little petrol there was accounted for an improbably high proportion of the economic action. The product was not diluted, and the distribution was orderly. The key challenge was how to match a controlled price, under the eyes of the law, to a large and impatient clientele whose demand clearly surpassed the quantity available. The ranking of people and manipulations of the add-on *(eeni)* approach that were discussed earlier were key to the process, at least in the western, Yoruba area of the country.

PRICES AND VALUE SCALES

Limits and frontiers in manipulation of scales are expressed in specific moral terminologies. There are three different judgmental terms for the match of value registers that result in a money price. First, there is *ojúlówó*, usually translated by English speakers as the "normal price." It was explained to me that, with *ojúlówó*, those who wanted that item could afford to buy it. Etymologically it comes close to the idea of "worth its monetary value." Add-ons and diminutions do not alter this judgment; *ojúlówó* refers to a base price, a fair price. It is possible for an item to be worth its value while being expensive beyond the reach of most people. In this case, people apply the idea of *wón* (expensive), with the connotation of "scarce." This judgment logically rests on another standard, of expected availability, and therefore on expert knowledge of supply to the market. Most people will keep a close eye on these two conditions for the market products in which they deal.

It is only beyond *wón* that negative moral implications enter into the judgment of price. If the price is thought to be unnecessarily high, or the add-ons demanded by the seller excessive, the buyer will start applying the concept of *ajeju*, or "unnecessary profit," "exploitation" (as the term translates into English). The Abraham dictionary (1958) derives *ajeju* from the verb *jẹ* (to eat), which ranges in meaning, throughout Atlantic Africa, from physical enjoyment to mystical predation. It is a dangerous accusation, bridging the ordinary world and the occult. Witches eat. *Ajeju* applies not to the market conditions in general but to a particular seller's demands. So within a local market in which s/he is well known, a seller has to try to remain within the rubric of *wón* and not veer beyond into the realm of *ajẹju*. Because no one knows what exactly is going on during a shortage, or why a particular dealer may suddenly have petrol while another does not, there is a premium on sellers performing *wón* (scarcity) to avoid being tainted by the term *ajẹju*.

Some experiences from the fuel shortage in Ibadan city illustrate a range of sellers' strategies for using familiar market categories to remain within the "expected" framework.[1] In all cases the "right price" was maintained. At one station customers were charged a premium of N200 to be allowed to stand in a shorter line, which advanced faster. Because the margin on the price, the length of the line, and the speed of service were all visible, this seemed acceptable to the impatient crowd. At another station, the operator (not the owner) would sell ten liters at the normal price but charged a premium on a complete fill-up of the tank. Again, a major gesture was made toward the right price, and the satisfaction of as many customers as possible under that price, before creating a qualitatively different measure to which to apply a different monetary calculus. A full tank is not a specific number of liters; it is a single unit, variable from vehicle to vehicle, and therefore on a different scale of measurement from the liter. At yet another station, to fill the tank the operator demanded that the driver buy some other good in addition to the petrol. He suggested that the customer buy "brake fluid"—at 30 percent higher than the usual price for that item. Here he stepped over the line between *wón* and *ajẹju* by asking for a price premium on both items. To express their scorn at the logical path this operator had embarked upon, the buyers taunted him. What would he do next: pour the break fluid into a plastic bag and keep the bottle for the next occasion? That is, would he take an additional margin on every single element in the transaction? The line between *wón* and *ajẹju*, however, is not fixed or easily predictable. Many ingenious premiums acquired by manipulating the value scales and their intersection are skillfully designed by the seller to fall within normal expectations for that product in one way or another. Taking advantage of multiple opportunities for small increments of gain—the sale of the full tank of petrol plus the sale of the brake fluid and keeping an empty bottle—can go a step too far.

Imaginative innovations, backed by threats of violence, can still fall

---

1. Customers and petrol sellers were interviewed by Olatunji Ojo in 1997 in Ibadan.

within the morality of equal access at the right price, plus variable add-ons. One friend told me that at the height of the shortage, when he had long ago stopped driving his own car in favor of public transport, the bus he was traveling in was mobbed by a crowd of taxi drivers who were waiting for fuel at a gas station. They asked the *passengers* on the bus — which clearly had acquired petrol, because it was running — to give them money for food. They claimed that they had earned it by their "suffering," by waiting in line for what in some cases was several days of lost income and increasing discomfort. In other words, those who get a commodity successfully may have to add another payment, even after the sale, to retain control over it. In this case those who had succeeded in gaining access would have to make a compensatory payment to those who had failed. Note that the taxi drivers did not steal the petrol from the bus driver, which they certainly could have done. As the story was told, they simply exacted an extra premium, to balance out their own unexpectedly severe deprivation. One added feature of this transaction was the threat behind it: to break the bus windows if their request was not met. Would they have done it? It's impossible to know because the passengers complied. They understood the claim and the terms under which it was being made. And yet it was also novel: to demand an add-on that was really due on one product but ask for it to be paid in another, between parties who did not transact together for the main product in the first instance. Possibly such a departure can only be created and affirmed under threat or, at least, duress. Possibly it implicitly invoked a profound Nigerian conviction that the oil belongs to them collectively in the first place, so that differential access can be subjected to a redistributive morality rather than a market logic. Thus do experiments in crisis, backed by threat, become known elements in the repertoire of people's expectations. Passengers learn, for example, never to travel in public transport without something they can offer in case of such a reasoned threat.

Finally, a note on social classifications and ranking. Shortages always throw categories of persons into relief. The bus incident could be understood as a confrontation between haves and have-nots. I do not know the whole range of verbal exchanges in this case — all the terms of challenge, response, or commentary — but status may have been at play. Status, however, does not necessarily invoke large groups by class, wealth, or social distance. In a niche economy organized around occupations, new specialties are being created and disappearing all the time, not least in the formal sector of law enforcement, where I counted eight different uniforms represented at roadblocks over the sixty miles between the countryside and the nearest major city. The claims people make, and the terms they make them in (short of armed robbery), often refer to the much smaller social differences, which I have argued are highly relevant to the economies of Atlantic

Africa. Such small increments and composites of status were in evidence in the incident that follows.

WAITING FOR PETROL

On June 27, 1997, I spent about five hours at a rural petrol station with a couple of hundred others (mostly young men) trying to buy petrol during a shortage that had already been quite severe for several weeks. By this time people had more or less stopped discussing the reasons for the shortage, and all conversation concentrated on the rumors about when and where a tanker might be making a delivery to a petrol station. The entire problem revolved around where to find any petrol at all. Those who had reliable contacts in the cities, and enough petrol to get there, took the risk of very long waits at urban petrol stations. The accuracy of information was at a premium. Mistakes would be very costly because every vehicle owner had saved just enough petrol to get to a station, but no more. Once there, if the rumor proved false or the supply inadequate, there would be no way of getting back. Abandoning a vehicle in an urban area probably meant returning later to find it stripped of tires, radio, and anything removable of any value, unless a guard could be hired. If one turned up with kegs rather than the vehicle itself, there was a strict limit to how much one could manage to transport away. The logistical problems intensified into Gordian knots. Meanwhile, people's incomes were severely affected. The farming economy was in serious straits because market access was very limited, and this for an area that supplied food to three major cities, each with several million inhabitants. Diesel for tractors was still available. It was rather the ramifying domain of transport of goods and people that was coming to a standstill. Rural taxi drivers and motorbike taxis were unable to work at all.

I was staying with a group of kin and friends who were quite privileged, in local terms. They were artisans and workers with several occupations, several kinds of vehicle, and wide networks for information gathering. They could afford to look at things with more equanimity and probably considerably less rage than did the thousands of drivers of dilapidated and imported secondhand pickups on whom the producers and consumers of three of Africa's largest cities depended for their food supply. The prolonged shortage and high add-on prices had eliminated most of them from even turning up at the petrol station. They couldn't get there, or move any filled petrol kegs out of the station, or get home again if they failed to buy. So they simply waited for conditions to change, losing income and neglecting their own customers, whom they would have to work hard to win back when it was over. So the crowd that turned up when rumor identified a particular station as waiting for a tanker was already self-selected.

News arrived that the owner of a petrol station far out into the country-side, about twenty-five miles north of the rural town where I was staying, had bought one tanker of petrol in Lagos, by working through old patron-age networks. Indeed, this is the only possible way that such a distant place could have been designated and actually receive an allotment. It seemed a miracle to me that it was not hijacked at any number of places along the route. Even when the vehicle broke down on the way and had to be repaired by local mechanics, the tanker and driver were treated respectfully. There seems to have been no replay of the bus incident, in which the sufferers took matters into their own hands by threat of force. Eventually the tanker arrived, having passed through quite densely populated areas and several large towns. Its passage of course alerted the customers, who then prepared to make the journey to the north. Local drivers who could trust leaving their vehicles overnight started to line them up at the petrol station. When the tanker finally arrived, it caused further problems when the brakes failed as the driver navigated the diminishing space, and it ran into the side of a car. It took all evening for this matter to get settled, so that the petrol could be off-loaded and preparations made for sales.

The next morning the people who had enough petrol to drive there—although in our case not enough to get back if we failed to make a pur-chase—started to turn up. For the most part, the buyers were representa-tives of the owners, not owners themselves. Our group, like most others, was made up of junior people who lost no status by being messengers, haulers of kegs, pushers of vehicles (when necessary), and the front line in the face of the police and military presence. Any senior people who at-tended wore robes, to make their status obvious, and did not stay very long. Messengers carried some identification with their seniors, so that status could operate appropriately. In our case, it was a letter.

Let me recount the narrative briefly and then return to analysis. The lines had already formed when we arrived. A few cars and pickups lined the sta-tion lot, and large numbers of motorcycles were ranged opposite them. In a sweeping curve was a long queue of lorry boys and other young men with fifty-liter plastic kegs lined up side by side. Some people had come from as far as twenty-five miles away, which was a very risky venture considering that the supply might run out or something else prevent sales. In a style one often sees in cases of an anticipated long wait—that is, when people will have to move around—it was the kegs that formed the neat and rigidly maintained line, while their owners milled around and presumably had slept at night.

The scene was, as one might expect, crowded, tense, hot, unpredictable on almost every score: the time anyone would start pumping, how much petrol there really was, or whether and how the five police and two soldiers would maintain order. The forces of the law were all armed—the soldiers with large rifles that seemed to get in the way in the cramped space around the pumps. The police were Yoruba-speaking, locally based, traveling in a vehicle, and included officers of obvious high status and middle age. The soldiers from the national army were very young, with little facility in either Yoruba or English, and there was no evidence of any vehicle for them. The police left early in the day after making their presence felt, leaving the soldiers basically stranded, to manage the crowds without a getaway strategy in case of serious trouble. A dignitary of the town did appear, in robes, at one point early on, to make an official representation of local authority, but no authoritative figure remained throughout the sales. Management was left implicitly to the skill of the station owner, in this case, a woman.

Minor violence did break out a few times, largely exacerbated by the military presence rather than resolved by it. At one point the soldiers lost all patience with the crowd pressing in. Lacking any terms to address them beyond military orders in very "bush" English, they started to wave sticks and belts, to chase people, to throw the front line of plastic kegs into the air and way over the pumps, jab at people with their rifles, and shout. A little blood was spilled when they jabbed a man in the leg. He retired to one of the mechanics' bays, complaining, while the lorry boys reassembled the line of kegs. At one point a scuffle even resulted in the station owner being hit in the face, which brought everything to a hushed halt for a good twenty minutes. As we left—which we did, with petrol, several quite orderly hours later—one member of our team said she had been afraid that someone might lose all patience and strike a match, as had happened in a couple of cases elsewhere, according to the newspapers, incinerating the entire station. I myself sat next to the pump as our kegs were filled, to get as close as possible to the transaction, and could imagine the possibility of that heady mixture of fumes and emotion exploding.

It was largely the quiet and methodical work of the station owner, who supervised the entire distribution, that kept the situation orderly. In the end there was no serious fighting, due at least in part to the skill with which she worked the repertoires for differential access throughout the whole day and night that it took, over several openings and closings, to sell the entire tanker-load to the assembled clientele. That day the government-mandated price of petrol stood at N11 per liter, as it had throughout the shortage. By now no petrol was actually sold by the liter, so that the parallel measurement scale of larger units could "mask" and legitimize the higher price. The unit of sale was the twenty- or fifty-liter keg, the latter selling for N1,700, or approximately three times the mandated price by the liter. It is worth noting that the petrol was sold at this price in the presence of the police and the army, who could certainly have cited the sale as a contravention of the law. They did not, and were just as certainly rewarded for their forbearance. Actually, this was a comparatively low price for this phase of the shortage, as everyone knew. As far as I heard, no one blamed the station owner; they were grateful for the supply.

The remarkable achievement was that, as far as I know and as people themselves discussed the event, the petrol was sold at the "same" price to all customers, even though in the end there was not enough to go around. It was understood that the station owner could not sell at changing or varied nominal prices to the group of customers who turned up for public sale. The transfer of money was very public, and the gestures of the owner and her assistants dramatized it further. The highest denomination naira bill is N50, so a one-keg sale involved counting out at least thirty-four bills—eighty-five if paid for in N20 bills. The station owner carried a huge hand-bag to hold all the money, and her employee counted each transaction in front of the first row of the crowd, so the chance of implementing differential nominal prices was very low. People did say later that they expected that she kept some petrol back to be sold under totally different circumstances, to her own business associates, but these transactions did not take place during the same sales episode. No one thought that holding and selling at a different price, under different conditions, for her own close customers was a problem, although it would have been unacceptably indiscrete to do so in public. After all, it was through personal connections that she had acquired the tanker in the first place.

We learned afterward that the supply had run out eventually, but that all social categories had been served at this same nominal price. Every couple of hours the station had closed: to reorganize things, mark stages in the distribution, and probably simply for rest. It had reopened to complete the sales to the smallest customers during the night. We never had enough petrol for me to go back the twenty-five miles to interview the station owner, but she was well known in her methods, so others were able to give their commentary on what we had observed and understood from our own participation.

TOWARD AN INTERPRETATION

I do not consider the following to be a complete account so much as a foray into subject matter that vitally concerns all analysts of globalization in local arenas. The importance must justify its schematic nature. Time and discretion in a sensitive situation, for which I had not really prepared myself adequately, militated against detailed investigations and interviews by someone as conspicuous as myself. I was the only white person and one of the very few women in a very large crowd. I knew some people, but not very many, and I was outside the range of my usual region for work. My "home team" was realistically concerned about my safety and kept trying to locate me somewhere on the fringes. I think that, in the end, I was more of a neutral presence than one might have expected. I was familiar enough to a few people as a researcher into the regional economy that the police and the soldiers made no particular attempt to identify who I was or why I was there, to dissimulate or otherwise change their behavior. I received no automatic preference, and when my status did enter into the situation it was in a way that I had not anticipated.

People appeared to be sorted into status categories and the time into episodes. A first group was served by filling up the actual vehicle tanks, and then the station closed for a while. As the morning wore on and the crowd edged its way forward, the soldiers, and possibly the employees of the owner, started quietly collecting access money. Filling up stopped and started, as the owner saw fit. It gradually became clear to me that she was not moving from high- to low-status customers in that order with absolute regularity. She was actually serving from all categories at the same time, although very disproportionately, and was making a point of keeping some prominent people waiting. This first episode set parameters in place: a constant nominal price, modified by variables of status, waiting time, dashes, and the presence of the authorities. The variables, and the timing of opening and closing the pumps, would be orchestrated by the owner rather than applied by some automatic derivation from a formula. Everyone apparently knew the formula. There was an extra charisma in performing it with panache and success.

Service to the customers placed them into three great categories. One group paid the nominal price, at no extra add-on premium and at the front of the line, because of relations of proximity or long-term reciprocity with the owner. For the most part this coincided with rank in the local hierarchy: the mayor, the military, the customs officials. Our team tried but failed to place itself in this category. One of the seniors who sent us was distantly related to the station owner's husband, a teacher at a school a couple of miles from the station. Before arriving at the station, we went on a detour to the school and called him out of class to present a note requesting that he intercede on our behalf, by writing a note to his wife to indicate our relationship and to plead our case. He agreed to write, knowing—as became clear later—that the chances of his wife paying any attention at all were minimal. When we arrived, one of our group duly pushed through the crowd to deliver the note, which she accepted. It did not take much of the morning to pass before we inferred that we would have to find other ways of getting into the line, besides the default position, which was simply to line our kegs up behind the others. This preferred category was clearly very limited in scope. Refusal was diplomatic however; it worked by passive elimination. A buyer of higher local status than we could claim suffered the same fate. A small businessman, with eventual political ambitions when electoral politics would open up again, arrived in robes and moved conspicuously to the center of the crowd. But that was as far as it went, and rather than suffer the indignity of having to wait so long as to fall obviously into a lower category, he decided to leave early in the day. He said as much. After milling around and greeting people for a while, he said he found it not worth waiting.

We were studiously ignored during the entire period when the first favored clients were served: the driver for the local government office, others in the commercial sector, and a couple of private cars. The local police were there for this stage of the sale only, leaving as the second kind of sale took over. Maintaining public order was then left to the two very young, non-Yoruba, soldiers. This second group paid a premium of one sort or another, not to the station owner herself but to surrounding employees and facilitators, including the soldiers. This was where we were able to fit into the scheme. Eventually, after several hours in the sun, I decided to break ranks and asked the owner in a personal way, without explanation or justification, whether we could be served soon. I was apprehensive about the response of the crowd, knowing that white people no longer had any right to privilege without imbrication in the complex long-term reciprocity of local status. In the event my fears were unfounded because the crowd around commented that after all I had stood in the sun since morning without a head covering, which is not good for a woman, if avoidable. In other words, I had paid appropriate dues in suffering, which was measured for me in the same terms as were applied to others: time waiting, and the strength of the sun. Of course, my presence and my patient waiting had been obvious to everyone all along, but the owner was discrete, and in accordance with public opinion, in her confirmation of our specific qualification to be moved into the second category of customer. She put me in the shade with a biscuit to eat and promised to get us into the line. At this point, one of the soldiers moved in and demanded "drinks" to help us forward. We obliged, and were now on the path forward.

It was still not a quick process, because now we were subject to the logic of lining up within our own category. The assistants did the triage, presenting each customer to the owner who stood right next to the pump with her large bag of money. When we eventually got to the front we had to negotiate the amount we would be allowed. This had been designated in advance by those controlling the triage. We would get one keg short of the amount we wanted. The maneuvers were subtle, but our one keg short turned out to be due to my strategy of offering the expected dash to the helper *after* the sale and not *before*. At this phase of the sale, the calibrations were very precise. The basic dash was a premium on access itself and had to be offered to both groups of helpers, civilian and military. Then volume was valued not so much in increments from one keg upward but in decrements from the amount desired. To get the full amount required additional money, paid at the right moment to the right recipient. In the end we had "paid" then: several hours of suffering, one access dash in drinks, a final dash to the helpers, and a diminution of our total allowance, all in addition to the nominal price that had tacitly been declared legal by the authorities and that would be charged to the entire clientele.

The crowd was orderly, especially considering the provocation from the soldiers. The final group of customers, comprised of local assistants to taxi drivers, motorcycle drivers, and other small operators, simply waited in line and paid in suffering. Apparently they were mainly served much later, into the middle of the night, especially after the soldiers left. The owner closed and reopened to make these final sales. In the end all three categories of customer were served, and not because there was enough petrol for everyone but because the owner played across the possibilities of combination of categories so skillfully.

The owner had effectively rationed the sale of this tanker of petrol in a way that allowed the play of the market, and of status differences, and at the same time had maintained the image of a stable and fair price, offered to everyone. Deviations were qualitative add-ons and exemptions: clientelistic exemption from waiting and anxiety; shortening of waiting or access to a greater amount through payment of a premium to a set of gatekeepers; and the spending of time in line. All were recognized; all were successful; and all preserved the sense that the owner herself had sold at a standard price and therefore had not profited in devious ways from the deal, through *ajeju*.

CONCLUSION

Linked registers — of commodities, measuring units, add-ons, and the social value of customers — provided a repertoire for combination and permutation under crisis conditions that allowed *both* the price rise occasioned by volatile political and economic conditions *and* the controlled access consonant with long-term relations, without departing from the ordinary, routine, workaday cognitive categorization of the market and the moral economy of commercial access. This was not rationing devised from a blueprint from above, and neither was it the free operation of supply and demand on the nominal price, either of which could have cut whole categories of people out of the market. To have allowed the nominal price alone to govern access would have been utterly unacceptable and would have threatened the station owner's ability to stay in business over the long run. It would also, of course, have been an even greater legal infraction, in full view of the forces of the law, whose retribution would probably have been far more unpredictable than the action of the crowd, if they had chosen to exert it. Small shifts and recombinations of elements from different registers preserved a sense that this particular sale fell within a certain normality. This skill of improvisation in a volatile situation was based on particular logics already in place and shared at the cognitive level: logics and skills that create the often-mentioned West African qualities of flexibility and resilience.

Such performances are as routine in general as they are extraordinary in each instance, in an economic life lived under volatile conditions. A great deal is at stake individually and collectively in every episode. I turn now to the even more mundane, routinized performances of everyday budgeting. One step at a time, we need to work toward the aggregative process by which scales and performances become institutions, institutions form into repertoires, and finally patterns of action are discernible. I turn first to institutions through which conversionary transactions are made and the way in which they are ordered into repertoires.

7
INSTITUTIONS
REPERTOIRES OF FINANCIAL OPTION

One must imagine that the market produced situations of glut and short-age throughout its history, and that each time they put the operators on improvisational frontiers similar to the one faced by the owner of the rural petrol station in June 1997. As Herbert (1984) points out, the imposition of trends on the historical data smoothes out of existence the most immediate challenges people faced for economic action. Commercial life was always on the edge of success and failure, even where the mediating criteria settled into a clear institutional form, such as *bilaba*. On performative frontiers, a variety of gainful pathways and points of conversion open up, as situations, trade partners, goods, and currencies change.

The issue that interests me here is their ordering, that is, the ways in which one or another viable transactional form can rise to dominance while others fade. Part of the answer is surely that there are political and religious vested interests in one or another configuration through which scales could be brought together. Scholars of Eastern Nigeria suggest that leaders made policy on certain issues, such as the kind of currency to be used in designated markets. My sense, however, is that with no concerted central political effort to *de*legitimate resolutions that had once proved viable, the possibilities can be (as it were) archived into a continuing repertoire. Thus a conversionary practice may be retained, even when not in current use. Some important components of a repertoire may be almost entirely in abeyance as concrete practices at any particular point in time, even though they may be perfectly accessible in some form for more elaborate mobilization should the context arise. This point was made by structuralists such as Leach (1965), with respect to political institutions, and Bloch (1975), with respect to ritual. Both show how a specific practice can be enacted in elaborated or restricted form, in public or private contexts, with differing implications. Only a detailed historical account can show these changes, and only a detailed ethnography can make clear the forms under which an institution remains generative over time.

The challenge in Africa is that the relevant history fits poorly a structural or developmental model of change over time. Economic experience has been a series of disjunctures attendant on extraversion. There was always a multiplicity of transactions and rarely a clear anchoring of stability. It might seem best, then, to look at *all* transactional forms as fluid, labile, open-ended. On the contrary, I think it is worth retaining the idea that some conversions become stabilized as institutions, as structuralists claim, but arc ratcheted up and down through situational shifts and struggles. Unlike structuralists, however, I propose that the repertoire is relatively open and the changes can be enacted and reversed quite quickly. The theoretical bases for bringing together the analysis of uncertainty and the analysis of institutions are weak, but the topic is crucial. I review some themes in development economics before turning back to anthropology.

THE OPEN MONETARY ECONOMY

The theories of the open economy and institutional growth offer a clear example of inadequacy with respect to theorizing "commercial but unbankable" popular economies, because the logics of the macromodel are discrepant with their own microeconomics. The macroeconomics predict recurrent turbulence, whereas the microanalytics gravitate to regularity — trends and equilibria. The defining features of an open economy are quite specific, although they have changed in relative emphasis markedly over the forty years since the concept was launched by Dudley Seers in the *Economic Bulletin* of the Economic Society of Ghana in 1963. Seers was originally proposing it as a "more modest" contribution to the development debate than the all-inclusive theories of Rostow on the one hand and the Marxists on the other, while sharing with them the same purpose of defining stages of growth and change in capitalist development. He proposed that "primary producing countries . . . [in] the middle of the present century" (1963, 57) constitute a meaningful category of analysis that would include much of Africa and Latin America. They have three qualities in common: currency backed by a major international power, few quantitative restrictions on imports, and low tariffs. Taken together, this set of characteristics causes them to respond "readily to external influences" (57–58).

The internal political dynamics of the open economy, according to Seers, typically encourage efforts at closure and government control, resulting from the difficulty of meeting the generally rising aspirations of the population when the prices for primary commodities fall, as they inevitably do. The main solution he saw was diversification, import substitution, and eventually new exports. But he was under no illusion that this was an easy path, or in some cases even possible. "A country may become "stuck" at some stage" (1963, 66), he warned. Seers's concept is taken up in almost identical terms by A. G. Hopkins ten years later. Hopkins's major departure was to work out some internal dynamics, including the fallout of the inevitable slumps. Colonial governments could not use the instrument of deficit financing to mitigate booms and slumps (Hopkins 1973, 171), so any extended period of poor terms of trade, such as between 1930 and 1945, deeply affected internal trade and production for the local market (253). There was less money to buy things, so local production contracted in volume and diversity. Hopkins implied, however, that although these conditions would be difficult to endure, it would not necessarily be advantageous to try to budge them. By using the term *dysfunctional elements* to describe protective modifications to the open economy regime (186), he implied that the system itself had a compellingly coherent logic that might be even more unstable to change than to put up with. He argued forcefully that the West African economy had, indeed, grown under open economy conditions, albeit fitfully.

Cooper pointed out that Hopkins offered no explanation of why these features are sufficient to describe the performance of open economies, occur together, appear under certain circumstances, are modified under others, or develop beyond them (1981, 7). In fact, these same features—with a different theoretical understanding of the market—could just as easily have been attributed to neo-Marxist dependency theory as to neoclassical economics. By 1993 Hopkins's view had crystallized further. In his major co-authored work on British imperialism he (implicitly) links the features of the open economy together into "the appropriate [analytical] model for Africa [which] is one of colonial rule with limited supplies of capital" (1993, 203). "The distinctive feature of Britain's overseas expansion [and thereby of the open economy] was that it integrated countries which lacked sizable capital markets of their own by offering them sterling credits and the facilities of the City of London" (313). By now, the "ideal-type" open economy has become one whose primary characteristic is that financial capital is managed in the great metropolitan centers.

In a new era, economists have taken the idea of an open economy and shifted their emphasis again on its key features. Financial dependence and primary commodity production are taken more or less for granted. Seers's "external influences" are foregrounded as the "external price shocks" of a newly dynamic world economy. The idea of "shocks" comes in after the sudden international price shifts of the mid-1970s, attendant on the almost simultaneous abandonment of the Bretton Woods financial system and the OPEC oil price hike, which brought massive windfalls and shortfalls to the smaller and less-diversified economies of the world. Vulnerability to "terms of trade shocks" now becomes the analytical entry point to a class of economies that are grouped—rather vaguely in the work of Bevan, Collier, and Gunning—as "many developing countries" (1990, 1), characterized as "controlled open economies" ("controlled" by virtue of the state's attempts to protect local industrial growth from ruinous competition at a fledgling stage, as well as by regulatory venality). The full roster of distinctive features they identify is "[f]inancial markets are often virtually absent, . . . economies are small, open and periodically hit by temporary trade shocks, and most of them are heavily regulated by government controls" (1). After the development of off-shore banking and other highly competitive innovations in global finance in the 1990s, Hopkins's view of financial extraversion as entailing key metropolitan centers "offering . . . facilities" to countries without capital markets has to be replaced by a more competitive, less managerial view of how world capital markets work. No longer a coherent situation, openness is now a dangerous and probably intractable condition for some nations in the global economy.

This macropicture presents local decision-makers with incoherent frameworks and intractable uncertainties. Microeconomic analysis that employs ceteris paribus assumptions then becomes problematic for answering key questions about how the world of employment, provisioning, and wealth creation is actually working. What is expected to happen in local economies that remain "stuck" (Seers 1963) over long periods of time, and chronically vulnerable to recurrent "shocks" (Bevan, Collier, and Gunning 1990)? Through what institutions of conversion can people "save," when investment in local banks or capital markets is inaccessible or where the value of the national currency is lurching downward? These macroeconomic dynamics evoke issues of intense human and theoretical interest. To elaborate a theory of economic construction under conditions of extraversion, one needs a theory of institution building that can address uncertainties of the magnitude that Atlantic Africa has faced. In the spirit of turning to the empirical case for guidance first, I look to Western Nigeria and then return to the theory of institutions as developed within a neoclassical framework.

WESTERN NIGERIAN MONETARY HISTORY AND MONEY CULTURE

Yoruba history reflects the experience that the theory of open economy would predict. Yoruba social structure is classically described as highly elaborated, with hierarchical town government, titles, large compounds, occupational societies, and age and cult associations. It is clear, however, that such a view of social life is a projection—perhaps by colonial rulers, perhaps by anthropology, and perhaps by their own leadership—from a very different existence. Under the pressures of trade and politics in the nineteenth century, the Yoruba suffered "[t]he experience of confusion—of communities racked by internal conflict or destroyed altogether, of families

broken up, or large-scale displacement, of radical changes in personal circumstances, of the norms of social life challenged or overthrown" (Peel
2000, 50). In terms of money, there were eras of penury and plenty. There
was a "scarcity of cowries" during the wars of the nineteenth century
(Oroge 1985, 79), cowrie inflation on the eve of colonial rule (Hopkins
1968), a massive reduction in the money in circulation when commodity
prices plunged during the Great Depression and again during World War II,
and *ko s'ówó*, or "no money," in the context of structural adjustment and military rule in the late twentieth century (Guyer, Denzer, and Agbaje 2002).
Interspersed between the troughs there have been peaks. Peel writes, "It
is fitting to call the 1920s something of a jazz age in Ilesha. . . . Trading
profits and debts soared to unprecedented levels. . . . The possibilities of
consumption rose equally dizzily . . . more men built houses for themselves" (1983, 140–41). During World War II, the discovery of gold deposits near Ilesha created a sudden and intense "gold-fever" (Falola 1992,
39). Peak prices reigned for commodities on the world market in the
1950s. They were followed by deep declines in the 1960s, then civil war
from 1967 until 1970, during which Yoruba farmers took up arms in revolt
against the tax level. The avalanche of national income from oil started to
filter through to the ordinary people in about 1974, lasting until 1981,
when oil prices dropped and the national debt crisis set in. The ten-year devaluation of structural adjustment started in 1986, not only affecting relative prices and the rewards for salaried work, but creating opportunities for
arbitrage and other financial dealing that set in motion a voracious demand
in the formal sector that siphoned money out of the popular economy
through bank frauds. The anthropological task is to understand the embodied memory, the cultural and social ramifications of such a history, and
their implications for "rationality."

The Yoruba cultural conception of money is that it is deeply intimate
to the person, something that makes a person effective, while its ultimate
sources and pathways are mysterious and unpredictable. At the same time,
however, there are quite varied and even contradictory ideas about specific
thresholds, conversions, and causalities in its use. Although money is fundamentally a good thing, the conversion of currency into assets can take a
whole range of changing forms with varying moral valence. Nothing in the
sources emphatically endorses one over the other in a transhistorical way.
Children, health, and money are grouped as a threesome of necessities for
the good life, but their prioritization and the interaction of investments in
each one are contingent. Whether a house or another wife or a loan on interest or a contribution to a religious organization is a good way to convert
one's steady gains, let alone the windfall of the moment, is not self-evident.
Falola writes that the "definition and uses of assets were to see significant

changes" (1995, 167) over time. Choice involved learning, judgment, and extrapolation from example (Barber 2000). In all kinds of ways, Adebayo (1999) points out, the action–money–person equation is fraught with inconsistencies and outright contradictions. Patience over the long term is valued in one proverb and opportunism in another. The injunction to acquire money by morally defensible means coexists with the willingness not to ask where it comes from in a particular case. The agreement that dependents are a good thing does not specify how many or what sort (more wives? in the past, more *ìwòfà* debt servants?), and in relation to what other potential uses for the money.

Part of the explanation for inconsistency lies, according to Adebayo, in the accretion of varied historical experience. Some of the modes of converting money into assets that were invented in the late nineteenth and twentieth centuries can be more or less accurately dated by their names and the circumstances of their innovation. *Ìwòfà* debt pawning (labor payment as interest on a money loan) may be very old, but it became widespread in the nineteenth century not through evolutionary growth processes in the economy and gradual enrichment but through innovation during a profound crisis. According to Oroge, "Iwofa was an institution that thrived largely on calamity. Wars, raids, famine, scarcity of cowries and imperative heavy expenses that could not be met by normal efforts were potent factors in the growth of the institution" (1985, 76). *Ìwòfà* became a "very important institution" that "proved to be very resilient" (99) to subsequent change. When I carried out fieldwork in 1968, my field assistant, then aged about twenty, remembered that as a boy he carried food to his father's *ìwòfà* at work on the farm, even though the institution had been outlawed by the colonial government in 1928. Without doubt, the practice could still be revived even now, and may even have been continuously practiced in some places, in a sub rosa fashion.

Of other named financial institutions that mediated monetary conversions, only *esusu*, "rotating credit," dates back before the wars of the nineteenth century. Others have been added, and each can be identified with a situation in the past that encouraged its creation and wide adoption. The literature mentions the following: *àjo* (savings clubs), *òsómálò* (a kind of trader who based sales on hire purchase), *s'ogún'dogóji* (high-interest money-lending, repayment at twice the loan), and various other kinds of loan—*fi d'ogo* (pledge), shading off into transactions that seem to wander ambiguously from pawn to sale, *pàrò-olówó* (conversion of assets into cash), and *pàrò eleru* (a kind of barter of secondhand goods) (Falola 1995). The use of material assets as collateral dates from the colonial period, accompanying and hastening the decline in human labor as interest on a debt. *Ìwòfà* was outlawed in 1928, during the "jazz age" (Peel 1984). Thus began the first great wave of "real" asset acquisition, and their use as collateral in the credit market. "The most common assets were gold ornaments, radios, expensive dandogo cloth made of velvet or wool, wristwatches, leather shoes and so forth" (Falola 1995, 173). The possibilities expanded: "The horse as a status symbol gradually gave way to the car . . . ; a house in town became more important commercially than one in the village; . . . imported goods like jewelry, radios, televisions (after 1957), wristwatches, books and newspapers, suits, shoes, and so forth, entered into the organization of credit" (167). The varieties of small credit and debt relations that mushroomed in Yoruba society during the colonial period were innovations on the nature of acceptable collateral in a context in which the land alone could not fulfill that function and where hardly anyone had a bank account. The conversion of cash into many kinds of more or less durable and ostentatious consumer goods became not so much "consumption" as a means of ensuring access to credit.

Throughout the twentieth century, house building has been a major channel for creating an asset out of money. Polly Hill (1962) was the first to describe how the slow addition of materials to a half-built house was a form of "saving" and "investment" in a context in which income and capital can easily be dissipated. There are yet other economically important assets that are created through house building because it usually demands collaborative work. Emigrants can test the social and managerial skills of potential collaborators at home by involving them in the long process of house building in the hometown. And the presence of a kinsman's house in the hometown improves the creditworthiness of the local family by dramatizing its connections abroad (Okonkwo 2002). Surely housing investment could be studied historically in the same way as *ìwòfà* or consumer collateral (see Arimah 2002).

Investment in local collective life may be termed traditional, but there have been peaks and troughs in the kinds of credit people extend and debt they undertake in these arenas. The range is wide, from investment in the public finance of town government, to pooling of funds through *egbẹ* (associations), hometown associations (see Trager 2001), *iṣákọ́lè* (payments to landowners for use of land), and interpersonal debt in ceremonial life (chieftaincy, naming, marriage, funerals, apprenticeship, freedom ceremonies). Berry (1985) captures the three great popular investments of the 1970s oil-boom years: education, apprenticeship, and political claims on the government. "Freedom" ceremonies became more frequent and more expensive by comparison with other life-cycle rituals, and enormous new effort was put into cultivating town identity and attendant political ritual. Over the same period, *iṣákọ́lè* for land has offered less and less return to the landowner, possibly since the Land Use Act of 1978 rendered "customary occupancy" legally ambiguous. At the same time, bridewealth payments have declined, from a peak sometime during the colonial period (Guyer 1996). Although we cannot date the creation of "traditional" payments, as can be done more or less accurately for other financial inventions, each clearly has its own history of expansion and contraction.

None of these financial institutions has completely disappeared. Even though Falola (1995) places them in a historical sequence, the older forms of *esúsú* and *àjọ* are still working. He writes of one of the new credit forms of the colonial period, *s'ogúndogóji,* which involved repaying double the principal, that "[n]o one wished to resort to this, except in desperate conditions" (174), whereas I hear that it is popular at the present moment (the early 2000s).[1]

The result is a ramifying set of options for converting money into assets, each of which may contain its own pathways for pursuing, for example, individual or collective gains, transfers from one person to another, security for the future, or more immediate returns. Both the roster of possibilities and their internal potentials can be differentially cultivated and emphasized: from one era to the next and, very importantly, by different categories of the population. Women traders make use of credit forms particular to them or to a passing situation they are facing; Christian sects may develop others, of their own. Once formed and named, institutions can be reinvoked. Repertoires consist of partially inconsistent financial transactional forms that are ideologically maintained but differentially highlighted in practice, which has implications for their internal organization.

To understand more closely the changing shape of asset acquisition, I look at the modest and mundane transactions and conversions of the hardworking farming community in the food-supply hinterland of Ibadan, where I have worked in three fieldwork periods: 1968–69, four months in 1987–88, and four weeks in 1997 (see Guyer 1997).

ASSETS AND LOANS IN IDERE, 1968–88

I worked in Idere in 1968–69 and 1988 — two periods of national crisis. When I did my dissertation research, the country was in civil war. This region was not directly affected, except by the presence a few miles away of a basic training camp for raw military recruits. But in spite of its distance from any theaters of battle, this region due west of Ibadan, close to the Benin border, did not thrive under the conditions of a wartime economy. Markets were accessible with great difficulty because trucks had been req-

---

1. I am grateful for this information to Salami Kabiru, who is currently undertaking a study of local credit institutions.

uisitioned for the army. The cities were under nighttime curfew, so commerce was hurried. Attractive illegal activities, such as growing marijuana or smuggling goods from Benin, were severely punished. In 1988, by contrast, there was peace. But the naira was declining in the midst of the structural adjustment program, and crises and protests were intensifying. In both periods the urban food market for which the farmers produced was under stress, but of different kinds. During the war, they faced difficulties of transport and circulation. Under the structural adjustment program, the urban markets were accessible but the clientele was poor because of the fall in real incomes and declining formal-sector employment. By that time, a transport revolution had brought farmers more deeply into urban market dynamics, so their standard of living was dependent on urban demand. The real value of their money incomes from farming had risen by about 25 percent over the twenty-year period as a result of the complex of influences exerted by market integration.

As part of a larger study of the food economy, I collected work and monetary transaction diaries for 15 men for the first growing period of six months (March to August) in 1968 and 19 men and 4 women in 1988, which can illuminate investment and the creation of assets. The data show a series of marked shifts in the earning and expenditure patterns over the twenty years, from deep involvement in the social debt nexus of ceremonial life to productive debts in agriculture. Farmers did not, however, abandon social expenditure; they changed the composition of resources, the timing, and the participation devoted to it, after the manner I invoked and then modified in the discussion of structuralism. What Berry has pioneered as "investment in social relations" (1989) could be reduced, rather than eliminated, when another competing institutional configuration was adopted into the repertoire.

I start with the monetary expenditures of my sample of farmers and group them into categories of goods according to social purpose. Table 7.1 summarizes the percentage of expenditure devoted to these different categories of goods during the two years (men only; I return to women).

A proviso: house building was in a passing hiatus at the time of the second study. With currency devaluation raising the prices of construction materials in 1988, people were postponing house building until they settled. During a short visit in 1997, when the exchange rate had been stable for about a year, it was clear that building had picked up again.

In general, the proportion of total money expenditure devoted to just living, to consumption in the narrowest sense, has stayed almost exactly the same over this twenty-year period. Change in the asset/debt/investment domain is almost entirely accounted for by a shift from ceremonial and gift conversions to investment in production. Two specific sets of changes, in-

Table 7.1. Percentage of Expenditure, by Category (March–August 1969, and 1988)

Category	1969	1988
Living		
Food, household items	13	21
Clothes	9	2
Medical	1	5
Travel	2	5
Other	3	1
Total	28	30
Lifetime assets		
Building	10	1
Schooling	8	10
Total	18	11
Social membership		
Ceremonies/gifts	35	11
Associations	5	3
Credit associations	8	3
Total	48	17
Production		
Farm inputs	2	1
Hired labor (cash)	4	3
Hired labor (debt)	Neg.	23
Tractor hire	N.a.	11
Total	6	38
TOTAL	100	100

Notes: N.a., not applicable; neg., negligible.

ternal to the two sets of institutional practices, show that this is a shift of emphasis only and not a change in the composition of the repertoire itself. One shift contracts the monetary infrastructure of social and ceremonial life, and the other elaborates the seasonal/annual debt cycle in agriculture.

First, ceremonial life. The costs of large ceremonial expenses are borne in two ways: from the savings of the central celebrants, and from numerous gifts and contributions from association members, close kin, congregation members, friends, and so on, all of whom are partners in ongoing gift exchange at one another's celebrations. In 1968, people expected that a gift given at one occasion would be reciprocated by a return gift that was of at least equivalent value. By 1987, as ceremonial life diminished as a proportion of total expenditure, the balance between sponsorship and participation internal to the rituals had radically altered. On average people spent three times the proportion of their total expenditure on ceremonies in 1968 compared with 1988. At the same time, individual central celebrants only spent half as much in the earlier year than twenty years later. Not only had the overall amount spent on ceremonies contracted, but much more of it now devolved on the main sponsor of the ceremony. Sponsors in 1968 benefited from the more frequent and higher-value ancillary contributions of others in the ceremonial debt nexus. In 1968, the farmers in my sample gave to a mean of nine celebrations over six months; no one fell below five. In 1988 the mean was only five contributions per farmer, and the amount of each contribution was considerably lower than in 1968.

In 1968, people were tied into an intricate nexus of monetary transactions with one another. Every person had an implicit account with a number of partners and groups, such that each knew exactly how much should be given: according to the occasion, the relative status of the celebrant, and the previous transactions between the parties. The multitude of credits and debts ensured that lump sums could always be generated for status occasions, and that every relevant relationship would be recognized, through the stepwise pooling process from juniors to their immediate seniors, and so on, to the central sponsor. The social mapping and accounting were so taken for granted that people were very surprised when they discovered that a particular very old woman, who had no children and very few kin, had made advance purchases for her own funeral. By comparison, in 1987–88, the whole ceremonial complex had been streamlined down to a disproportionate burden on the central celebrant, who had to be able to raise lump sums from his/her own resources. People still attended ceremonies, now streamlined to the weekend (Guyer 1993). But they had cut down notably on giving money.

Seventeen men gave figures for their central payments for several kinds of ceremony they sponsored in 1987: naming ceremonies for children, marriage, funerals, and apprenticeship freedom ceremonies. This averaged N422, or about $100 at the then-exchange rate, which would be approximately half of their six-month (first season) income, or probably about one-fifth of their annual income from agriculture. By comparison, I have records for 24 central ceremonial payments for 1968. They averaged £4 sterling, or about one-sixth of the payees' six-month income, probably — given the seasonality of income — about one-twelfth of their annual income. The total ceremonial cost in 1968 would be very much higher than this, augmented by all the contributions of all the guests and minor participants. So the balance of responsibility has shifted, as the amount as a proportion of income has diminished.

Does this indicate changes in the quality of "investment in social relations" as assets? An article by Lawuyi and Falola (1992) helps to address this question. They show exactly how the new money shortages under structural adjustment have allowed discrete elements of a ceremonial to be reduced in monetary obligations without loss of the symbolic representation of their meaning. Formulae exist within the institution so that people should not fail to "make appropriate payments" (1992, 225). "Debt repayments are not subject only to the whims of the market economy but to the criteria of moral assessment" of creditor and debtor (226). Ceremonial participation can be cut down by pruning elements out, or substituting for them, without necessarily changing the key meanings. To contract the *range* of kin implicated in the ceremonial debt nexus is another step in institutional contraction. Even though contraction has taken place under changeable circumstances, it has not been itself a disorderly or unprincipled change.

There is no less credit and debt nowadays, but it prioritizes a different domain: a shift to agricultural expenditure on hired labor and tractor clearing of fields, both of which involve innovations around existing credit institutions. In the long-established system of hired labor, work that is negotiated at the beginning of the year, from March onward, can be paid for any time before Christmas, after the harvest, when the laborers *(oníṣẹ́ or Àgàtú)* return home to the Benoue region. More labor is used now than in the past, so most farmers are in debt to laborers for most of the year. To this has been added a novel component. In the past it was almost impossible for anyone to borrow money for production; all loans gravitated to the social and ceremonial system, where the constraints imposed by frequent mutual need and the risk of reputation loss could be relied on to ensure repayment. So when the hire of tractor services was institutionalized around 1980 as a "cash on the barrel" niche in the economy, farmers with no money before the season were unable to benefit. In recent years, women traders have taken the pledge system that was developed earlier in the cocoa region and now advance cash as *èdà* to farmers to pay for tractor hire in March. In return they collect a certain number of bags of the high-value, nonperishable egusi-melon seed at harvest time. The relative dependability of the urban market, in a time of rising prices, has made it possible to adapt this old kind of credit from the export crop sector to the food sector. *S'ogúndogójì* has also seen a new lease on life, alongside the first successful experiment in formal-sector banking for small producers—the community banks (discussed in chap. 9). Invented earlier in the century, *s'ogúndogójì* now offers the sure availability of short-term credit, albeit at a high interest rate.

If we look at these social and financial asset dynamics together, there is a dimension other than the ceremonial/production contrast that an "open economy" perspective encourages us to bring out. The dual shift—away from constant ceremonial contribution and toward seasonal peaks in agricultural debt repayment—places individual cash income and asset acquisition into sharper lifetime peaks and troughs than in the past. Less expenditure falls within a matrix of recurrent social debts that build up and are cashed out slowly and predictably over the life cycle of political ambition. The two temporal patterns of income earning and expenditure—life-cycle/

ambition buildup versus seasonal cycles — correspond to two sets of institutions, each consonant with a particular mode of instability. In 1968, farmers' worry was not with prices per se but with whether goods could be transported to market at all, because of the war. The rewards for involvement in the long-term monetary social indebtedness that reaffirmed status and membership were fairly clear for a partially enclosed economy. One could never become influential or hold office without cultivating not just a farm but a constituency of supporters.

After the devaluation of 1986, the prices themselves were the cause of instability. Some items changed a lot more than others; consumer prices rose, and the government put substantial price tags on health and education services. In fact, the whole system of monetary equivalencies was in disruption and showed no signs of settling. The short seasonal contract of credit and debt for work done offers flexibilities, whereas the long haul of multiple exchanges becomes a calculative nightmare. Any instabilities that would reduce market access again, by undermining the transport or marketing infrastructure, might well encourage a small return to frequent social payments, on the life-cycle/ambition path. This possibility remains embedded in the way that elements in the repertoire of credit and debt institutions have been foregrounded, and components reshaped, in intricate ways that have preserved their recognized cultural form. Nothing has been eliminated from the available repertoire of monetary investments.

INSTITUTIONS

In all branches of social theory, institutions are seen as in some sense stable, or at least stabilizing. Douglass North writes, for example, that "institutions reduce uncertainty by providing a structure to everyday life" (1990, 3); Mary Douglas sees them as conventions that meet the "common interest in ensuring coordination" (1986, 46). Social anthropologists have concentrated on large phenomena, "total prestations," that have names, mythical charters, rules, and "structural durations" (Gluckman 1968). However limited or comprehensive their reach, institutions are seen as collective creations that filter, buffer, assign meaning, consolidate powers, and in general shape the random instabilities of life. How they arise in the first place and then survive the "slings and arrows of outrageous fortune" have been treated in rather formulaic ways. As a critique of North's rationalism, Mary Douglas has put the formation of institutions into analytical slow motion, arguing that they do not spring up easily. "The conditions for stable conventions to arise are more stringent than it may seem" (1986, 46). According to her, these conditions include the stabilization of domains of cognitive classification for persons, things, situations, temporalities, and all the transitive verbs among them. The effects of intermittent disruption after institutions have been formed were not, however, explicitly addressed.

Yoruba social and economic life and scholarly work have taught similar compelling theoretical lessons about institutions to many analysts, without those lessons gaining adequate profile in the theoretical literature. Yoruba institutions are small, multiple, combinatorial, and internally complex enough to expand and contract under varying circumstances. In his study of "the past in the Ilesha present," John Peel (1984) gives an example of how stabilization may combine with indeterminacy. The concept of repertoires, the process of foregrounding and backgrounding, is basic to his argument. He takes narrative forms as a repertoire of conventions. Each narrative convention is indexed to one of three different concepts of time: the static precedent, the cyclical, and the linear. Because these are nonconsonant models of time, the match between convention and situation, made in performance, is indeterminate and therefore historically changing. In one era the application of a convention that is indexed to the "static precedent" might be plausible to invoke in several different domains of life, from chieftaincy disputes to family economy, whereas in another it has been beaten back into a single domain (say, chieftaincy affairs). It may be internally altered in other ways as well—reduced in richness of allusion or in the social identity of those who are entitled to mobilize it. The cultural and social negotiation, or outright struggle involved in making these shifts, evokes the same aesthetic of composition and allusion that Barber (1991, 2000) describes for oral performance more broadly. Yoruba skill at repertoire creation and mobilization may be consummate, but it is certainly not unique. All these processes are invoked, if not formally analyzed, in the recent anthropological literature on institutions, such as Parker Shipton's (1995) comprehensive list of the repertoire of forms of "savings" in rural Gambia.

Juxtaposing the anthropological approach and the premises of institutional economics throws into relief how deeply grounded economics is in a world that indexes to equilibrium and systemic coherence or to development through slow, incremental, directional change. Rather than allowing for elements to be moved around in a kaleidoscope of skillful ways, Douglass North's institutional theory "orients" them to given baselines. The "efficiency" that is normally identified in economics with equilibrium is here also identified with a "set of constraints [that] will produce economic growth" (North 1990, 92). From this definition it follows that "the single most important point about institutional change, which must be grasped if we are to begin to get a handle on the subject, is that institutional change is overwhelmingly incremental" (89). Discontinuous change through war, revolution, conquest, and natural disaster is secondary and ultimately settles again "to produce a new equilibrium" (91).

This intellectual "homing instinct" toward equilibrium, systematicity, and slow directional growth is eminently understandable, but it has far-reaching implications for the struggle to deal accurately with Africa. African realities have to be wrenched out of their true historical sequences, and their most salient characteristics have to be backgrounded, in order to make them amenable to neoclassical concepts. With an evolutionary theory, it becomes impossible to envisage a precolonial past when regional markets and money management institutions might have been at least as flourishing — if not more so, as Fairhead and Leach (2003) argue for Sierra Leone — than they are now. "Efficiencies" instead have to be seen as a result of cumulative challenges of "the expansion of trade and increased specialization" from a starting point of "developing societies with weak institutions" (Ensminger 1992, 28, 18). Such a speculative history distorts the empirically established sequence of events. Shocks have to be treated one at a time, not as the actual concatenations and successions that are the logical implication of open economy theory and the actual experience of African peoples.

Human empathy and comparative knowledge both suggest how varied are the possible ways in which recurrent shocks and institutional repertoires may be shaken into comprehensible visions of the world. Or not. The neoclassical and institutional literature is often evasive. Granovetter writes that "social structure [may become] . . . more dispersed and disconnected," where "there is less capacity for collective action in sanctioning malfeasance, and economic action must be conducted via highly personalized relations." He also writes, in the same article, that "personalized economic relations emerge slowly" (1993, 26, 27). So recurrent shocks should eventually put *all* relations at risk. Where is any equilibrium here, and what is it, in sociological terms? The logic of theories that index to Western experience would predict eventual total social incoherence for any society that was subjected for any length of time to the conditions expected in small open economies.

African historical experience, by contrast, can show how instability may be domesticated: yes, institutions are stabilizing elements — but they are not composed into integrated systems. Rather they are ordered as a multiplicity. Such a world was envisaged (minus the depth and recurrence of crisis) by philosophical pragmatism. William James points to the kind of structural parsimony and openness of category construction that may help a great deal in the understanding of novel and perhaps ephemeral configurations that can be put together from existing familiar conceptions. He wrote in 1907:

> It *may* be that some parts of the world are connected so loosely with some other parts as to be strung together by nothing but the copula *and*. They

might even come and go without those other parts suffering any internal change. This pluralistic view, of a world of *additive* constitution, is one that pragmatism is unable to rule out from serious consideration. But this view leads one to the farther hypothesis that the actual world, instead of being complete "eternally," as the monists assure us, may be eternally incomplete, and at all times subject to addition or liable to loss. (1964, 112; emphasis in the original)

It bears attention, then, to compare these insights with the history and sociology of Atlantic Africa, and to see how experience and analytics are related to each other. America was re-creating itself under conditions of uncertainty after the Civil War, when Pragmatism addressed the current realities (Menand 2001). The stable, cumulative, and systemic concept of institutions is a reflection of a later Western world, more sure of its direction. It becomes, however, blunt and illogical when applied to a reality that seems, to those who live it, altogether less settled. Like pragmatists, they have to apply reason and judgment to horizons of contingency rather than applying a narrow calculative rationality to given variables.

8

BALANCES
HOUSEHOLD BUDGETS IN A GHANAIAN STUDY

Crises may be averted by a dramatically skillful performance from a familiar repertoire of transactional institutions. There is a dose of charisma in it. But does this same combinatorial juggling of multiple independent scales — for things and people, in quantities and qualities — figure at yet more mundane levels of popular economic practice, as people pull out the everyday routine performance of making an economic living and a social and spiritual life? Is reasoning a complex combination of rational calculation and charismatic aspiration? If so, there should be evidence of it in aggregate accounts of daily practices, such as survey data. Anthropologists generally steer clear of standardized surveys, where the framing of the problematic and the choice of concepts strongly shape the findings toward specific policy purposes. They characteristically find, like Polly Hill in the work I address here, that "the gulf between social anthropologists and economists is so terrifying that even the simplest anthropological ideas are liable to disappear into thin air when one is pursuing economic survey work in the field" (1957, 8). But sometimes the results can surprise their makers, as they do in the present case of Ghanaian family budgets. Whereas the specialists in method may then turn back to the drawing board to review the adequacy of the research instruments in the face of unusual results, anthropologists might reasonably turn to the field to try for a different interpretation. Possibly the respondents were interpreting the questions from their own vantage points. People say *something* true about themselves, but on assumptions that probably differ from those of the investigators. The less routinized is formality in their lives, the more likely are respondents to construe questions from their own standpoints in their own social landscape. They are saying something, but perhaps something *else*.

Ironically, to take this tack means accepting the economists' data with more confidence than they sometimes do themselves. The designers of the survey I reanalyze here, the Ghana Living Standards Survey of 1991–92, describe their methods and point out their deficiencies considerably more frankly than do most anthropologists. In the present study, for example, they point out that the aggregate income of respondents was only two-

CHAPTER EIGHT / 132

thirds (64 percent) of the amount they claimed to be spending (Ghana Statistical Service 1995, 57–60). Such very large difficulties necessarily qualify confidence and reduce enthusiasm for arguments based on small statistical variations. And yet, noting the economists' concerns as I go along, I want to push as far as possible the experiment of listening for "another voice" in the data as they are reported, without trying either to vilify or modify their shortcomings (see Bledsoe 2002; Bledsoe et al. 1999).

To prefigure my eventual argument: I suggest that when these Ghanaian respondents come up with answers to questions about their money expenditures, they are speaking about their performances of scalar judgment from an understood position and aspiration along a social gradient. The matrix in which expenditures are embedded is more plausibly understood as a status gradation than as the class differentiation (based on access to resources) or the life cycle (based on age/stage of domestic dependency) that is presumed in standard budget methodology. As a gradation, the social scale emerging from the Ghana budget data is cognate to the ritualized ranking system of Igbo society in the late nineteenth and early twentieth century addressed in chapter 4 and to Lloyd's finding for urban Yoruba in the 1970s, that they see "society as a ladder up which individuals have risen to various levels of success" (1974, 225). Expenditure at any one level reflects both the upward and the downward glance: to ambition on the one side and responsibility on the other. The data suggest that over a large range of middle incomes, the balancing of these inspirations for the good life is so highly consistent that one may see a single principle of calibration at play. But this is a conclusion. I start with the problem and the data set, accepting both "as is" for the moment (see the appendix), and working from there.

The problem of interpreting what she called "some puzzling spending habits" reflected in Ghanaian budget findings was first raised by Polly Hill in 1957. Expenditure patterns appear not to follow Engel's Law. Over a wide range of income between the very wealthy and the very poor, households apparently do not reduce the proportion of expenditures devoted to food as total expenditure rises. After a few years of intensity in the early 1960s (Poleman 1961; Lawson 1962; Davey 1963), the debate died down without resolution, and—as far as I can figure out—the "puzzle" has never been systematically addressed again. Indeed, when the same finding was noted again in a national study in 1987–88 (Glewwe and Twum-Baah 1991), it evoked hardly any commentary. And yet the very same "habits" are evident in the much more comprehensive Ghana Living Standards Survey (GLSS) carried out in 1991–92. For the national sample as a whole[1]— urban and rural, northern savanna and southern forest, from 290,000 cedis

1. The data are from Ghana Statistical Service 1995, table A9.27, p. 169.

to 640,000 cedis per household — across four quintiles the proportion of expenditure devoted to the major commodity categories is almost identical. Food and beverages account for 53 percent of total expenditure, clothing and footwear between 9 and 11 percent, housing between 8 and 11 percent, and so on. Even the highest quintile, with a total mean expenditure of 844,000 cedis, differs by relatively little: 45 percent on food and beverages, balanced by increased proportions only for transport and "miscellaneous goods and services." Those in this highest quintile probably own a vehicle of some sort and make a wider array of contributions. The numbers are also, of course, affected by the limitlessness of the upper reaches of the highest quintile, where a few extremely wealthy households can affect the means. All in all, these data produce the same picture of uniformity first noticed by Polly Hill.

Economic analysis has focused on two possible frontiers of explanation and exploration: first, that the class-based assumptions of Engel's Law are valid if one could eliminate problems of method, and second, that the life-cycle dynamic is still important enough to affect the distributions. Because both the social class and the life-cycle approaches ultimately turn out to apply poorly to the Ghana data, I review both frameworks of interpretation before coming back to my own exploration in terms of the social gradient.

SOCIAL CLASS APPROACHES AND THE GHANA CONTROVERSY OF THE 1950s AND 1960s

The puzzles from the past were generated by applying the methods and interpretations from Western budget studies to Ghana. A classic budget analysis was published by pioneer methodologists Prais and Houthakker in 1955, using data from English research from the 1930s (that is, before the welfare state provisions instituted after World War II). They compared a working-class sample (1937) with a middle-class sample (1939), chosen by a combination of income and occupation criteria that would reflect a modal concept of each social class. The working-class sample was chosen from manual workers who were registered for unemployment insurance, which would certainly exclude the very poor and the intermittently employed; the middle-class sample had as its base civil servants and teachers, reflecting a professional rather than a strictly income-based concept. The mean expenditures of the middle class were double those of the working class.

The results showed the operation of Engel's Law, which had been defined in Germany a hundred years earlier. Comfort, status, and nonfood consumption are disproportionately expanded as income rises. Middle-class expenditure on food was sharply lower (23 percent) than in the working class (39 percent) — not static in absolute terms, but certainly growing far more slowly than the total budget as incomes rose. Over and above food, the two classes maintained the same proportion of expenditure on clothing, housing, and travel. The particular middle-class advantage was that its members doubled the proportion of total expenditure devoted to household goods, health, and education/recreation compared with that of the working class. All the rest of the middle-class gain from higher income was devoted to household help, to the tune of having ten times as great an expenditure for this item as the working class.

It is important to note that Prais and Houthakker considered structural as well as quantitative differences between the two classes. They interpreted expenditure as not only a function of current income but of access to capital that can smooth out the effects of short-run fluctuations in income and allow prediction of long-run career plans. Without secure employment and access to formal financial institutions, "a working class household will be acting in a perfectly rational manner if it discounts its expected future income stream" (1955, 155–56) and devotes surges in income to consumption. They expected that by instituting greater predictability, the welfare state would reduce these qualitative differences to something more like a smooth curve, still — of course — following the same direction of declining proportion of income devoted to food and a rising proportion devoted to investment in health, education, and status markers.

With the expectation that the same would apply in Ghana, Hill found that the results of the first budget study were "very surprising [although they] . . . excited no comment": "the proportion of total consumer expenditure devoted to food is extraordinarily constant (57–58%), and independent of the actual size of total expenditure" (1957, 3). Not only that, people in the higher-expenditure groups were buying *cheaper* food staples than were the poorer households — demonstrating the sarcastically termed Cassava Law. After considering artifactual possibilities, Hill suggested that the pattern reflected a reality, namely, that richer households feed more people in kind than are counted as household members. They give away meals much more often, and they prepare feasts.

One counterargument was that no one should expect Engel's Law to apply because "the entire group of comparatively low incomes which were surveyed is below the poverty line" (Crossley 1958, 13). Hill's rejoinder was dismissive: "Ghana is not the Far East and such a preposterous suggestion must be at once disposed of" (1958, 16). And in fact, no subsequent study has shown high enough levels of nutritional deficiency in the low-income groups to support the idea that high demand for food as income rises was simply making up for chronic deficiencies in the lower-income classes (e.g., Poleman 1961, 151).

Subsequent economic studies postponed addressing Hill's interpretation directly. They put priority on methodological issues such as capturing the relevance of household size to consumption patterns, the substitution of (more expensive) fresh for dried staples, the challenge of imputing value to home production, the need to weight the demands that children of different ages place on the budget, and so on. Even so, Lawson and Poleman both confirmed the original finding of "the constancy of the figure [the proportion spent on food] throughout virtually the entire expenditure [income] range," extending over a fivefold difference between the extremes (Poleman 1961, 143). But both also concluded that without sorting out the methodological problems, "the real economic indicators may be concealed" (Lawson 1962, 39). At best, "some [factors were] clear-cut, some obscure" (Poleman 1961, 144). Dutta Roy and Mabey (1968, 64) argued that household size and composition could indeed account for the constancy effect; the better-off households were simply larger. In a much smaller, rural study, Davey (1963) found otherwise — that there was no evidence of differential household size across the income scale. But by taking greater care with the seasonality of income, and weighting the consumption of children, his study yielded a pattern more consonant with Engel's Law; expenditure devoted to food fell from two-thirds to one-half as total expenditure doubled (1963, 18). Much later, however, working on a national sample, Glewwe and Twum-Baah reconfirmed all the same patterns: "Irrespective of welfare level or area of residence, about 60 percent of total expenditure is on food" (1991, 64). Finding that "Engel's method did not give very accurate results" (16), they applied adult equivalencies and still found that "food shares are only weakly (negatively) correlated with total household expenditure" (18). The latest study abandoned weighting because "there is at present no agreement as to what would constitute a suitable adult equivalency scale for Ghana" (Ghana Statistical Service 1995, 5). Far more attention was devoted to all the other methodological problems: the estimation of the value of home-produced goods and the recording of extra-household transactions in kind and in cash.

Still, an approach to the constancy of consumption proportions had only been deferred, not solved. Hill's suggestion was left aside, largely because there was no quantitative empirical basis for it. Except by working very precisely with small samples, that is, anthropologically, it would be extremely difficult to capture all the small, irregular, and often spontaneous transactions that are clearly escaping the categories of the surveys. We know from field research that food is devoted to guests, celebrations, laborers, kin next door, children staying over, travelers' snacks on more frequent trips, and so forth, without being distinguished as gifts or remittances. We know that people are suddenly posed with helping with school fees or health costs or taxi fare for someone outside their household. What we don't know from our own perspective is how this adds up. Poleman (1961, 161) was particularly dismissive of Hill's framing of the problem, not only because of the methodological challenge of testing it but also because her interpretation implied that people could not better themselves by their own efforts. Whether and how people "better themselves" in a particular system of differentiation has been at the core of the issue from the beginning. One next step to take is to address the domestic cycle, to ask whether the life cycle of dependency and social investment embedded in kinship is cutting across the income variable.

DOMESTIC CYCLES AND THE CONSUMER MODEL

One hypothesis I explored early on was that expenditure patterns were based on one or the other of two economic models of the life cycle: one based on basic needs and the other based on basic ambitions. The first comes from Chayanovian (1966) analysis, based on the domestic cycle of total consumption requirements, with a changing combination of dependents and workers. We would expect both a higher total expenditure and a higher proportion devoted to food over the middle years of total household population, when there are few adults and many dependents, perhaps from ages 30 to 49 of household heads. As a result of the "self-exploitation" or the "drudgery" of the adults, the proportion of income devoted to food would have to rise at this stage in order to keep absolute per capita food consumption levels stable. The second life-cycle model originates in the Modigliani theory of savings and investment, where people borrow in youth, begin to save in middle age, and dissave toward the end of the life cycle. This model assumes a stable absolute level of food consumption, which would therefore decline proportional to the total, starting precisely in the middle years. Wherever there is no formal financial infrastructure, people cannot conveniently smooth their consumption over the life cycle in this way, by saving money for a rainy day and for old age, but Sara Berry's (1989) concept of investment in social relations can suggest an African proxy for this rationale. In early adulthood, people's social investments are still subsidized by their elders; then they invest heavily in early middle age, which pays off as regular donations from others in old age.

Economists who have examined the lifetime "savings and investment" patterns for populations without financial assets (means of banking, access to credit) have more or less abandoned the life-cycle model because of the apparently minimal effects. It simply does not emerge from the data as they have collected them. More realistic to them is a model of decision making focused on vicissitudes at closer term time horizons. Deaton argues that "[i]n the presence of borrowing restrictions [i.e., no banks], the behavior of saving and asset accumulation is quite sensitive to what consumers believe about the stochastic process generating their incomes. . . . Assets play the role of a buffer stock, and the consumer saves and dissaves in order to smooth consumption in the face of economic uncertainty" (1991, 1223).

Pushing the idea of short-term risk and time horizons further, Meghir suggests—exactly as Prais and Houthakker had done for the English middle and working classes—that income uncertainty is a key differentiating factor. In Meghir's case, it is between "less developed countries" and developed economies. He argues that the source of vulnerability needs to be defined as either idiosyncratic or aggregate. Communities that expect households to suffer idiosyncratic risk—from illness, bad harvests, and so on—may develop risk-pooling institutions, as Udry's work in Northern Nigeria showed (1990). Aggregate risk, where everyone is subject to the same instability at once, may work differently. The question of how is not deeply pursued. Meghir's own commentary rather peters out on aggregate risk. At the end of a paragraph, before the discussion moves elsewhere, he makes the following crucial remark: "if most of the risk is aggregate, this would explain the absence of risk-pooling mechanisms. The absence of markets to insure against aggregate uncertainty could be an important reason behind the low growth rates of some developing countries" (1992, 277). In other words, frequent external shocks from negative market conditions may militate against the development of collective local institutions that support both income smoothing at the household level and longer-term social investments at the community level. The patterns of people's strategies would then be so varied as to appear haphazard in the aggregate.

Because I have suggested from the outset of this collection of essays that recurrent shift of circumstance is a persistent—not an incidental—feature of Atlantic African economies, we need to pursue variation to the very end of the logic. When he develops the concept of assets as a "buffer stock" against uncertainty, Deaton claims that a "crucial assumption of the buffering model is that consumers are impatient, so that assets are a necessary evil" (1992, 264). But through long-term *habituation* to high aggregate risk such as the collapse of market prices or political instability, assets must surely shift from being a necessary evil to being a moral imperative and an absolute good. This is rather tentatively prefigured by Meghir: the "large extended families of Cote d'Ivoire . . . [p]resumably [channel] a large part of savings . . . into investments in both agricultural tools and, more importantly, education . . . [and investments that enable] diversifying the activities of its members" (1992, 278). That variety or diversity in investment strategies is considered highly positive is an argument made most notably by Sara Berry in several publications (1985, 1989, 1993). But once the

concept of investment is used for almost anything that offers some purchase or claim on the future, then the old consumer classifications really
break down. Tools; education; gifts in cash and in kind, large and small; ancillary expenses to social participation such as transport and clothes for fes-
tivals: they burst all the boundaries between consumption and savings that
underlie Western budget analysis. Classifying investment goods "in kind"
into conventional consumption categories completely masks the process of
investment and the expectation of return. Ideally, one would conduct research in people's own categories: for money, objects, relationships, time
frames, and all else. To our shame as anthropologists, as far as I know, no
one has ever tried to do this consistently, although Polly Hill argued long
ago that Akan economic concepts do include "the distinction between capital and other cash [spending money]" (1962, 6). The interim solution is to
see everything as investment.

The patterns for a life-cycle interpretation of either consumption or investment for our own sample are weak. Although total household expenditure follows the age curve of the household head, the proportions devoted to the different categories of use vary little (see fig. 8.1). So we return
to inferring people's conceptual schemes from a series of different analyses
and turn back to Polly Hill's suggestion: that people in the upper quintiles
are spending such high proportions of their higher incomes on food because they are giving it to others in a manner that has been misidentified as
consumption.

One last emphatic point: an anthropological approach cannot stop at

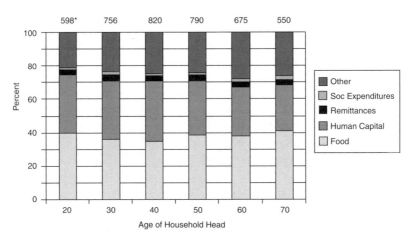

*Mean Household Expenditure in Thousand Cedis

Figure 8.1. Distribution of mean expenditures per household, by category and age of household
head. The numbers at top indicate mean household expenditure in thousand cedis.

the concept of risk aversion to explain in kind and miscellaneous "investments," because this gets at only short time frames and the shallow pragmatics of "getting by." As Mary Douglas (1986) has argued, pragmatics that work are impregnated with larger meaning and force. They are complementary, cumulative, expressive, and efficacious on a larger scale. They invoke elements of the "small" transactional institutions I discussed in the previous chapter. In contexts in which financial institutions and the state have never identified all the meaningful forms that investment can take, we then must infer how patterns in the data reflect the respondents' own aggregated intentionalities as they work at framing social life and economic careers in a particular time and place.

THE GHANA LIVING STANDARDS SURVEY

The GLSS was one of a series of national household budget studies carried out in poor countries, under the auspices of the World Bank and the national statistical services, to monitor the effects of structural adjustment. Three rounds were carried out between 1987 and 1992, and it is the last— September 1991 to September 1992—whose results I use.

Ghana comprises major ethnic, religious, and ecological variations, all of which are included and coded in the national sample. To experiment with placing people's intentions into socioeconomic contexts that can be related to ethnography and history demands more uniformity than this national sample represents. So I chose only those administrative regions in which 50 percent or more of the population was Akan-speaking by primary language and over 50 percent of the terrain was defined as forest. This gave us the Western, Eastern, Ashanti, and Brong Ahafo regions (see fig. 8.2).[2] Sixty-one percent of households in the combined region are Akan-speaking. A series of preliminary explorations suggested that the Akan and non-Akan within the region do not differ systematically from each other in expenditure patterns. Nor does migrant origin seem to make a difference; the households whose heads are defined as "born in this region" differ very little in their budgeting from those "born elsewhere." There are some major towns in this combined region but not the national capital. With regard to religion, the great majority of the population is Christian or animist. So the subsample is a zonal one. It is not culturally or economically homogeneous, but the people do share social and geographical space and historical conditions.

To take this subsample means sacrificing about half of the national sample. We end up with 2,336 households, comprising 10,312 individuals,

2. The Central region is very predominantly Akan but not forested, because of the coastal area, so it was excluded.

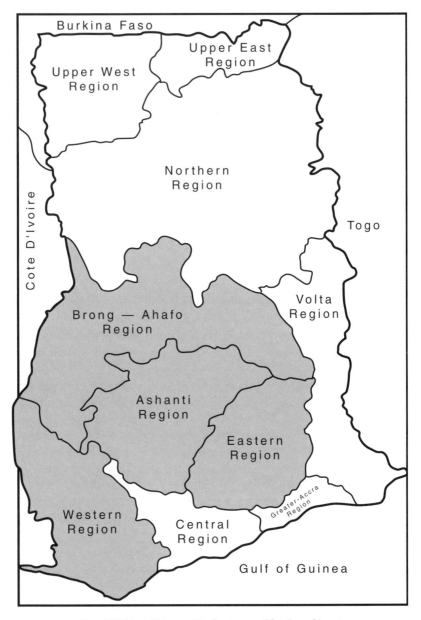

Figure 8.2. Map of Akan and the forest area of Southern Ghana.

out of the national sample of 4,552 households with 20,403 members. The social variables to which the presentation is restricted are gender of household head, age of household head (in ten-year intervals), and single-person versus multi-person households. It required more intervention to regroup the consumption categories to reflect what we could imagine as an "investment" logic rather than a "consumption" logic. The official report groups expenditures into many intermediate categories for special tables and then into ten major ones for publication. These ten reflect conventional commodity types: food and beverages; alcohol and tobacco; clothing and footwear; housing and utilities; household goods; operations and services; medical care and health expenses; transport and communications; recreation and education; and miscellaneous goods and services. We decided to regroup the intermediate variables in a different way, into four large categories, leaving as "other" those that were too ambiguous to recategorize by our own criteria. Following the idea that every expenditure could be treated as an investment in the future, of one sort or another, we supposed concentric circles of social commitment. The first is food, in the innermost circle, assuming it to be primarily devoted to the daily reproduction of close relations. The second is human capital expenditure, including all items that would enhance close relatives' own value in the future. The third is remittances, thought of as those expenditures that sustain the dispersed membership of the extended household. Fourth, there is social expenditure, as all money and goods devoted to organizations or to social status in a wider social world, presumably devoted to the long cycles of social reproduction. Everything else was considered as "other." None of the intermediary categories composed by the architects of the survey was unpacked; they were just regrouped. (The details are given in the appendix.) With these very simple, and reversible, changes, I extend Polly Hill's question about food-by-income-level by including other investments, and in relation to social variables other than income level. Does the proportion of expenditure devoted to food show any *other* surprising patterns than across the income quintiles, for example, by gender or age of household head, or by level of autonomy (single/multi-person households)?

First, we repeat Polly Hill's analysis: the proportion of total expenditure devoted to food, by income quintile. In the full national sample, as noted earlier, the variation is very small over the first four quintiles. For our subsample, Engel's Law seems slightly more relevant, although hardly at all over the three middle quintiles (see fig. 8.3). The highest quintile is always a problem, in any case, because of the undefined upper limit, which raises the mean. So our subsample shows a slightly higher gradient to the curve than the full sample, especially when mapped against the proportion of expenditure devoted to human capital. The proportion devoted to food

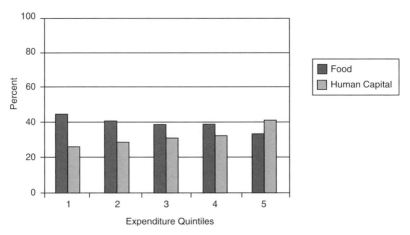

Figure 8.3. Percentage of household expenditure on food and human
capital, by expenditure quintile.

varies very slightly inversely with the proportion devoted to human capital. The result, however, is too small to obviate further exploration of how household expenditures can vary by a factor of two over the middle three quintiles — exactly the same as the difference between Prais and Houttakker's middle-class and working-class samples — while the effect on the proportion devoted to food is only 2 percent (in contrast to the English 16 percent), and to human capital, 5 percent. The Ghana sample's expenditure on food only differs by 10 percent between the top and the bottom of the social scale, whereas the total expenditure level in the fifth quintile is more than 600 percent of that in the first.

THE EPIPHANY OF SINGLE-PERSON HOUSEHOLDS

Our first analyses — by gender, age, and migrant status of household head — were producing a picture almost as inconclusive about internal variations as the tables in the official report and the quintile analyses. No correlations were significant (see the appendix). At this point, I turned to a tactic I advocated long ago (Guyer 1981), that is, to try looking at households as dense networks of relationship among individual persons. Ethnographic work supports this view. Clark (1994, 337) writes of Akan children making their own incomes and cultivating their own support networks. She also emphasizes (335) that, in general, people's sense of obligation to one another is based on their experience of trustworthiness and not on the ascriptions of kinship. So I turned to single-person households, assuming of course that these were not isolated hermits but rather persons whom the research definition of a household would place outside the unit. This category turned out to contain far more members than I expected. Sixteen percent of all households were comprised of a single person (277 male and 97 female). Although these individuals are a very small minority, less than 4 percent of the individuals in the whole subsample, they offer two things. First, on the cautionary side, they provoke reservations about household-level analysis when such a small group can be represented so disproportionately. But second, on the positive side, this category can offer a notional benchmark for how one adult person uses his/her money, against which to compare the per capita expenditure in multi-person households. With the "wealth in people" model in mind, I would have predicted that single-person households should be, although not isolated, at least poor, with little disposable income. This turned out to be very far from the truth. The single-person households in the GLSS have a mean expenditure that is almost *two and a half times* the per capita expenditure in multi-person households.

In fact, the people "living alone" comprise an astonishing category, which also scrambles the life-cycle approach of the consumption/savings model. First of all, the major categories of expenditure are distributed quite similarly between single-person and multi-person households (fig. 8.4), in spite of differences within each category by gender. More than 70 percent of the men in single-person households are *under* 50 years old (the largest group is between 20 and 29). As one might predict, they are mostly bachelors. By contrast, about 70 percent of the women are *over* 50 (the largest group being between 60 and 69). As one might expect, they are divorcees

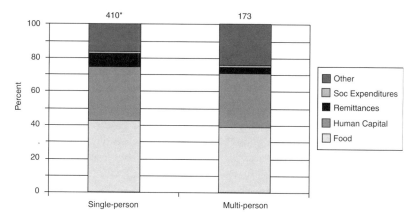

*Mean per capita expenditure in thousand cedis

Figure 8.4. Distribution of mean expenditures per capita, by category and single- or multi-person households. The numbers at top indicate mean household expenditure in thousand cedis.

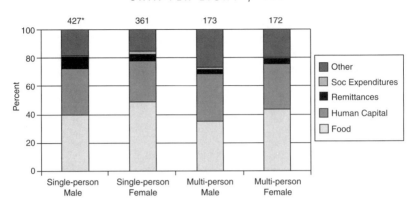

*Mean per capita expenditure in thousand cedis

Figure 8.5. Distribution of mean expenditures per capita, by category and single- or multi-person households, by gender of household head. The numbers at top indicate mean household expenditure in thousand cedis.

and widows. *And yet* the personal economies of the two categories are quite similar to each other, even in the absolute levels. Mean total expenditure for single men was 427,324 cedis and for single women 361,485 cedis (85 percent of the male level), by comparison with per capita expenditure in multi-person households of 173,602 cedis in male-headed households and 171,569 cedis (99 percent of the male level) in female-headed households (see fig. 8.5). As *households,* the single-person units have lower mean expenditure, but as *individuals* they appear better off. My subsequent thinking was definitively shaped by this combination of findings about single-person households: their improbable level of economic well-being, their heterogeneity of marital status, age, and gender, and their astonishing similarity in expenditure levels and patterns. Total expenditure must then reflect (or determine) an aspect of personal status that is not reducible systematically to age, gender, or (most probably) access to resources in any conventional sense.

One could wonder whether this is the quantitative representation of haphazardness, or, in another theoretical frame, what Bourdieu argued as the product of homogenizing methods: "the 'mass' of the dominated, a contingent, disorganized multiplicity, interchangeable and innumerable, existing only statistically" (1984, 468). Perhaps more to the point is Theodore Porter's argument that some populations do not submit their characteristics to formal methods until certain changes have already been institutionalized: "an adequate statistics for bureaucratic purposes [in nineteenth century France] had to await the remaking of the country" (1995, 37) along modernist lines. Conventional methods do presuppose people's subjection to common disciplines of economic life, generally set by national and class structures. And yet, surely social and economic life in Southern Ghana is lived in some kind of disciplined fashion, possibly of a sort that can be excavated from people's answers to questions, even though conventional analyses may miss it.

EXPENDITURE AND THE SOCIAL GRADIENT

The food expenditures of the single-person households are a particularly striking example of a pattern that emerges in other breakdowns of the population. Even with their higher total per capita expenditures and even with no one else at home to feed, the single people spend 42 percent of their total on food, by comparison with a mean of 38 percent for the multi-person households. On the face of it, there could hardly be a more emphatically complementary finding to Polly Hill's claim of 1957. People are spending per capita proportions on food irrespective of other variables that one would think *for sure* would have a profound effect, such as who is in the household. It would take another round of more focused analyses to establish whether this effect of constancy is produced by single people purchasing food in lieu of cooking, purchasing higher-cost items, giving food away, or buying items for someone else—and therefore their whole family—to cook and eat together. Whatever the explanations, they have to apply to 20-year-old bachelors and 60-year-old widows.

The multi-person households follow the same pattern as the single-person households with respect to the effect of the gender of the household head. The means for male- and female-headed households are very similar to each other, in absolute and proportional expenditure per capita. Gender does show its influence in two ways: more spending by female heads on food and less on "other items" than men, and also a lower coefficient of variation for every category of expenditure than men.[3] In other words, women consistently follow less diversified strategies than men, although always within the same general parameters as men. This picture is striking, given the importance accorded to men's social investment in elderhood (see Manuh 1995). It surely means that women are also investing, albeit in ways that may not be distinguished by standard budget methods. From the survey, the gender differentials are small.

The lack of a striking gender differential may reflect the powerful status of women in Akan society and economy, and their age-old pattern of lead-

---

3. The coefficient of variation for total expenditure is 91 percent for male-headed households and 72 percent for female-headed households, a difference that may also be a function of the sample size.

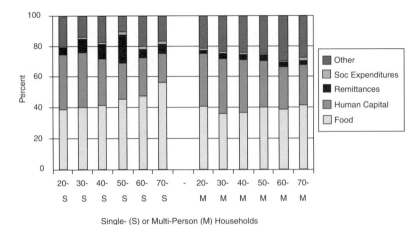

Figure 8.6. Distribution of mean expenditures per capita, by category and age of household head, for single- and multi-person households.

ing their own residence units, even when married (see Clark 1994). If these women are also of different age and marital status among themselves, I think we can go a little further and ask whether age as well as gender of household head is better considered only marginally relevant to household management (as measured in the survey), across the board. Figure 8.6 summarizes the findings. Although there are some small changes over the life cycle — primarily declining proportions of expenditure devoted to human capital with age in both single- and multi-person categories — I would argue that any pattern of change across the ages is far from dramatic.

These figures show a remarkable constancy in the internal balance of the budget, per capita, regardless of *any* major standard sociological feature of the household: size, composition (single/multi-person), age of head, gender, and expenditure quintile. Polly Hill's "puzzling" finding for income quintiles applies to all the conventional variables. How to make sense of this: probably that the poor person lives a diminished, but otherwise similarly balanced, version of the good life to the better off. Correspondingly, I would expect any single expenditure category to comprise a whole variety of household "types," by standard demographic and sociological variables. Ethnography can fill in some of the gaps here. People do expect certain intermittent expenses to be picked up by those who are better off. Kin and friends offer the occasional school fee, medical expense, or meal to someone outside their own household, all of which are so routine an expectation as to figure in the donor's budget simply as "education," "medicine," and "food" rather than as "gifts" or "remittances." But the quantification is not useless. It can add definition to Poleman's concern that *any* redistributive model implies that "people cannot better themselves by their own efforts" (1961, 161). In fact, in the gradient modal there is no leveling, since the well-off still live at absolutely higher levels of per capita expenditure on every item. At any level, people are consuming, receiving, and distributing—not amorphously, but strictly and almost *precisely* proportional to their capacities.

So with my previous chapters in mind, I hazard that money ranks people on a scale corresponding to profiles of achievement and good fortune (or self-realization), rather than structural ascription. Achievement is graded and profiled. People move up and down in increments, recognized in small nuances by others, who then make claims, but claims that are adjusted quite precisely to the means. So this is not a model of "sharing." It reflects a political economy of recognition whose implications will vary by historical circumstance. If everyone's expenditure level falls, even faithful implementation of a proportional "rule" can result in absolute deprivation at the bottom. Amanor argues that this has been increasingly the case in Ghana as structural adjustment conditions have intensified: "The breakdown in the lineage results in various types of fragmented households coming into being. Youth begin to fend for themselves" (2001, 118). The social gradient can become steeper, its ranks harder to scale, its interrank transactions greater or smaller, and conflict more or less acute. In hard times, some more institutionalized modes of claiming and giving may sharply reduce in amounts and frequency (as shown in chap. 6). But these pressures can be brought to bear without the fundamental notion of a social gradient, with contant spending ratios, necessarily being breached.

ETHNOGRAPHIC INSIGHTS

As with the analyses based on historical and anthropological evidence, I have wanted this analysis, which is based on economic evidence, to "stand alone" first, before deconstructing or qualifying the evidence. Data can tell "a truth" without that being either "whole" or "nothing but" *the* truth, let alone reflecting directly and in their own terms the realities of those who furnished them. Once a plateau of understanding has been reached, however, the next stage beckons. If, as I have argued, a lot of transactions that are better understood anthropologically as asymmetrical exchange up and down the social gradient are being classified as *commodity purchases* understood tacitly as taking place *within the household,* are the standard definitions adequate to the task? With characteristic bluntness, Polly Hill (1957, 8) noted the difference between economists' and anthropologists' definition of the Ghanaian household as "terrifying." Forty years later, the problems were clear to the designers of the GLSS, and—given the demands of national representativeness and comparative and panel analysis — they chose a very reasonable course. For the GLSS, the household was defined in terms of shared residence and cooking, with no explicit expectation of a common budget. In fact the enumerators were to make as great an effort as possible to elicit information from as many members of the household as possible. Thanks to their precision, it is clear that the household unit and its members' transactional patterns are overlaid rather than isomorphic. The large expenditures of single-person households suggest that individuals spend much more of their money across household boundaries than can be identified after the fact.

When I argued earlier (Guyer 1981) that we should analyze the persons and the relationships of domestic economies rather than prioritizing the units, Akan kinship had been a prime example of the extreme difficulty of working with households as units. Yet I was still unprepared for the extraordinary consonance between my own inferences from the GLSS and newly published ethnographic work. Three related conclusions are worth reviewing: the complexity of the household, the multiplicity of criteria of worth, and their composition into a scale of social value.

Gracia Clark writes that "[i]t is not entirely clear that Asante *have* households in the usual sense of the term. . . . If shared residence is debatable, a shared budget is almost unspeakable" (1994, 334, 340). Each individual negotiates for resources within a broad field of relationships, each of which is individually cultivated and judged according to its reliability. Status does not derive from household or lineage directly, and access to resources depends largely on skill and past performance. Clark organizes her entire exposition on the basis of multiple sources of identity, each with its own hierarchical scale, which are composed together to bring "complete fulfillment." People "attempt to manage the way in which all these axes of domination interpenetrate . . . to accumulate power through using their position in one system to leverage dominance in another." Through "interminable, not always explicit, negotiations" (370) they build independence and prestige. The mutual imbrication of several scales of value — gender, number of children, education, lineage, occupation, and so on — in producing personal position through mutual transactions is stated another way by Berry: "individual accomplishment is inseparable from interaction with others, and . . . there is no time limit for either" (2001, 200). In other words, accomplishment is individuated. It is not recognized, however, through any single external referent but rather through endless and inescapable transactions with others who are in the same domain, and on the same scale, of advance. One can rise and fall, but at every step there are ways forward and backward, which define the incentives and cautions for advancement through increments at whatever age and stage of life. Stucki writes that for both men and women, "Given the importance of wealth (ahonya) and personal achievement it is not surprising that there are numerous Asante proverbs that emphasize personal initiative, while others associate poverty with failure and even madness" (1995, 45).

McCaskie's vivid evocation of Asante under colonial rule includes a letter written to Meyer Fortes that evokes, in the religious domain, exactly the logic of multiple scales of value ultimately composable into a continuous gradient that I have tried to express here for the monetized domain of life. It is a philosophy, an aesthetic, a profound skill with respect to living a ranked, competitive, aspirational social life. The letter says: "The fetishes were brought to the 'Ahemfie' where they were lined up according to their order of importance which is calculated from the point of view of their time of coming and potence [*sic*]. There were a great many fetishes, varying in sizes, some tall, others short; some covered in muslin, other bare; some small, others big" (2000, 195).

The enormous variety of descriptive criteria is reduced to two principles — one fixed by chronology and the other volatile according to power — to produce a momentary performance of a single scale of value. It is interesting to discover, later, that an archaeologist (Stahl 2002) working in Southern Ghana finds equally compelling the concept of a "gradient" of objects of similar materials that have different uses and values.

So what does quantification add to such rich evocations of multiplicity arranged into scales? The great contribution that quantitative evidence can bring to the economic domain is a window into the scalar *properties* of the enormously complex judgments people make on a daily basis. Using "quantities of money expended" as an external measure of the value of persons does two things. It preserves the *relational* foundation to the logic of the social gradient, as emphasized in the ethnography, because people are spending money on themselves and others. At the same time, the "quantities" give that logic a momentary simplicity and precision (like the relative potency of the fetishes). The numbers suggest that it is the *proportion* of the budget expended on each social category that is more or less constant along the social gradient, or perhaps the *ratio* of one kind of expenditure to another. So one can see that the system is by no means a *leveling* kind of redistribution. The asymmetrical claims of people at different points on the scale must therefore be seen as crucial to the workings of differentiation. Two properties that are otherwise difficult to support empirically can be inferred and put back on the agenda for greater ethnographic precision.

Provisional though my interpretation is, it tracks that of others, and it brings important implications. Another economist has independently argued an interpretation similar to that of Polly Hill, but forty years later and using data from other budget and nutrition studies in economies with limited formal institutions. Bouis concludes, of the puzzling results of studies carried out in Kenya and the Philippines, that "underestimates of . . . nonfamily meals occurred, underestimates which were systematically related to a household's income" (1994, 21). The history and practice of interhousehold monetary and in-kind transactions are absolutely critical to understanding how these practices are constituted, both with and without the presence of formal financial institutions. The history of the formal financial institutions has been to invade the social domain, to submit insurance, savings, investment, contributions, and so on to the disciplines of organizations, including nonprofit philanthropy, and to put them into the circuits of the capital market, rather than leave them to spontaneous social processes. And a delimited household unit has been central to the formal concept of social life. One might even look back at Engel's Law in the West itself and explore whether the lower proportion of money income spent on food as income rises might also reflect a rising implication of household expenditure in frameworks for capital management in national financial institutions. Households begin to have savings in banks, pension funds, insurance and taxation, and investment in formal assets such as real estate, philanthropic contributions, and membership in associations. All of this costs money, even as it provides services. In other words, the sharpness of Engel's Law in the West may result from the differential "bankability" of households in the formal sector rather than from their consumer preferences as families.

CONCLUSION

In an economy such as Southern Ghana's, expenditure is based on people's careers, which are guided by a single broad pathway forward, applicable across many differences, including all the unforeseeable contingencies of the life course that crosscut sociological variables. The social and cultural map of how to start from wherever one is and advance — step by step through conversionary transactions, working the repertoires, creating the niches — is accessible to, and enacted by, everyone. And at each step a person is on both the receiving and the giving end: of expectations to give social support in return for material transfers (food, school fees, medical costs) looking upward, and the converse looking downward, all along the finely discriminated ranking that connects the two ends of the gradient. Apart from the outer limits of the expenditure spectrum, where a class dynamic may prevail, a wide range of the Ghana popular economy conforms to a social gradient model, and not a class or a kinship model, of the economic order. This model is deeply monetary in origin and expression. Polly Hill argued forcefully in another work that "cash economies always tend to operate in a manner which raises the rich and depresses the poor" (1986, 72). Her position echoes Douglas and Isherwood, who write from a different theoretical standpoint: "a free market in individual transactions always seems to result in an uneven distribution of influence and wealth" (1979, 40). I want to stress, however, that the social gradient cannot be seen as an ahistorical, structural, sui generis construct. In the long run, historical experience with the conditions of extraversion and long periods of inconvertibility with European currencies has shaped it. In the short run, it operates under the particular circumstances of the moment. The Ghanaian economy at the time of the Ghana Living Standards Survey was struggling under the stresses of the time: the reduced incomes and the increased instability of the 1990s, to which I allude in the next chapter.

PART IV

CONCLUSIONS AND DIRECTIONS

The dynamics I have presented in parts 2 and 3 of this book continue to play out in the popular economies of Atlantic Africa. In the present, people are also faced with the challenge of fixity. Conceptually, reduction comes with the world religions, the state, and international codes, all of which are particularly intensely active at present. The modernist project of state building, to which mastery of money and measurement are crucial, is still a real project, even when parts of the economic world seem to be moving in other directions. The religions attempt to bring their own blueprint approaches, whose implications could be more comprehensively extrapolated from the economics of Atlantic Africa's two "coasts"—the Muslim and Christian economic worldviews. But this would be another canvas altogether. My more modest point in this section is simply to pinpoint some strategic empirical and conceptual issues in the study of (secular) formalization, when we take advantage of anthropology's foundational commitment to address paradoxes and originalities in the social, cultural, and—in this case—economic worlds. In practice, fixity comes in a multitude of separate forms rather than as a comprehensive blueprint. And it is dangerous. The African world remains fraught with uncertainties produced by its relationship to the world as well as by any properly indigenous forces.

9

FORMALITIES
FIXING DEBT AND DELAY

Formalization is the modern state's counterpart to conversion. Legal texts and conventional quantitative measures bring different value scales and different modes of measurement into relationship with each other. The difference, in theory, is that the value relationship is treated officially as a permanent reduction to a particular systemic logic, not as a performative moment to be re-created at every transaction. A written statement—announced to the public and archived in perpetuity—is a testimony to the temporal duration of a set of provisions, and it is used as the touchstone to sanction them. Atlantic Africa has been endowed in the literature with a celebrated recalcitrance to this kind of reductionism and fixity. Mbembe (1989) writes of "indocility"; Berry (1993) writes of negotiability; and Fabian notes the intractability of Kongo political practice to the systematizing mind: "What looks paradoxical or simply confusing from the outside . . . may express a cultural preference for a state of anarchy, be it in religion, economics or politics" (1990, 25). Peter Ekeh goes further, to suggest that what he calls a "fragmentation of moral perspectives" arose historically, in the era of the slave trade, along with the kinship polities that alone offered some protection from "the barbarism of predatory state institutions" (1990, 682). Although not necessarily thinking that "fragmentation" adequately represents the process, I also am convinced that the history of trade is relevant to the scales, repertoires, and performances through which such qualities have emerged in gainful transactions. There can be no gain without mediating value scales, and under "open economy" conditions, relentless commercial pressures favor the elaboration of flexible methods and indeterminate conditions. Looked at from the vantage point of the "indociles," formal reductionism can become a kind of dangerous monopoly. It may guarantee a service, but at a price that can spin out of the buyer's influence. The tangible form of reductive monopolies is the document.

Of the spirit of capitalism, Max Weber wrote that "Commercialism involves, in the first place, the appearance of paper" (Swedberg 1999, 43). An official paper fixes a relationship, usually among several different value scales: the identity of the parties (including those who will enforce the contract in case of default), the kind and quality of the goods and services at issue, the monetary value, and the timing. From the earliest phase, modern economic policy documents presumed the prior existence of a wide range of scalar values and the possibility of fixing their relationship over specified durations. The famous Statute of Artificers of England in 1563 (Minchinton 1969), considered the first mercantilist policy document, contains measures for people (by age, sex, marital status, relationship, occupation, and location in administrative units), for money wages, for the severity of penalties, and — above all — for time. The hours of the day, the months of the year, the timing of the great fairs on the religious calendar, and the calendar of justice are all invoked. For example, the justices of the peace were to meet to assess the labor situation "before the 10th day of June next coming, and afterward yearly at every general sessions first to be holden after Easter, and at some time convenient within six weeks" (Minchinton 1969, 5). For conceptualization, the statute depended on the existence and plausibility of all these measures, and for implementation, it depended on existing institutions of law and order. The introduction of such economic documents into African transactions, with the history and experience described so far, must have important and ramifying implications.

I highlight three implications in this chapter. First, the document *mandated* equations (at least, in principle). In the public sphere, for example, one adult person equaled one head-tax payment per year. To implement such a policy required the definition of an adult, a payment and a year, and a force of law to reproduce the transaction, exactly as written, in every case in the same way. In commodity trade, the relationship between quality, money, and export status required official scales for all three qualities and an official service to implement them. Context is relevant only as it is defined in the founding document. Any changes over time require changes in the document if they are to affect the enactment of its provisions. Under volatile conditions, when the context can change rapidly, the predictability achieved by formalization is a very sharp double-edged sword. As a monopoly, it ensures the goods but at a "price" that may be far higher than was expected in the first instance. The struggle to capture the power of the commitments contained in documents has a very long history of its own in Atlantic Africa, ranging all across the horizon of legality.

Consequently, and secondly here, one particular danger was a reductive mastery of a measure for time. The spirit of capitalism also depends on the equation "time is money" (Weber, quoting Benjamin Franklin, in Swedberg 1999, 43, 53). Benjamin Franklin's homily lays out the exact logic: every unit of time has an opportunity cost in the money income forgone by doing one thing versus another. Visible adherence to a regimen of punctuality and probity over the use of time therefore stands symbolically for a person's value in the market for credit, itself indexed to the exact passage of time. But there is a condition that Weber, and Franklin, already took for granted. As with the Statute of Artificers, the existence of a unique quantitative measure for time is assumed. Every modern document assumes the modernist concept of incremental units of time, which alone allows the quantitative equation of time with money. Documents are dated precisely. Contracts begin and end. Financial instruments mature on particular dates. Interest on capital is indexed to time, to give interest *rates*. By contrast, time had figured sparsely in the value scales of the African past, being "understood" in the way that other scales were used. A modernist spirit of time measurement was triply sensitive then, in Africa. It was new; it was (in theory) fixed, rather than just added as another element to the pragmatic repertoire of scales, to be adapted, improvised, and performed, like any other; and it was enforced under conditions in which the context of a transaction, over time, was particularly uncontrollable.

Third, and disconcerting for any analytical methods derived from formal-sector assumptions, these interventions have become so specific and focused that they are more accurately seen as piecemeal and reactive than systemic. The state was never called on to rationalize economic logistics in Africa in the way in which wars forced them to do so in Europe. Its management activities were always run "on a shoestring" (Berry 1992). The most "efficient" colonial domination involved defining separate legal subdivisions of the population, which produced rigidities that generated their own contradictions (Mamdani 1996). In Africa, also, Western formal interests themselves have had to submit to the unstable conditions of the open economy, under which acceptance of comprehensive binding commitments without escape clauses can hardly be the best way to prosper. Formal banking was extremely slow and tentative in becoming established. For only perhaps a single decade after Independence was policy built on the assumption of incremental progress toward building coherent formal institutions. Military interventions and dictatorial politics intervened. The neoliberal policies of structural adjustment after 1980 were intended to substitute the systemic order of the market for the systemic order of the state. But the question of how to rebuild formal institutions was hardly raised in the international institutions that were promoting markets until the landmark World Bank world development report of 1997 titled "The State in a Changing World."

Much has been written about the rise of informality in the world economy, but one thing is clear. The "neoliberal" moment has not necessarily *decreased* formalization so much as *extended* it *piecemeal*. Every NGO has to be registered; every multinational requires an export license (among a mountain of other documents); every international financial institution links to national government bodies and financial institutions, to banks, and eventually to their customers. There is a premium on "legal engineering"— the production of innovative but workable documents for all manner of situations. Within each national context then, there is no guarantee that situationally negotiated legal provisions add up in any systemic sense. To give a concrete example: Frynas (2000) writes of the dense intersection of legal and jural frameworks applied to the relationship between communities and oil companies in the Niger Delta. The terms for some mediations end up having no clear status at all in national law and so are dubiously actionable in court. For the people, bringing a case requires enormous documentation, much of it almost impossible to acquire, so for the judges, hearing a case demands unusual levels of interpretation. Hence my title of this chapter, "Formalities," in the plural, to mirror the "conversions" of the beginning. It leaves open the question of the systematicity of the "formal sector."

Formality is experienced by the population in its plural and concrete forms, as "papers," rather than as an enduring generalizable principle. In the Nigerian countryside where I worked, people held onto all kinds of official papers: the registered map of a plot of land for a cooperative farm, an identity card for the last elections, a record book for land rent payments, the results of a court case, and an invitation to take part in a loan scheme. As policies rose and fell, the documents' utility waxed and waned, even though each was written as if it set up a continuing commitment. Bank accounts were extremely difficult to manage. Branch banks could close without warning because they had no money. Clerks and tellers could delay transactions until it suited them. Exchanging currencies involved accepting a heavy discount. Even the local branches of international banks implemented measures that would seem exceptional, at least to the standard middle-class account holder in the West. Traditional rulers had their loans forgiven; prominent people were offered loans for celebrations, such as the funeral of a parent. Recent experiences in Western finance suggest that naiveté is perhaps misplaced. The piecemeal constructs with arcane loopholes and idiosyncratic implementations are present in the center as they are in the geographical and legal peripheries, as I showed in the discussion of conversion. In the peripheries, however, they are not concealed.

Now that Pietz (1985) has illuminated the history of the original fetishes of the fifteenth-century Atlantic trade as fixers of specific contracts, one can see how documents may play this role in the literal, and not only metaphorical, sense in the present. Managing gains through creative manipulation of monetary multiplicity, number, and commodity classification is entirely familiar in Atlantic African history. Documents, by contrast, may be openly negotiated and agreed to (like a commodity sale), without any of the backward and forward linkages being clear to all parties equally. The entailments cannot be assumed at the time or contained over the long run. They become, then, more powerful, perhaps more mysterious, and may conceal far more gain than any of the marginal scalar manipulations of the past. The law may "forge the impression of consonance amidst contrast, of the existence of universal standards that, like money, facilitate the negotiation of incommensurables across otherwise intransitive boundaries" (Comaroff and Comaroff 2001, 39). But the experience on the ground includes loopholes, obsolescence, nonconsonance, and straightforward cheating, as well as opportunities for popular empowerment. In the West, an institutional infrastructure for treating formalities as incremental to a systemic logic is already in place. In Africa, what is being created is more plausibly a coral reef of separate formalities that coexist with — and shade into — conversionary modes of exchange. The modernist struggle is still aimed at forging national coherence, but the struggle now seems much tougher than it did at Independence. For progressive political as well as critical academic reasons, it is the document, at least as much as the commodity, on which anthropology needs to focus ethnographic attention as the fetish of the modern economic era (see Riles, forthcoming). Financial institutions are now more mysterious, more varied, and more powerful than the secret societies they in some ways resemble.

As one contribution, I turn to time and the economic document. Disjunctive temporality is fundamental to my argument in this book. To my knowledge, there is no comprehensive study of the economic philosophy and practice of time and the calendar in Africa (although see Diagne and Kimmerle 1998), so, until corrected, I continue on the assumption that the little historical record that exists does reflect popular perceptions. It is a rather dangerous assumption. It could seem extremely bizarre, for example, that equilibrium and progressive models of time would have flourished in the West during a century of unprecedented carnage and mortal danger such as the twentieth century was. But theoretical economic time is not a model *of* but a model *for*. It purports to fix conditions for the future, not reflect the sedimentation of the past in the present. One should not preclude the possibility that African temporal constructions contain some kind of abstract "logic of the procedures through which knowledge [of the calendar] is applied to practical situations" (Gell 1992, 300), although they do not — so far — seem implicated in any comparable drive to reconstruct the future as time measurements in modern economic practice. The temporalities of monetary transactions in Africa is a topic crying out for study. This chapter can only indicate directions of exploration.

MEASUREMENT AND THE PASSAGE OF TIME

The gains embedded in conversions in Africa were dependent on time but did not, on the whole, measure it. The passage of time was embedded in other diacritics. Tiv conversions anticipated future transactions through the medium of directionality. The important point was that things should go and come from a particular horizon; the timing would be implicit in that. To anticipate the purchase of cattle, one took Munchi cloth and oriented northwestward; to anticipate acquisition of a wife, one took the cattle and turned northeastward. The different concepts of "one hundred" along the trade routes northward from the coast in some sense covered time passed as well as distance; both were a function of the standard journey. The Igbo insistence on special numbering for bridewealth created the "illusion" that the passage of time did not change the value of the exchange, in case of repayment, even if the material content might have to be altered in light of the time factor. The Yoruba savings institution of *esúsú* (rotating credit) was based on the very short durations of days or weeks that defined contributions and payouts, with the longer duration of the credit cycle as a simple multiple, depending on the number of members. In uncertain times, when circumstances might change between the first and last payout, the number of members per group could be kept low without changing any other provisions. In fact, I have not come across any mode of financial management in nonformalized Atlantic Africa that was explicitly based on the passage of time, except where time was measured in agricultural seasons (see Shipton 1991, 1995). Even there, and even now, the terms and timing of repayment of a debt, and therefore the gains for being a creditor, are not treated as inflexibly attached to the inexorability of the Western calendar. Interest is an amount, not a rate.

Credit would be the most obvious place for temporal precision of one kind or another to be expressed in a commercial civilization, perhaps even in the abstract and modular terms that Gell (1992) encourages us to look for. Gareth Austin's historical review of indigenous credit institutions in West Africa is the most comprehensive. He writes that there was a practice "probably common in both precolonial and colonial times, of fixing the total amount of interest to be paid while leaving the duration of the loan open" (1993, 108). In very few cases could he find a specification of the duration of repayment for the most widespread form of debt institution, labor pawnship (107). Interest rates "could be very elastic in the short term" (108). Annualized and modeled by an outsider, they were rarely lower than 100 percent, but no one counted in this way. Time was in thresholds and not increments. There might be an effective statute of limitations, after which sanctions would be imposed. Gracia Clark (1994, 178), for example, writes of the Asante differentiation between commercial advance and cash loans, the one turning into the other if the implicit time limit was exceeded. After long periods, indebtedness takes on personal qualities until "[t]he donor . . . writes it off gradually over the years if the relationship proves satisfactory. These blend almost imperceptibly into the popular forms of pre-mortem inheritance" (1994, 181). There is a sequence. In Ewe society, the next temporal threshold for defining the dispensation on a debt is death; the next one the burial of the debtor's body and the inheritance of the debt (Austin 1993, 109–10); and so on, through temporal punctuations rather than measured increments. Debt forgiveness may only be possible in the temporal realm of the living, carrying much more serious implications if carried over into the infinite time of the spiritual realm after death. Nevertheless, forgiveness seems to be possible, depending on intermediate steps that are more nuanced than in modern financial debt. Berry reports that "Stool debts declined in the latter part of the colonial period, not because they were repaid or sold to private creditors, but because they were written off" (2001, 54). In fact, Shipton writes of The Gambia that the creditor's forgiveness is the proper moral solution to an untenable situation in which the mere passage of "linear and inexorable time" could result in interest "accumulating ad infinitum as time passes" (1991, 130).

Although Gambian practice is deeply influenced by Islam, which I have treated throughout as a coastal presence rather than an intrinsic force within Atlantic Africa, the situation described by Shipton is very similar to that described by Austin and others. Reflecting a similar calculus to the rationale I have suggested to be implicit in Akan budgets, he writes that the benchmark concept is an acceptable *ratio,* in this case of total interest to principal, which may be reached sooner or later, more or less indifferently (Shipton 1991, 130).[1] "Time and money are not necessarily understood as linked in linear function. . . . The complex calculations and negotiations involved in Gambian interest charges are not all easily amenable to conventional western economic analysis" (131). Perhaps they are recalcitrant because they were created as an obverse to Western economy. They were created by a monetized economy, which simultaneously rendered untenable a standard modernist institutional control.

Given the shortcomings of the record, another way of analyzing "time and money" would be to start with calendrics and then follow out the implications for monetary transactions. McCaskie's study of the Asante calendar is a model of "breaking the chronological stranglehold of the European sources, and . . . placing those sources in a more appropriate interpretative perspective" (1980, 185). The Akan calendar was based on concurrent counting of a six-day and a seven-day cycle, "giving a simple combinatorial

1. The cognitive and moral bases for thinking in ratios remain one of the puzzles for which I have found no direct evidence. Adam writes that the artisans of Ibadan did not think in fractions. Verran's approach to whole/part logics might provide an answer, if scholarship pushed on to such tangible instantiations of cognitive worlds as "outcomes of collective goings-on" (2001, 220), as Gell (1992) also advocates.

cycle of forty-two named days" (181). Laid over the forty-two-day cycle was a sequence of "bad days," when some key social activities were prohibited, and a fewer number of "good days" that were auspicious, resulting in complex judgments about the appropriateness of activities on particular days which proved impenetrable to visiting European merchants and diplomats. McCaskie ends with a plea that now applies more powerfully to economic life than to diplomacy: "The reconciliation of the 'rational' and the 'irrational'" through the study of "the beliefs which under-pinned action" (1980, 195).

It is remarkable how little time comes into the analysis of African credit and debt, given the centrality of the numerical time–money equation under capitalist logic. Monetary calendrics lie at the heart of Western — and any modern state-run — financial institutions. Incremental time remains the baseline measure against money, especially for the cumulative gains of interest on capital. The punctuations of weekly wages, monthly rent, annual taxes, twenty-five-year mortgages, and so on create moments of synchronization, horizons for planning, and also opportunities for arbitrage, for the insertion of qualitative thresholds where costs can be raised or lowered. Knowing how this timescape is laid out, and how it gets reworked, demands specialist technique. Yet the profoundly important reshaping of time (see Thompson 1969), and the naturalization of that reshaping, seems reproduced in our own thinking about the wider political-economic and cultural process that is modern reductionist commensuration (see Espeland and Stevens 1998). The constant reconstruction of temporal punctuations seems now far more naturalized in analytical work than the question of money itself. One wonders whether this is partly an artifact of presentist methods rather than anything more profound. Ethnographers hardly address time horizons, although in all chronically turbulent economies, the passage of time matters crucially. The kind of ethnography advocated by Gell would be one way to proceed. He recommends bringing together the analysis of ritual/meaningful categories with "the ponderous entropic time of real-world events," including "the analysis of language and cognition" (1992, 326, 327).

Temporality is possibly the most important and most difficult of all measures to fix in the "real world"— to define in language and to realize under entropic conditions. So the analysis of economic documents "at work," over time and in relation to their temporal commitments, would be a particularly illuminating point of entry into the study of transactional formalities in the popular economies of a turbulent world. Conversions give the illusion that the *terms* of a transaction do not change over time. Expectations of changes in context and content are built in, so time is neutralized. Modern documents about transactions give a different illusion, namely, that time is intrinsic and valued in uniform increments, whereas the *contexts* of transactions are assumed to be neutral and unchanging. Africa could hardly afford to be convinced of this latter view of the world.

TIME AND FORMALITY

The capacity of Nigerian enterprise to create and discover disjunctures in the architecture of formality is legendary, especially under the Abacha government that was still in power when I started this book. The "419" advance fee frauds and the Abacha government's retention of a dual exchange rate for the naira on the international foreign exchange market were thought of as part of the same syndrome of mediating, by tapping into, the cracks in the edifice or spaces in the coral reef of formalities. European businesses made their own points for arbitrage, generally within the letter of a badly loopholed law. They wrote penalty fines for delay on construction projects that would never be completed on time. They took advantage of lax, nonimplemented, or forward-dated legal restrictions on their activities. They made agreements with communities that failed to specify delivery dates or conditions of operation. And so on. Under the downward jolts of devaluation and the venality of the Abacha government, enormous advantage was taken of the capacity to delay payment, often with impunity.

Three examples suffice. In 1997, the *Daily Times* announced that "Consumers' bill runs to N12bn. NEPA threatens blackout. Mass disconnection imminent." Twelve billion naira should be about $130 million. NEPA is the Nigerian Electric Power Authority. It is a parastatal, and yet 60 percent of the debt was owed by "the public sector which included federal and state ministries, parastatals and agencies" (*Daily Times*, Jan. 20, 1997, 5). That is, almost two-thirds of the debt that threatened blackout was owed by one branch of government to another. The shortfall was accounted for by two factors. First, top officials were working temporal arbitrage with funds by delaying payment. Then the shortage of money within organizations resulted in mid- and lower-level officials being paid their salaries on an unpredictable schedule. So they sold the services of their organization to the consumers by adding an additional cut for themselves. Sometimes they even sold it on their own private account, at their own rates. The article quotes the new district manager at Onitsha advising "consumers to report NEPA staff seen illegally tampering with the authority's installations or using his position to the detriment of consumers." It would not necessarily be an exaggeration, then, to think that 80 percent of the debt problem derived from the imperatives of speculative arbitrage on the timing of debt payment.

The *Daily Times* of January 14, 1997, offered another angle on the same dynamic: "NITEL duped of N2.5 Billion. Illegal tapping of telephone lines." In somewhat smaller type the article notes that Government House in Enugu, the center of the fraud, owed NITEL about $600,000. NITEL is the telephone company, and N2.5 billion is about $30 million. Apparently NITEL employees had given "419 fraudsters" access to phone lines, and allowed them to take "advantage of the delay in the delivery of bills" to escape altogether. This time the loss was total, probably fueling the inability of NITEL to pay NEPA, and so on down the line. The logic seemed pervasive. An investigation into the People's Bank, another government venture, revealed that a sum of N2 million (about $25,000) had been converted by a branch manager and an accountant into a "seven-day call deposit agreement" in a private account in Pan African Bank in Port Harcourt (Olatunde 1993, 14). The interest on seven days was worth the risk of delays on the legitimate business.

It is not difficult to find examples of massive gains from the kinds of arbitrage made possible by formalities. The incentive to do as the People's Bank manager did was starkly obvious. The gain from seven days in one account versus seven days in another was enormous. It would be rewarding to extend the study and to analyze these transactions in as detailed an ethnographic fashion as Bohannan analyzed conversions, adding the regional and international backward and forward linkages discussed in chapter 2. The story of just a few dated documents and the temporal arbitrage they permit across the formal/informal divide (and back), in the face of the "ponderous entropic time of real-world events" (Gell 1992, 326), would go far toward illuminating the generative nature of this new analog of conversions in the world of big money. Although Gregory is certainly right in emphasizing the "tendency of those with power to impose their standards of value on others with different standards" (1997, 257), under entropic conditions it is not always possible for them to foresee all the ramifications. Under conditions that people are persuaded to see as stable, it may be that "the temporary conversion of goods into money on the part of the borrower always involves shame of some kind" (229). By contrast, under conditions that people expect to shift at any moment and where conversion can bring short-run gains, the morality of shame may operate altogether differently.

The logical questions to end on here are not how and why formalities are subverted so that they work like conversions. More mysterious, for the entropic world, is how and when they do not—how and why operators in the popular economy do invest in financial fixity over time—given the circumstances of West African economic history. Trusting the rational–legal framing of economic life can be dangerously irrational for individual actors. In some sense, it is the formalities that seem to work at face value that become the most challenging of all to understand. Here, I can only go part way, to indicate one empirical case to which the question applies. It is too important a topic to speculate about without evidence, so I leave it begging further study.

FAITH IN FORMALITY: AN UNPREDICTED AND IMPROBABLE STABILITY

The time and money mediation of measurement scales has to be bridged in mundane as well as "big money" contexts. According to Crump (1981, 212), a nonbanked sector of a commercial economy can only function and grow if it maintains a positive balance of payments with the formal sector. The interpenetration is intimate. Delays in official payment filter down eventually to the vast informal sector that provides food, local transport, and the basic demands of life, forcing the kind of ripple effect of debt and insecure repayment described by Obukhova (2002) for news vendors. Sudden currency change causes momentary disruption and even panic by putting the terms of credit or sales-advance repayment into question (Clark 1994, 272–74; Adesina 2002). Yet in many places, here and there, people seem to have been "irrational" enough to observe the required temporal conditions laid down in official documents, and further, to have created documents for themselves.

In the midst of the currency instabilities and national banking scandals of the 1990s, a very large number of Nigerians put money into a new government banking project, the community banks. The classic banking link, first created in Florence in the Middle Ages, between a community's savings and its capacity to grant credit, had never been successfully forged in local Nigeria. During the colonial period, the withholding of credit from the holders of savings was by government design. Post office savings banks were founded in 1908. Forty-eight years later, in 1955, the World Bank noted that "the savings are entirely invested outside of Nigeria" (International Bank of Reconstruction and Development, quoted in Mabogunje 1995, 286). Subsequent schemes were for credit only, more like officially sponsored rotating funds than banks. Commercial banks had never managed to make enough profit operating with the small savings and credit of the rural areas and the popular economy. People also distrusted the banks. They had lost money exchanging their savings at the time of currency change from the pound to the naira in 1973 and then from old to new notes in 1984. Bank personnel had proved far from evenhanded. In any case, the early 1990s saw the continual devaluation of the naira, unpredictably downward toward an unknown fate. So it was counterlogical for ordinary people — who, it was said, were otherwise saving "in the roofs, the ground and tieing our money around our waists" (*Community Banks Newsletter* 2, no. 3, p. 8) — to contribute to deposits totaling 930 million naira (Mabogunje 1995, 291) in 1,358 banks (Onugu 2000, 102) by 1995. Of course, this amount does not approach the sum owed by one set of 419 fraudsters to the telephone company in Enugu. A certain proportion of the founding deposits was also put up by wealthy individuals for their hometowns. Even so, the growth was still remarkable for a new and untried institution, during inflationary times, in a delay/arbitrage financial culture.

Even more surprising, the community banks have outlived one of the most turbulent decades in Nigerian economic history. They have survived three presidents, military and civilian rule, the corruption of the Central Bank of Nigeria (under whose auspices they function), a national bank collapse, continuous devaluation of the naira, the devaluation of the franc cfa in all the surrounding countries in the franc zone, and the great expansion of the parallel exchange market for international currency (Adesina 2002). In 1999 there were still "a little over 1,000 Community Banks in operation spread across the country" (Chawai 1999, 1)

The community banks were announced on January 1, 1990, by then-President Babangida. Minimum capital for each unit was set very low, N250,000, one two-hundredth of the requirements for conventional commercial banks. They were to be unit banks, owned by and responsive to the needs of local communities, offering loans that were guaranteed by people's preexisting commitments to the community. Restrictions on shareholding prevented anyone not living in the community, including sons and daughters living away, from owning more than 5 percent of the shares, and there had to be at least fifty shareholders. The sense of ownership of the banks was intended to be broad-based, otherwise they risked turning into the personal patronage outfit of the wealthiest citizen.

Compliance was not complete. The *Community Banks Newsletter* suggests some imaginative extensions: a community bank that granted loans on the personal guarantee of the traditional ruler (2, no. 3, p. 6); others that ceded influence to the wealthy, who in one way or another ensured the initial share capital (2, no. 9, p. 4). It is worth noting that these instances date from the run-up to the canceled national elections of 1993, when the party campaigns were up and running. Everyone of importance was worried about attracting their local vote to the party of choice. Some community bank chairs wanted to put the fund into the international exchange market (12, no. 12, p. 1). Still, at the end of the year, stern messages were going out from the national board about keeping their sights on development projects that would bring returns rather than on relationships that would build patronage or investments to bring speculative gain.

Much went as planned. The question is: how? and why? (under the circumstances). There were investments in the kind of enterprise for which small-scale credit is usually intended—workshops, farms, and so on. It is also clear that many communities had highly localized problems that they had been unable to address and were jumping on the community bank as the opportunity to do something about them. For example, a community in the east with a strong masquerade tradition had been unable to afford to put on the annual festival, which then meant that their sons and daughters in the cities came back more rarely, sent less in remittances, and were generally more disengaged from community life than the residents preferred. So the community bank loan was intended to revitalize an institution that would serve as a monetary pooling device and perhaps attract tourists as well. Most importantly, it lent itself to re-creating the centrality of the hometown in the financial management of its diaspora, now scattered all over the world (*Community Banks Newsletter* 2, no. 11, p. 2). Financing the revival of masquerades was just one of a very varied collection of enterprises, from football leagues to house building and a museum fund, all of which seemed to bear on the most urgent of community needs in the aftermath of structural adjustment's effects on the educated middle class. Individual loans are also granted, with apparently considerable success at generating business for the banks as well as the clients (Onugu 2000; Trager 2001). Commerce was by far the largest sector to benefit from loans (45.7 percent), but these "other activities" accounted for the next largest category, at 15.8 percent (Onugu 2000, 104).

Without further research, I can only suggest questions about the mediation of time and money in formal community banking. Like the literature on African debt already alluded to, it is remarkable how little the time factor comes into the published descriptions of community bank credit. Only once did I come across an allusion to an interest rate in the newsletter and the booklets about community bank functioning: 13.5 percent paid on savings at one local bank, to induce people to deposit their money (*Community Banks Newsletter* 2, no. 6, p. 6). Depositors have to have money in the bank for three months in order to qualify for a loan, which cannot exceed double their deposit. The overwhelming impression is given, however, that loans are very short term by comparison with bank loans in Western financial practice. Trager writes of the Ilesha Community Bank running a "daily contribution scheme" (2001, 165), which is similar to *esúsú* or *àjọ* and deliberately focused on competing for the clientele of those two institutions. Another sponsors the hajj by demanding 75 percent of the cost to be saved by the pilgrim, then granting the final 25 percent on loan at half the current interest rate (*Community Banks Newsletter* 2, no. 11, p. 2). Onugu suggests that the emphasis on commerce also results from the banks' inclination toward short-term returns.

Enthusiasm to *have* a bank may, however, have been greater than the enthusiasm to use it. The loan capacity of the banks is still "underutilized" by community members. At 23 percent of deposits, it falls below the ideal range of 30–70 percent of deposits on loan at any one time. Onugu argues that "the bank operators are involved in capital flight through placements, are risk-averse or loan-shy, or are involved in direct trading . . . [resulting in] the inability to recover funds placed in distressed merchant banks in the cities" (2000, 106). In other words, bank portfolios are composed with a complex of time frames, deposit mobilization, and investment returns in mind, with only the shorter time frames focused on loans to the community itself. Longer-term investments are made outside.

Depositors presumably keep their money in the bank. At the end of 1996, Onugu reported the total deposits of the twenty community banks he studied as 178 million naira, or $2.1 million (using the parallel exchange rate). For rural communities in a very badly run economy, at one of its worst moments, this is a large amount of money. How does this formality work for the shareholders and the depositors, and over what time horizons? What is an account as an asset? Probably it is one of many credit, debt, and asset acquisitions that people are engaged in, some with official documents, some with local documents, and others on the time frames and conditions embedded in existing financial institutions and conversions. The same people who save and borrow in the community banks are engaged in other debt nexuses, such as borrowing on the local credit market against an asset such as a machine or a vehicle. I learned in 1997 that many loans in the "informal" credit sector are now documented and witnessed, which allows the lenders access to formal credit of their own.

In brief, people cultivate investment repertoires, of which their fully formalized bank accounts and credit commitments are only a part. To study them is an intellectual problem analogous, at the end of the twentieth century, to studying the intricate scales and thresholds on the Ubangi–Congo confluence at the end of the nineteenth. The difference is that now it is possible to do ethnographic research into the apparent paradoxes. To reconjure the nineteenth century, one was sitting in the museum, *kwa* in hand, gazing at a beautifully handwritten acquisition list that claims a buyer needed two *kwa* to purchase a "bell" and one to purchase "ten spear-heads," and suspecting — because we are looking at them and touching them — that the amount of metal in the currency and the quality of the workmanship that produced such elegance and flexibility were similar to the object it was supposed to be buying. How could this be? Or maybe *kwa* too, like Georges Dupré's (1995) *mandjong*, were stamped out of sheet metal in European factories and then refashioned by local blacksmiths, eager to take their own portion of a seigniorage margin whose principles were well understood (Van Leynseele 1983, 90)? On the face of it, and until laboratory analysis is carried out, *kwa* seem counterlogical to any theory of money.

Although Equatorial ingenuity surpasses the imagination for the moment, Nigerian ingenuity with formalized transactions is a fact of the present—one that affects the welfare of millions and is creating the social order of the future. Much of what is clearly illegal seems perfectly logical, under the circumstances. The coral reef of formality creates loopholes and opportunities. It is the legal pathways of monetary circulation and asset acquisition that seem more paradoxical. With its capacity to embrace the unexpected, and its inclusive ambitions bequeathed by founders such as Morgan, anthropology would seem well positioned to study the culture, experience, and structured relationships of this, one of the most generative processes of our era, namely, the struggle for the gains embedded in the formalities that define time, money, and their mutual implications. It is no longer diversity but uniformity that seems so unlikely as to be bewildering.

10

BEWILDERMENT REVISITED

These chapters, as "lines on the page," seem very spare and sparse by comparison with the lived complexities, the more massive asymmetries, and the analytical gridlocks that provoked them. One advantage of spareness is that it also reveals what is absent, rather than cluttering the canvas so completely that the last thing one needs is yet another idea, other than a mantra-like conclusion that "only history will reveal . . ." Critics will doubtless see far more absent, and just wrong, than I do. My conclusion here is limited to prefiguring the next move along this line of thinking. In these studies, I have mined material that is already in the archive and rearranged it in a new way. The material is familiar. It is quite literally, as the cartoon caption in chapter 5 puts it, "general knowledge." Only the juxtapositions, the abstractions, and the suggestion that all these "anomalies" form a single configuration have been added to cast the material in a different light.

There is a lot more to be done. There are two related problems, reflecting macro and micro components of economic theory. First, on the anthropology of macroeconomic logics: Our subdiscipline has always been about "thinking other" than capitalism, either by looking far back into the past or way out into the world. The originalities that we find remain the bedrock of our own capacity to "think other" of economic processes. Ethnography has allowed the playing off each other of two critical approaches: the Marxist moral-political critique of commodity exchange from within and the empirical understanding of other forms of exchange from without. The continuing richness of the intellectual juxtaposition of internal critique and external understanding permeates the newest as well as some of the oldest work in our field (see Graeber 2001). The literature on the Maori *hau,* the *kula,* the *potlatch,* the *moka,* wampum, the prestations of caste, and so on, provides important landmarks for sounding out ideas about other phenomena.

By comparison, "thinking other" from the borderlands *between* the capitalism of the core and the "remotely global" (Piot 1999) has been conceptually very difficult. The "articulation" approach of the 1960s and 1970s faded with the structuralism on which it depended. The idea of studying "process" became problematic when it tended to be confused with the teleology of trends. The trouble is in the inevitable paradox. Several different theoretical approaches to economic borderlands must offer *some* purchase on *some* issues, while at the same time *none* of them offers enough to move beyond an "only history will reveal . . ." sense of indeterminacy. When events turn very surprising, the theory seems a particularly weak reed to lean on. In Africa, scholarship has been anchored by three powerful analytical traditions that, in the end, have served to block key realities from view. The first is the progressive monetary reductionism of practical economics, in which the value of conventionalized variables is established on a numerical scale from zero to infinity in an expansive and encompassing quantitative model. Neither the relevant variables nor numerical practice in West African exchange is well captured by conventional economic approaches. In an extroverted position in the world, the creation of margins on transactions has involved configuring value scales rather than reducing them all to number. Number was only one — albeit far more important a one than culture theory so far accords — of the measurement scales at play. Scalar multiplicity has been fundamental, shaped by the "non-bankability" and the institutional ramifications of European mercantilist policies that, for several centuries, have lain at the heart of varying modes of legitimized exploitation of the African continent's resources, largely in the service of development elsewhere.

The second is the philosophical commitment of economic thinking to what Mirowski (1989) calls "conservation principles," in which a key parameter is held constant so that the variability of others can be gauged. In classical theory, it was the material — such as labor — that fixed the value of commodities. In neoclassical theory, it was the assumption of the constancy of utility: "there can be no divergence between the anticipation and the realization of utility" (Mirowski 1989, 273). In the calculative practice that linked theory to the world, for much of the era of theoretical construction it was the centrality of gold and its stability as a standard for conversion and as a reserve. And during the whole history of modern economies, up to very recently, it was the nation-state and its capacity to create and enforce an increasingly dense set of systematically related regulatory measures with respect to property and transactions, all of which have precise and legally enforceable temporal durations. All these could be "taken as given," or naturalized, and theory proceeded from there. Mirowski summarizes: "causal explanation requires invariance, but plausible invariance requires institutional stability" (397). In West Africa, by contrast, nothing has been consistently constant; everything is referential. And analysis can only go so far by pretending that this is not the case. The imperative to surpass conservation principles derives from the experience of turbulence.

The third is the cultural particularism of anthropology. The study of economic life in Africa certainly needs more language-based study, more critical examination of philosophical concepts in practice. The main problem, however, is a familiar one: that institutions, practices, cultural constructions *must* be historicized because they represent not (or not only) ancient fundamental principles but the long-term sedimentation of experience. Even without the kind of direct evidence that historians would prefer to have, we must assume that centuries of African discourse about economic experience — between specialists and populations, dominators and the dominated, and across linguistic frontiers — shifted and clarified the ideas that make institutionalized transactional practices and their sanctions plausible and therefore predictably enactable. The reference point that makes this or that practice plausible may be explicitly historically encoded (as I showed in chap. 5 on commodity classifications in Western Nigeria), even where the nature of that coding also shares logics with other and older qualities of culture and society. Recent works make a parallel point about historical sediments and repertoires for the less explicit, secret mysteries of spiritual life (Ferme 2001; Shaw 2002). My commitment to stay focused on the concreteness of history justifies making only sparse and selective recourse to a theoretical framework that is otherwise attractive, namely, constructivism. The fact that expectations of unpredictability and relativity seem to permeate West African constructions is not used, in the first instance, to support a *general* constructivist argument about indeterminacy. A general constructivist theory fits Africa better than others, if only because it is far less likely than others to make Africa look like a pathological departure from a standard model based on Western experience and institutions. However, to make this argument would short circuit the more fundamental consonance we can show, and therefore the linking dynamics we can suggest, between *particular* experience and *particular* constructions.

These three conditions of West African popular economic practice breech the assumptions of conventional theoretical traditions: multiplicity of scales, including but not reducing to number; their endlessly reflexive mutual referentiality rather than common reference to a constant; and their construction through experience — "action and reflection" as Graeber writes (2001, 91–115) or "intelligence" as Morgan put it — rather than age-old cultural principles or instrumental political imposition. And behind and informing them all, there is an entertainment of asymmetry in exchange, and the accommodation of gain on a ranking principle, rather than the veil of equivalence. A transaction is a moment when correspondences are agreed upon. It emanates from valuational ranking and established potentials for tropic linkage, but it does not erase the asymmetries from which it originates and which motivate it in the first place. These conditions are consonant with, even though not entirely reducible to, the centuries-long experience of Atlantic Africa with European mercantilism: with trade monies, built-in thresholds, revaluation of goods at those thresholds, and temporal uncertainty. Before returning to the analytical issues in anthropology, let me discuss this "consonance" in more detail.

What was mercantilism? The standard histories of economic theory consign it to the forerunner of classical theory, in turn the forerunner of neoclassical theory. Economic history gives it a different role (Heckscher 1935). It was not "a" theory in the sense of an internally coherent set of propositions. It was a political and economic program for building the nation-state out of the feudal domains and religious empires that preceded it. The most important goals were the production of internal uniformity in measurement and the destruction of barriers to exchange within national boundaries. And in accordance with the promotion of internal trade and improved government control and access to national resources was control of the money supply (thought of in gold). Loss of money to the nation through any means, particularly over-importing goods, was to be avoided. Balance of trade was fundamental. There was always a large challenge here with respect to places either not able or not willing to pay for European goods in gold. Buying from them was a problem because the money would not come back. The famous "commodity currencies" of West Africa were a solution to the problem. Whatever manillas, cowries, and outdated guns were in Africa, they were definitely commodities and not money in Europe, so their use to "buy" ("barter") African goods did not entail loss of European control of money circulation and therefore posed no challenge to national stores of wealth.[1] Thus were one-way thresholds created and/or modernized in the geography of trade. And trade itself, linked as it was to the surges of political exigency, cultural taste, and technical inventions, created the uncertainties that placed those thresholds under recurrent pressures. It is this condition that is now depicted by the concept of "the open economy."

One might think that mercantilism is the "ancient history" of modernity. But the imperatives of mercantilism have never completely disappeared from the political practice of Western economic decision-making. The "national interest" can still be invoked to protect markets, control the balance of trade, define some currencies as inconvertible, restrict access to financial instruments that depend on national and now international legal institutions, and so on. For example, newly available official sources on British policy toward Biafran independence from Nigeria in the late 1960s

---

1. Silver Maria-Theresa talers — minted in exclusively in Austria from 1751 to 1936 — are a fascinating exception to Europe's avoidance of the use of precious metals for exchange within Africa. See Gervais 1982.

consistently return to the effects of changes in oil policy on the British balance of payments.

The result of accretions from mercantilist to fiscal and now monetarist Western political economic practice is incoherent, above all when experienced from the receiving end. Monetarism—the control of the national economy through the money supply—is particularly out of reach for African governments. They do not control the international exchange rate, nor the more arcane fictional units of financial markets, nor even their own vast informal sectors, which pursue their transactions outside the frameworks of fiscal policy and banking disciplines. This macrosituation deeply affects the microdynamics. In metropolitan centers, people are protected from the experience of incoherence and turbulence by the sheer density of private and professional effort that goes into producing daily predictability: in material life and in the ideologies that undergird the crucial but elusive quality of "confidence." In Atlantic Africa, there has been very little institutional buffering at the macro level, and people have a long history of facing head-on the implications of an uncontrolled currency supply, fictional financial units, and emergent transactional institutions.

One can therefore claim an analytical position on these borderlands and "think other" about the microconstructs that arise within them. There is no a priori reason why an abstract appreciation should not be possible, on the basis of propositions that reflect specific history and experience rather than general propositions of psychology and culture established ahead of all empirical engagement. If the topic is gain, then the most profound microeconomic questions are about reasoning.

There is rising anthropological interest in rationality (as science, as the Enlightenment intellectual tradition), but it has yet to make major inroads into microeconomics. For several decades the analysis of representation and expression has been polarized from analysis in terms of reason, in part because of anthropology's alienation from the increasingly parsimonious definition given to reason, as "rational choice." Cultural analysis has made significant contributions to the study of social reproductive power while avoiding directly addressing the plans and strategies that value and desire must surely generate (Gudeman 2001). Concentration on the symbolic bases for value is important in avoiding the methodological reductionism of quantification that simply reproduces the reductive political-economic process in the present world. The continuing work in Melanesia on "equality" (Robbins 1994) and "equivalence" (Foster 1990) keeps alternatives and vistas open for thought. The radical and liberational horizons of Graeber (2001) and Hart (2000), in different ways, reposition alternatives in a political field. But we need to increasingly incorporate attention to thought and calculation.

In like manner, one needs to "think other" precisely about number, measurement, and money in the awkward and dangerous present because they are such powerful constructions in a quantified and insurgently commercial world. Gains of one sort or another constitute one of the frames for thinking about that world, both by theorists and actors. Jean Lave (1988) has pioneered this effort, writing on "price arithmetic" in Western supermarkets. More recently Miyazaki (2003) writes on Japanese stock traders' utopian rationalism, which they apply to all manner of otherwise "nonrational" domains such as religion and private life. In a particularly rich conjuncture of macro, cultural, and rational analyses, Maurer (2002) explores the meaning of the "Gold Coin for Pilgrimage Expenses" *(koin emas)* produced by the World Gold Council in the immediate aftermath of currency collapse in Indonesia in the late 1990s. During the crisis people had realized the value of their gold jewelry and coins as an asset, and especially to finance the religious imperatives of life, such as the pilgrimage to Mecca, whose spiritual and temporal horizons are unaffected by the short-run vicissitudes of the world economy. Its uses have since ramified, so that it is best defined now by the Indonesian concept of *aspal* — a term that literally combines the roots of *authentic* and *fake,* that "puts the real, the fake and the relation between the two under erasure" (Maurer 2002, 64). The terrain that would seem ambiguous by the analytical categories that distinguish commodity from token is rendered clear by an indigenous concept that avoids engaging with the distinction, even to mediate it.

From these vantage points, all the classic dualisms leave spaces unilluminated: use and exchange value do not exhaust value dynamics in a monetarist economy; gift and commodity do not exhaust the forms of exchange. The new anthropology of exchange is taking anthropology's classic homing instinct for anomaly and originality to look at crises and interstices, choosing topics that seem ambiguous, transitional, ephemeral, or contradictory, and probing most deeply the realities of experience on that terrain. Apparent paradoxes in foundational writing about political economy, such as those Caffentzis (1989) explores in John Locke's philosophy of money, may be re-envisioned by placing the propositions within a wider frame of historical and political reference. Locke was concerned with "reducing the entropy" (Caffentzis 1989, 122) in monetary forms, in words, and in civil government. Atlantic Africa was already engaged with the same political-economic world as Locke, dealing with the same entropic inventions of British merchants, with different methods. The world over, powerful thinkers and small actors struggle to make sense, because the human mind cannot — in the event or for long — simply "stand bewildered in the presence of its own creation," as Lewis Henry Morgan (1977, 467) momentarily found his own mind to be. African monetary practices present a challenge to theories that attempt to "reduce entropy" in standard ways that depend precisely on the institutional forms Locke promoted — unambiguous law, a purist approach to money, and a central bank — but only succeeded in implementing at home. However, African practices also provide a geographically broad, historically deep, and experientially rich source from which to contemplate how people have not been utterly "bewildered" in the creation of their own transactional orders at the interface with the "unmanageable power" unleashed by the "advent" of what Morgan called "civilization" but we might prefer to call "modernity."

All my analyses were undertaken by Shobha Shagle, Ph.D., and developed in discussion with her and with Caroline Bledsoe.

The Ghana Living Standards Survey (GLSS) was one of a series of household budget studies undertaken in Africa during the period of structural adjustment in the 1980s and 1990s. As of 1993, Living Standards Measurement Surveys had been conducted in eleven countries, under the auspices of the Poverty and Human Resources Division of the World Bank, by national teams and international consultants. Their purpose was to "collect individual, household and community level data to measure levels and changes in the living standards of the population, and to evaluate the effects of various government policies on these indicators of living standards in developing countries." This literature has been "expanding very rapidly" (Sender 2001, 37). It would clearly be worth a major effort for anthropologists to engage with this entire project, now folded into the crucial process of qualification and implementation for funds under the Heavily Indebted Poor Countries (HIPC) process of debt relief. The present initiative was experimental and therefore focused on one particular comprehensive survey. The sheer pragmatic and intellectual plausibility of working on such a data set was very much in question, and the process stalled several times.

The household was defined narrowly as "any person living alone or any group of persons staying together and sharing the same catering arrangements" and membership as applying only to those living in the household for at least nine of the last twelve months (Ghana Statistical Service 1995). Income and expenditure data were collected from household heads but did address individuals, who were themselves the source of information wherever possible. One problematic method is that the data were extrapolated to the entire year from the sixteen days of monitoring and the informants' own statements about annual amounts. The analysts address this problem of extrapolation, for the population as a whole, to represent an entire annual cycle, but one may lose the precision when working with subpopulations. One indication of the problems that can accrue from extrapolation is the finding that total reported income is only two-thirds of total reported expenditure (Ghana Statistical Service 1995, 60). In a bad year it is possible that people are doing some dissaving, but this gap is so wide that it must be an artifact. This appendix traces out our techniques so that our findings can be subjected to critique.

Just to revisit out logic: my purpose was to infer from the quantitative findings the social, cultural, and historical constructions with respect to valuation, which anthropologists would assume would motivate the expenditures reported by the subjects to the enumerators. To optimize our perceptions, we had to redefine the population, regroup the variables, and make some unusual categories for analysis. We did not try to compensate for problems that an anthropologist might see in the conduct of the survey itself and which derive from the imperatives for panel data replicability, international comparison, and secure placement in the disciplinary literature in statistics and economics. Some of these procedural decisions would be very difficult in the Ghana case: the definition of a household, the choice of key household informants, the documentation of multiple income and expenditure decision-makers within households, sampling, extrapolation over an annual cycle of data generated over four weeks, and so on. But to address these challenges would be a completely different analysis. We chose to assume that something important about value was conveyed across the interface of the interview, supposed that this might not be randomly distributed, and proceeded with analysis on those assumptions. The key steps were as follows.

CHOICE OF A SUBSAMPLE

A national study in almost any country in Africa comprises several ethnic groups and several economic–ecological zones. In Ghana one can control the "noise" produced by these variations in ethnicity and economy without reducing the sample to an unworkable level. There is one very large ethnic cluster, the Akan-speaking peoples, whose homeland overlaps one major ecological zone, the forest, and there is one cosmopolitan primate city that can be excluded. Out of the ten regions of the country, we defined as our zone of enquiry all those regions in which 50 percent or more of the population was Akan-speaking by primary language and over 50 percent of the terrain was defined as forest. This gave us the Western, Eastern, Ashanti, and Brong Ahafo regions. The Central region is very predominantly Akan but not over 50 percent forested, because of the coastal area, and therefore we excluded it. Taken together, 61 percent of the households in the combined region are Akan-speaking. A series of explorations suggested that the Akan and non-Akan did not differ systematically from each other in expenditure patterns, and neither did the categories "born in this region" from "born elsewhere." So we take this to mean that we can interpret the population as a zonal one, sharing social and geographical space and historical conditions and, by virtue of that, certain commonalities of economic culture.

This subsample comes to about half of the national sample: 2,336 households, comprising 10,312 individuals, out of the national sample of 4,552 households with 20,403 members. Sixty-six percent of the households in the subsample were male-headed, with a mean size of 4.7; 34 percent were female-headed, with a mean size of 3.9. What seems a high proportion of 16 percent of households comprised a single person (277 male and 97 female).

VARIABLES

Population

The only groupings we use here are (a) gender of household head; (b) age of household head in ten-year intervals; and (c) single-person versus multi-person households.

Expenditures

The official report groups expenditures in intermediate categories and then in ten major ones: food and beverages; alcohol and tobacco; clothing and footwear; housing and utilities; household goods; operations and services; medical care and health expenses; transport and communications; recreation and education; and miscellaneous goods and services.

Our interest was in expenditure by social destination rather than primarily by commodity, so we regrouped the variables into four large categories and left as "other" those that were too ambiguous to recategorize by our own criteria. By anthropological standards, ambiguities remain and must come into the interpretation, but we started out with simple assumptions that any social scientist in any discipline might find plausible. We supposed concentric circles of social commitment: (1) food, in the innermost circle, as if primarily devoted to physical reproduction of household members; (2) human capital expenditure, as all items enhancing the long-term value of the household's members; (3) remittances, as expenditure sustaining an extended household; and (4) social expenditure, as all money and goods devoted to organizations or to social status in a wider social world. Everything else was considered as "other." The variable groupings are as follows.

1. *Food* (created by GLSS)

2. *Human capital expenditure*

(a) Educational items: school and registration fees; contribution to parent–teacher associations, uniforms and sport clothes; books and school supplies; transportation to and from school; food, board, and lodging at school; and other (variable obtained from IE21.ssd file, sec. 2A).

(b) Frequent nonfood items: recreation; health and medical care; transportation; communication; miscellaneous goods and services (variable obtained from IE29.ssd file, sec. 9 2A).

(c) Less frequent nonfood items: furniture; appliances; clothing and footwear (variable obtained from IE28.ssd, sec. 9 A1).

3. *Remittances.* Data from three questions from section 11A, aggregated: cash sent/given to individual; food value sent/given; other goods (variable taken directly from file IA34.ssd, created by GLSS).

4. *Social expenditure.* Data from five questions from section 11D: includes taxes; contributions to self-help projects; celebrations; gifts and other miscellaneous expenditures.

ANALYSIS

All analyses were carried out using EpiInfo. We proceeded with caution about making arguments that depend on small differences and variations. In fact, although we ran correlations, regressions, and significance tests for several variables, nothing was persuasive. We proceeded with means only, having found the pervasive constancies more interesting that the minimal differences.

We tested for significant differences in expenditure patterns by the gender, age category (in twenty-year groups), and migrant/nonmigrant status of the household head. T test was used to assess differences by gender and migrant/nonmigrant status of household heads, whereas F test was used to compare differences in expenditure by age categories. The only significant differences we found were for total expenditure, the proportion devoted to social expenditure, and the proportion devoted to human capital, as follows: Male-headed households had significantly higher total expenditures than female-headed households (mean of 767,013 vs. 640,520 cedis). Household heads in the 40–59 age category had higher total expenditures (807,657 cedis) than did either of the other two groups (20–39 age category, 689,353 cedis; 60–79 age category, 633,658 cedis). The proportion of total expenditure devoted to social expenditure was slightly higher among male-headed households (.015) than among female-headed households (.011). Household heads in the age group 60–79 (.018) devoted a greater proportion to social expenditure than did households whose heads were in either the 20–39 (.012) or 40–59 (.013) age category. The proportion devoted to human capital expenditures was highest when the age of the household head ranged between 20 and 39 years (.32). However, all these differences are small enough to disappear with per capita analysis.

REFERENCES

Abraham, R. C. 1958. *Dictionary of modern Yoruba*. London: University of London Press.

Achema, Jonah. 1997. A matter of cash: Nigeria's economy runs on a cash and carry basis as most business houses prefer cash to cheques. *Newswatch,* Jan. 27, 29–30.

Adam, Susanna. 1995. *Competence utilization and transfer in informal sector production and service trades in Ibadan, Nigeria*. Bremen: Bremer Afrika-Studien.

Adebayo, Akanmu G. 1992. Pre-colonial institutional frameworks for money-lending and loan repayment among the Yoruba. *Paideuma* 38: 163–75.

———. 1994. Money, credit, and banking in precolonial Africa: The Yoruba experience. *Anthropos* 89: 379–400.

———. 1999. Kòs-é-mánì: Yoruba view of money and the development of financial institutions in southwestern Nigeria. In *Credit, currencies and culture: African financial institutions in historical perspective,* ed. E. Stiansen and J. I. Guyer, 146–74. Uppsala: Nordiska Afrikaninstitutet.

Adejobi, Oyin. 1981. *Articulated lorry.* Trans. Karin Barber. Originally performed and recorded in Yoruba as *Ajagbe ejo.*

Adesina, Charles Olutayo. 2002. Growth and change in the Ibadan underground foreign exchange market during devaluation. In *Money struggles and city life: Devaluation in Ibadan and other urban centers in Southern Nigeria, 1986–1996,* ed. J. I. Guyer, L. Denzer, and A. Agbaje, 75–91. Portsmouth, N.H.: Heinemann.

Ake, Claude. 1981. *A political economy of Africa*. London: Longman.

Akiga. 1965. *Akiga's story: The Tiv tribe as seen by one of its members.* Oxford: Oxford University Press.

Akin, David, and Joel Robbins. 1999. *Money and modernity: State and local currencies in Melanesia.* Pittsburgh, Pa.: Pittsburgh University Press.

Alexandre, Pierre, and Jacques Binet. 1958. *Le groupe dit Pahouin (Fang-Boulou-Beti)*. Paris: Presses Universitaires de France.

Amanor, Kojo Sebastian. 2001. *Land, labor and the family in Southern Ghana: A critique of land policy under neo-liberalism*. Research Report No. 116. Uppsala: Nordiska Afrikaninstitutet.

Amin, Samir. 1976. *Unequal development: An essay on the social formations of peripheral capitalism*. New York: Monthly Review Press.

Amogu, O. O. 1952. The introduction into and withdrawal of manillas from the "Oil Rivers" as seen in the Ndoki district. *Nigeria Magazine* 38: 134–39.

Aniakor, Chike. 1996. Household objects and the philosophy of Igbo social space. In *African material culture,* ed. M. J. Arnoldi, C. M. Geary, and K. L. Hardin, 214–42. Bloomington: Indiana University Press.

Appadurai, Arjun. 1986. Introduction: Commodities and the politics of value. In *The social life of things: Commodities in cultural perspective,* ed. A. Appadurai, 3–63. Cambridge: Cambridge University Press.

———. 1990. Disjuncture and difference in the global cultural economy. *Public Culture* 2, 2: 1–24.

Apter, Andrew. 1992. *Black critics and kings: The hermeneutics of power in Yoruba society.* Chicago: University of Chicago Press.

———. 1997. Africa, empire, and anthropology: A philological exploration of anthropology's heart of darkness. *Annual Review of Anthropology* 28: 577–98.

Ardener, Edwin W. 1950. Extract from a letter to Prof. Firth (July 27). Found in the collected papers of G. I. Jones. Box C2. Department of Social Anthropology, Cambridge University.

Arimah, Ben. 2002. Houses as assets and as homes: Urban construction and devaluation in Ibadan. In *Money struggles and city life: Devaluation in Ibadan and other urban centers in Southern Nigeria, 1986–1996,* ed. J. I. Guyer, L. Denzer, and A. Agbaje, 39–61. Portsmouth, N.H.: Heinemann.

Arrighi, Giovanni. 2002. The African crisis: World systemic and regional aspects. *New Left Review,* May–June 15, 5–36.

Aryeetey, Ernest, and Christopher Udry. 1995. The characteristics of informal financial markets in sub-Saharan Africa. Manuscript.

Austin, Gareth. 1993. Indigenous credit institutions in West Africa, c. 1750–c.1960. In *Local suppliers of credit in the third world, 1750–1960,* ed. Gareth Austin and Kaoru Sigihara, 93–159. London: St. Martin's Press.

Balandier, Georges. 1961. Phénomènes sociaux totaux et dynamique sociale. *Cahiers internationaux de scoiologie* 30: 22–34.

———. 1968. *Daily life in the kingdom of the Kongo from the sixteenth to the eighteenth century.* London: George Allen and Unwin.

Bangura, Yusuf. 1994. Economic restructuring, coping strategies and social change: Implications for institutional development in Africa. *Development and Change* 25: 785–827.

Barber, Karin. 1982. Popular reactions to the Petro-Naira. *Journal of Modern African Studies* 20, 3: 431–50.

———. 1991. Multiple discourses in Yoruba oral literature. *Bulletin of the John Rylands University Library of Manchester* 73, 3: 11–24.

———. 1995. Money, self-realization and the person in Yoruba texts. In *Money matters: Instability, values and social payments in the modern history of West African communities,* ed. J. I. Guyer, 205–24. Portsmouth, N.H.: Heinemann.

———. 2000. *The generation of plays: Yoruba popular life in theater.* Bloomington: Indiana University Press.

Barber, Karin, and Bayo Ogundijo. 1994. *Yoruba popular theatre: Three plays by the Oyin Adejobi company.* African Studies Association Press.

Barnes, Sandra. 1987. The urban frontier in West Africa: Mushin, Nigeria. In *The African frontier: The reproduction of traditional African societies,* ed. I. Kopytoff, 255–81. Bloomington: Indiana University Press.

Bascom, W. R. 1951. Social status, wealth and individual differences among the Yoruba. *American Anthropologist* 53, 4: 490–505.

———. 1952. The Esusu: A credit institution of the Yoruba. *Journal of the Royal Anthropological Institute* 82, 1: 63–69.

Basden, George. 1921. *Among the Ibos of Nigeria*. London: Selley, Service and Co.

Barth, Fredrik. 1967. Economic spheres in Darfur. In *Themes in economic anthropology*, ed. Raymond Firth, 149–74. London: Tavistock.

Bates, Robert H. 1990. Capital, kinship, and conflict: The structuring influence of capital in kinship societies. *Canadian Journal of African Studies* 24, 2: 151–64.

Bayart, Jean-François. 1999. L'Afrique dans le monde: Une histoire d'extraversion. *Critique internationale* 5: 97–120.

Belasco, Bernard. 1980. *The entrepreneur as culture-hero: Preadaptations to Nigerian economic development*. New York: J. F. Bergin.

Bernstein, Peter L. 1996. *Against the gods: The remarkable story of risk*. New York: John Wiley.

Berry, Sara S. 1985. *Fathers work for their sons: Accumulation, mobility, and class formation in an extended Yoruba community*. Berkeley: University of California Press.

———. 1989. Social institutions and access to resources. *Africa* 59, 1: 41–55.

———. 1992. Hegemony on a shoestring: Indirect rule and access to agricultural land. *Africa* 62, 3: 327–55.

———. 1993. *No condition is permanent: The social dynamics of agrarian change in sub-Saharan Africa*. Madison: University of Wisconsin Press.

———. 1995. Stable prices, unstable values: Some thoughts on monetization and the meaning of transactions in West African economies. In *Money matters: Instability, values and social payments in the modern history of West African communities*, ed. J. I. Guyer, 299–313. Portsmouth, N.H.: Heinemann.

———. 2001. *Chiefs know their boundaries: Essays on property, power and the past in Asante, 1896–1996*. Portsmouth, N.H.: Heinemann.

Bevan, David, Paul Collier, and Jan Willem Gunning. 1990. *Controlled open economies: A neoclassical approach to structuralism*. Oxford: Clarendon Press.

Beveridge, William H. 1928. *British food control*. London: Humphrey Milford.

Bledsoe, Caroline H. 2002. *Contingent lives: Fertility, time and aging in West Africa*. Chicago: University of Chicago Press.

Bledsoe, Caroline H., Jane I. Guyer, Barthelemy Kuate Defo, and Shobha Shagle. 1999. Anthropological vision and research logic: An epi info primer. Program of African Studies Working Paper Series No. 7. Northwestern University, Evanston, Ill.

Bloch, Maurice. 1975. *Death and the regeneration of life*. Cambridge: Cambridge University Press.

Bohannan, Paul. 1955. Some principles of exchange and investment among the Tiv. *American Anthropologist* 57, 1: 60–70.

———. 1959. The impact of money on an African subsistence economy. *Journal of Economic History* 19, 4: 491–503.

Bouis, Howarth E. 1994. The effect of income on demand for food in poor countries: Are our food consumption databases giving us reliable estimates? *Journal of Development Economics* 44: 199–226.

Bourdieu, Pierre. 1977. *Outline of a theory of practice.* Cambridge: Cambridge University Press.

———. 1984. *Distinction: A social critique of the judgment of taste.* Cambridge: Harvard University Press.

Braudel, Fernand. 1981. *The structures of everyday life: Civilization and capitalism, 15th–18th century.* Vol. 1. New York: Harper and Row.

Busch, Lawrence. 1995. The moral economy of grades and standards. Paper presented at the Conference on Agrarian Questions, Wageningen, The Netherlands.

Busch, Lawrence, and Keiko Tanaka. 1996. Rites of passage: Constructing quality in a commodity subsector. *Science, Technology and Human Values* 21, 1: 3–27.

Caffentzis, Constantine George. 1989. *Clipped coins, abused words, and civil government: John Locke's philosophy of money.* Brooklyn, N.Y.: Autonomedia.

Cain, P. J., and A. G. Hopkins. 1993. *British imperialism: Crisis and deconstruction, 1914–1990.* London: Longman.

Carrier, James, ed. 1995. *Occidentalism: Images of the West.* Oxford: Clarendon Press.

Carruthers, Bruce, and Wendy Nelson Espeland. 1991. Accounting for rationality: Double-entry bookkeeping and the rhetoric of economic rationality. *American Journal of Sociology* 97, 1: 31–69.

Castells, Manuel. 1996. *The rise of network society.* Malden, Mass.: Blackwell.

Chawai, Alhaji Zakari Isa. 1999. Address to community banks. *Community Banks Newsletter,* Jan.–June, 1–2.

Chayanov, A. V. 1966. *The theory of peasant economy.* Homewood, Ill.: Richard D. Irwin.

Clark, Gracia. 1994. *Onions are my husband: Survival and accumulation by West African market women.* Chicago: University of Chicago Press.

Collier, Paul. 1993. Africa and the study of economics. In *Africa and the disciplines,* ed. R. Bates, V. Mudimbe, and J. O'Barr, 58–82. Berkeley: University of California Press.

Comaroff, Jean, and John L. Comaroff. 1990. Goodly beasts and beastly goods: Cattle and commodities in a South African context. *American Ethnologist* 17, 2: 195–216.

———. 1999. Occult economies and the violence of abstraction: Notes from the South African post-colony. *American Ethnologist* 26, 2: 279–309.

———. 2001. Millennial capitalism: First thoughts on a second coming. In *Millennial capitalism and the culture of neoliberalism,* ed. J. Comaroff and J. Comaroff, 2–56. Durham, N.C.: Duke University Press.

Cooper, Frederick. 1981. Africa and the world system. *African Studies Review* 24, June–Sept., 1–84.

———. 2001. What is the concept of globalization good for? An African historian's perspective. *African Affairs* 100: 189–213.

Crossley, M. 1958. Some puzzling spending habits in Ghana: A comment. *Economic Bulletin* (Economic Society of Ghana) 2, 3: 13–16.

Crump, Thomas. 1981. *The phenomenon of money.* London: Routledge and Kegan Paul.

Dalton, George. 1965. Primitive money. *American Anthropologist* 67, 1: 44–65.

D'Andrade, Roy. 1990. Some propositions about the relations between culture and human cognition. In *Cultural psychology: Essays on comparative human development, ed.* James W. Stigler, Richard A. Shweder, and Gilbert Herdt, 65–129. Cambridge: Cambridge University Press.

Davey, P. L .P. 1963. Household budgets in rural areas. *Economic Bulletin* (Economic Society of Ghana) 7, 1: 17–28.

Deaton, Angus. 1990. Saving in developing countries: Theory and review. In *Proceedings of the World Bank annual conference on development economics,* 61–96. Washington, D.C.: World Bank.

———. 1991. Saving and liquidity constraints. *Econometrica* 59, 5: 1221–48.

———. 1992. Household saving in LDCs: Credit markets, insurance and welfare. *Scandinavian Journal of Economics* 94, 2: 253–73.

De Boeck, Filip. 1998. Domesticating diamonds and dollars: Identity, expenditure and sharing in southwestern Zaire (1984–1997). *Development and Change* 29, 4: 777–810.

De Cecco, Marcello. 1984. *The international gold standard: Money and empire.* New York: St. Martin's Press.

de Maret, Pierre. 1981. L'évolution monétaire du Shaba entre le 7è et le 18è siècles. *African Economic History* 10: 117–49.

Diagne, Souleymane Bachir, and Heinz Kimmerle, eds. 1998. *Time and development in the thought of Subsaharan Africa.* Atlanta: Rodopi.

Dike, K. O. 1956. *Trade and politics in the Niger Delta, 1830–1885.* Oxford: Clarendon Press.

Dike, Onwuka, and Felicia Ekejiuba. 1990. *The Aro of south-eastern Nigeria, 1650–1980: A study of socio-economic formation and transformation in Nigeria.* Ibadan: University of Ibadan Press.

Dorward, D. C. 1976. Precolonial Tiv trade and cloth currency. *International Journal of African Historical Studies* 9, 4: 576–91.

Douglas, Mary. 1958. Raffia cloth distribution in the Lele economy. *Africa* 28: 109–22.

———. 1982. *In the active voice.* London. Routledge and Kegan Paul.

———. 1986. *How institutions think.* Syracuse, N.Y.: Syracuse University Press.

Douglas, Mary, and Baron Isherwood. 1979. *The world of goods.* New York: Basic Books.

Drewal, Henry, and Margaret Thompson Drewal. 1983. *Gẹlẹdẹ: Art and female power among the Yoruba.* Bloomington: Indiana University Press.

Dupré, Georges. 1972. Le commerce entre societés lignagères: Les Nzabi dans la traite à la fin du XIXè siècle (Gabon-Congo). *Cahiers d'études africaines* 48, 4: 616–58.

———. 1995. The history and adventures of a monetary object of the Kwele of the Congo: Mzong, Mondjos and Mondjong. In *Money matters: Instability, values and social payments in the modern history of West African communities,* ed. J. I. Guyer, 77–96. Portsmouth, N.H.: Heinemann.

Dupré, Marie-Claude. 1995. Raphia monies among the Teke. In *Money matters: Instability, values and social payments in the modern history of West African communities,* ed. J. I. Guyer, 39–52. Portsmouth, N.H.: Heinemann.

Dutta Roy, D. K., and S. J. Mabey. 1968. Household budget survey in Ghana. Technical publications series, no. 2. Institute of Statistics, University of Ghana, Legon.

Eglash, Ron. 2002. *African fractals: Modern computing and indigenous design.* New Brunswick, N.J.: Rutgers University Press.

Ejizu, Christopher I. 1986. *Ofo: Igbo religious symbol.* Enugu, Nigeria: South Dimension Publishers.

Ekeh, Peter. 1990. Social anthropology and two contrasting uses of tribalism in Africa. *Comparative Studies in Society and History* 32: 660–700.

Ekejiuba, Felicia. 1972. The Aro system of trade in the nineteenth century. *Ikenga* 1, 1: 11–26.

———. 1995. Currency instability and social payments among the Igbo of Eastern Nigeria, 1890–1990. In *Money matters: Instability, values and social payments in the modern history of West African communities,* ed. J. I. Guyer, 133–61. Portsmouth, N.H.: Heinemann.

Eltis, David, and Lawrence C. Jennings. 1988. Trade between Western Africa and the Atlantic world in the pre-colonial era. *American Historical Review* 93, 4: 936–59.

Ensminger, Jean. 1992. *Making a market: The institutional transformation of an African society.* Cambridge: Cambridge University Press.

Enwerem, Iheanyi M. 2002. "Money-magic" and ritual killing in contemporary Nigeria. In *Money struggles and city life: Devaluation in Ibadan and other urban centers in Southern Nigeria, 1986–1996,* ed. J. I. Guyer, L. Denzer, and A. Agbaje, 189–205. Portsmouth, N.H.: Heinemann.

Espeland, Wendy Nelson, and Mitchell L. Stevens. 1998. Commensuration as a social process. *Annual Review of Sociology* 24: 313–43.

Fabian, Johannes. 1990. *Power and performance: Ethnographic explorations through proverbial wisdom and theater in Shaba, Zaire.* Madison: University of Wisconsin Press.

———. 1993. *Out of our minds: Reason and madness in the exploration of Central Africa.* Berkeley: University of California Press.

Fadipe, N. A. 1970. 1939. *The sociology of the Yoruba.* Ibadan: Ibadan University Press.

Fairhead, James, and Melissa Leach. 2003. *African American exploration in West Africa: Four nineteenth-century diaries.* Bloomington: Indiana University Press.

Falola, Toyin. 1992. "An ounce is enough": The gold industry and the politics of control in colonial Western Nigeria. *African Economic History* 20: 27–50.

———. 1993. "My friend the Shylock": Money-lenders and their clients in southwestern Nigeria. *Journal of African History* 34: 403–23.

———. 1995. Money and informal credit institutions in colonial Western Nigeria. In *Money matters: Instability, values and social payments in the modern history of West African communities,* ed. J. I. Guyer, 162–87. Portsmouth, N.H.: Heinemann.

Fardon, Richard. 1984. Sisters, wives, wards and daughters: A transformational analysis of the political organization of the Tiv and their neighbours. Part 1: The Tiv. *Africa* 54, 4: 2–21.

Ferguson, James. 1988. Cultural exchange: New developments in the anthropology of commodities. *Cultural Anthropology* 3, 4: 488–513.

———. 1992. The cultural topography of wealth: Commodity paths and the structure of property in rural Lesotho. *American Anthropologist* 94: 55–73.

Ferme, Marianne. 2001. *The underneath of things: Violence, history and the everyday in Sierra Leone.* Berkeley: University of California Press.

Fernandez, James. 1980. *Bwiti: An ethnography of the religious imagination in Africa.* Princeton, N.J.: Princeton University Press.

Fernandez, James, and Renate Fernandez. 1975. Fang reliquary art: Its quantities and qualities. *Cahiers d'études africaines* 15: 723–46.

Fortes, Meyer. 1970. *Kinship and the social order: The legacy of Lewis Henry Morgan.* Chicago: Aldine.

Fortes, Meyer, R. W. Steel, and P. Ady. 1948. Ashanti survey, 1945–46: An experiment in social research. *Geographical Journal* 110, 4–6: 149–79.

Foster, Robert J. 1990. Value without equivalence: Exchange and replacement in a Melanesian society. *Man* (n.s.) 25: 54–69.

Frynas, Georg Jedrzej. 2000. *Oil in Nigeria: Conflict and litigation between oil companies and village communities.* Munster-Hamburg-London: LIT.

Gell, Alfred. 1992. *The anthropology of time: Cultural constructions of temporal maps and images.* Oxford: Berg.

George, Sandys. 1935. Letter to the inspector general of police (Feb. 4). MSS.Afr.s.1556/7(a). Rhodes House Library, Oxford University.

Gervais, Raymond. 1982. Pre-colonial currencies: A note on the Maria Theresa thaler. *African Economic History* 11: 147–52.

Geschiere, Peter. 1997. *The modernity of witchcraft: Politics and the occult in postcolonial Africa.* Charlottesville: University Press of Virginia.

Geschiere, Peter, and Birgit Meyer. 1998. Globalization and identity: Dialectics of flow and closure. *Development and Change* 29, 4: 601–15.

Ghana Statistical Service. 1993. Rural communities in Ghana: Report of a national rural community survey carried out as part of the third round of the Ghana Living Standards Survey, 1991–92.

———. 1995. *Ghana living standards survey: Report on the third round* (GLSS3). Accra, Ghana.

Gleick, James. 1995. Dead as a dollar. *New York Times Magazine,* June 6, 26–30, 35, 42, 50, 54.

Glewwe, Paul, and Kwaku A. Twum-Baah. 1991. The distribution of welfare in Ghana, 1987–88. Living Standards Measurement Survey No. 75. Washington, D.C.: World Bank.

Gluckman, Max. 1968. The utility of the equilibrium model in the study of social change. *American Anthropologist* 70, 2: 219–37.

Graeber, David. 2001. *Toward an anthropological theory of value: The false coin of our own dreams.* New York: Palgrave.

Granovetter, Mark. 1993. The nature of economic relationships. In *Explorations in economic sociology,* ed. Richard Swedberg, 3–41. New York: Russell Sage Foundation.

Green, M. M. 1947. *Ibo village affairs.* New York: Praeger.

Gregory, C. A. 1982. *Gifts and commodities.* New York: Academic Press.

——. 1996. Cowries and conquest: Towards a subalternate quality theory of money. *Comparative Studies in Society and History* 38, 2: 195–217.

——. 1997. *Savage money: The anthropology and politics of commodity exchange.* Amsterdam: Harwood Brace.

Grey, R. F. A. 1951. Manillas. *Nigerian Field* 16, 2: 52–66.

Gudeman, Stephen. 2001. *The anthropology of economy, community, market and culture.* Oxford: Blackwell.

Guyer, Jane I. 1981. Household and community in African studies. *African Studies Review* 24, 2/3: 87–137.

——. 1988. Dynamic approaches to domestic budgeting: Cases and method from Africa. In *A home divided: Women and income in the third world,* ed. Daisy Dwyer and Judith Bruce, 155–72. Stanford: Stanford University Press.

——. 1989. The multiplication of labor: Historical methods in the study of gender and agricultural change in modern Africa. *Current Anthropology* 29, 2: 247–71.

——. 1992. Small change: Individual farm work and collective life in a Western Nigerian savanna town, 1969–88. *Africa* 62, 4: 465–89.

——. 1993. Wealth in people and self-realisation in Equatorial Africa. *Man* (n.s.) 28, 2: 243–65.

——. 1995. Introduction: The currency interface and its dynamics. In *Money matters: Instability, values and social payments in the modern history of West African communities,* ed. J. I. Guyer, 1–37. Portsmouth, N.H.: Heinemann.

——. 1996. Lineal identities and lateral networks: Anthropological approaches to marital change, based on research in a rural Yoruba community. In *Nuptiality in sub-Saharan Africa: Anthropological approaches to demographic change,* ed. Caroline Bledsoe and Gilles Pison, 231–52. Oxford: Oxford University Press.

——. 1997. *An African niche economy: Farming to feed Ibadan, 1968–88.* Edinburgh: Edinburgh University Press for the International African Institute.

Guyer, Jane I., LaRay Denzer, and Adigun Agbaje, eds. 2002. *Money struggles and city life: Devaluation in Ibadan and other urban areas in Southern Nigeria, 1986–1961.* Portsmouth, N.H.: Heinemann.

Guyer, Jane I., and S. M. Eno Belinga. 1995. Wealth in people as wealth in knowledge: Accumulation and composition in Equatorial Africa. *Journal of African History* 36: 91–129.

Hanks, Willliam. 1990. *Referential practice: Language and lived space among the Maya.* Chicago: University of Chicago Press.

Hansen, Karen Tranberg. 2000. *Salaula: The world of secondhand clothing and Zambia.* Chicago: University of Chicago Press.

Harms, Robert. 1981. *River of wealth, river of sorrow: The Central Zaire basin in the era of the slave and ivory trade, 1500–1891.* New Haven: Yale University Press.

Harris, Jack. 1942. Some aspects of slavery in southeastern Nigeria. *Journal of Negro History* 27, 1: 37–54.

Hart, Keith. 1981. On commoditization. In *From craft to industry: The ethnography of proto-industrial cloth production,* ed. Esther N. Goody. Cambridge: Cambridge: Cambridge University Press.

———. 1986. Heads or tails? Two sides of the coin. *Man* 21, 4: 637–58.

———. 2000. *The memory bank: Money in an unequal world.* London: Profile Books.

Hashim, Yahaya, and Kate Meagher. 1999. *Cross-border trade and the parallel currency market: Trade and finance in the context of structural adjustment.* Research Report No. 113. Uppsala: Nordiska Afrikaninstitutet.

Heckscher, Eli. 1935. *Mercantilism.* Vol. 2. London: George Allen and Unwin.

Henderson, Richard N. 1972. *The king in every man: Evolutionary trends in Ibo society and culture.* New Haven: Yale University Press.

Herbert, Eugenia. 1984. *Red gold of Africa: Copper in precolonial history and culture.* Madison: University of Wisconsin Press.

———. 1993. *Iron, gender and power: Rituals of transformation in African societies.* Bloomington: Indiana University Press.

Hibou, Béatrice. 2000. The political economy of the World Bank's discourse: From economic catechism to missionary deeds (and misdeeds). Etude CERI No. 39. Paris: Centre d'Etudes et de Recherches Internationales.

Hill, Polly. 1957. Some puzzling spending habits in Ghana. *Economic Bulletin* (Economic Society of Ghana) 10: 3–11; 11: 3–7.

———. 1958. Some puzzling spending habits in Ghana: A rejoinder. *Economic Bulletin* (Economic Society of Ghana) 2, 4: 16–17.

———. 1962. Aspects of indigenous West African economies. Conference Proceedings. Nigerian Institute of Social and Economic Research, Ibadan.

———. 1970. *Studies in rural capitalism in West Africa.* Cambridge: Cambridge University Press.

———. 1972. *Rural Hausa: A village and a setting.* Cambridge: Cambridge University Press.

———. 1986. *Development economics on trial: The anthropological case for the prosecution.* Cambridge: Cambridge University Press.

Hogendorn, Jan S., and Henry A. Gemery. 1982. Cash cropping, currency acquisition and seigniorage in West Africa. *African Economic History* 11: 15–27.

Hogendorn, Jan S., and Marion Johnson. 1986. *The shell money of the slave trade.* Cambridge: Cambridge University Press.

Hopkins, A. G. 1966. The currency revolution in south-west Nigeria in the late nineteenth century. *Journal of the Historical Society of Nigeria* 3, 3: 471–83.

———. 1973. *An economic history of West Africa.* New York: Columbia University Press.

Humphrey, Caroline, and Steven Hugh-Jones. 1992. *Barter, exchange and value: An anthropological approach.* Cambridge: Cambridge University Press.

Hunter, Sam, and John Jacobus. 1977. *Modern art: Painting/sculpture/architecture.* Englewood Cliffs, N.J.: Prentice Hall.

Inikori, J. E. 1977. The import of firearms into West Africa, 1750–1807: A quantitative analysis. *Journal of African History* 18, 3: 339–68.

Isichei, E. 1973. *The Ibo people and the Europeans: The genesis of a relationship.* New York: St. Martin's Press.

———. 1978. *Igbo worlds: An anthology of oral histories and historical descriptions.* Philadelphia: ISHI.

Jackson, Michael. 1989. *Paths toward a clearing: Radical empiricism and ethnographic enquiry.* Bloomington: Indiana University Press.

Jaja, E. A. 1977. *King Jaja of Opobo, 1821–1891*. Lagos: Opobo Action Council.

James, William. 1964. *Pragmatism*. 1907. Reprint, New York: Basic Books.

Janzen, John. 1982. *Lemba: A drum of affliction in Africa and the New World*. New York: Garland.

Jeffreys, M. D. W. 1954. Some Negro currencies in Nigeria. *South African Museums Association Bulletin* 5, 16:405–16.

Johnson, Marion. 1970. The cowry currencies of West Africa. Part 1. *Journal of African History* 11, 1: 17–49.

———. N.d. Cloth strip currencies. Manuscript.

Johnson, Samuel. 1921. *The history of the Yorubas*. London: Lowe and Brydone.

Jones, G. I. 1956. Report on the position, status, and influence of chiefs and natural rulers in the eastern region of Nigeria. Collected papers. Box A3. Department of Social Anthropology, Cambridge University.

———. 1958. Native and trade currencies in Southern Nigeria during the eighteenth and nineteenth centuries. *Africa* 28, 1: 43–54.

———. 1963. *The trading states of the Oil Rivers: A study of political development in Eastern Nigeria*. London: Oxford University Press.

———. 1989. *From slaves to palm oil: Slave trade and palm oil trade in the bight of Biafra*. Cambridge African Monographs No. 3. Cambridge University African Studies Center.

———. Collected papers. Department of Social Anthropology, Cambridge University.

Julien, Eileen. 1992. *African novels and the question of orality*. Bloomington: Indiana University Press.

Kelly, Raymond C. 1993. *Constructing inequality: The fabrication of a hierarchy of virtue among the Etoro*. Ann Arbor: University of Michigan Press.

Kriger, Colleen E. 1999. *Pride of men: Ironworking in nineteenth-century West Central Africa*. Portsmouth, N.H.: Heinemann.

Kula, Witold. 1986. *Measures and men*. Princeton, N.J.: Princeton University Press.

Laburthe-Tolra, Philippe. 1977. *Minlaaba: Histoire et société traditionelle chez les Beti du sud Cameroun*. Paris: Honor Champion.

———. 1981. *Les seigneurs de la forêt*. Paris: Presses Universitaires de France.

Latham, A. J. H. 1971. Currency, credit and capitalism on the Cross River in the pre-colonial era. *Journal of African History* 12, 4: 599–605.

Lave, Jean. 1988. *Cognition in practice: Mind, mathematics and culture in everyday life*. Cambridge: Cambridge: Cambridge University Press.

Law, Robin. 1992. Posthumous questions for Karl Polanyi: Price inflation in pre-colonial Dahomey. *Journal of African History* 33: 387–420.

———. 1995. Cowries, gold, and dollars: Exchange rate instability and domestic price inflation in Dahomey in the eighteenth and nineteenth centuries. In *Money matters: Instability, values and social payments in the modern history of West African communities*, ed. J. I. Guyer, 53–73. Portsmouth, N.H.: Heinemann.

Lawson, Rowena. 1962. Engel's Law and its application to Ghana. *Economic Bulletin* (Economic Society of Ghana) 6, 4: 334–46.

Lawuyi, Tunde, and Toyin Falola. 1992. The instability of the Naira and social payment among the Yoruba. *Journal of Asian and African Studies* 27, 3–4:216–28.

Leach, Edmund. 1965. *Political systems of highland Burma: A study of Kachin social structure.* Boston: Beacon Press.

Lederman, R. 1998. Globalization and the future of culture areas: Melanesianist anthropology in transition. *Annual Review of Anthropology* 27: 427–49.

Leith-Ross, Sylvia. 1972. The small coins: Nigeria, 1907–1969. Manuscript. MSS.Afr.s.1520. Rhodes House Library, Oxford University.

Leonard, Robert D. 1998. *Manillas: Money of West Africa.* Chicago: Chicago Coin Club.

Lloyd, Peter. C. 1974. *Power and independence: Urban Africans' perception of social inequality.* London: Routledge and Kegan Paul.

Lovejoy, Paul. 1974. Interregional monetary flows in the precolonial trade of Nigeria. *Journal of African History* 15, 4: 563–85.

Mabogunje, Akin. 1995. The capitalization of money and credit in the development process: The case of community banking in Nigeria. In *Money matters: Instability, values and social payments in the modern history of West African communities,* ed. J. I. Guyer, 277–95. Portsmouth, N.H.: Heinemann.

MacGaffey, Janet, and Remy Bazenguissa-Ganga. 2000. *Congo–Paris: Transnational traders on the margins of the law.* Oxford: James Currey.

MacGaffey, Janet, with Mukohya Vwakyanakazi et al. 1991. *The real economy of Zaire: The contribution of smuggling and other unofficial activities to national wealth.* London: James Currey; Philadelphia: University of Pennsylvania Press.

MacGaffey, Wyatt. 2000. *Kongo political culture: The conceptual challenge of the particular.* Bloomington: Indiana University Press.

Mamdani, Mahmood. 1996. *Citizen and subject: Contemporary Africa and the legacy of late colonialism.* Princeton, N.J.: Princeton University Press.

Mann, Adolphus. 1887. Notes on the numeral system of the Yoruba nation. *Journal of the Anthropological Institute* 16: 59–64.

Manuh, Takyiwaa. 1995. Changes in marriage and funeral exchanges in Asante: A case study from Kona, Afigya-Kwabre. In *Money matters: Instability, values and social payments in the modern history of West African communities,* ed. J. I. Guyer, 188–201. Portsmouth, N.H.: Heinemann.

Mason, Roger. 1998. *The economics of conspicuous consumption: Theory and thought since 1700.* Northampton, Mass.: Edward Elgar.

Maurer, Bill. 2002. Chrysography: Substance and effect. *Asia Pacific Journal of Anthropology* 3, 1: 49–74.

Mayne, C. J. 1946–55. Annual reports on the Calabar Province. MSS.Afr.s.1505. Rhodes House Library, Oxford University.

Mbembe, Achille. 1989. *Afriques indociles: Christianisme, pouvoir et état en société postcoloniale.* Paris: Karthala.

———. 1996. Une économie de prédation: Les rapports entre la rareté matérielle et la démocratie en Afrique subsaharienne. *Foi et développement,* no. 241, 1–8.

———. 2001. *On the postcolony.* Berkeley: University of California Press.

McCaskie, Thomas. 1980. Time and the calendar in nineteenth-century Asante: An exploratory essay. *History in Africa* 7: 179–200.

———. 1995. *State and society in pre-colonial Asante.* Cambridge: Cambridge University Press.

———. 2000. *Asante identities: History and modernity in an African village.* Bloomington: Indiana University Press.

Meghir, Costas. 1992. Comment on A. Deaton, Household saving in LDCs: Credit markets, insurance and welfare. *Scandinavian Journal of Economics* 94, 2: 275–79.

Meillassoux, Claude. 1964. *Anthropologie économique des gouros de Côte d'Ivoire: De l'économie de subsistance à l'agriculture commerciale.* Paris: Mouton.

———. 1977. *Terrains et théories.* Paris: Anthropos.

———. 1978. "The economy" in agricultural self-sustaining societies: A preliminary analysis. In *Relations of production: Marxist approaches to economic anthropology,* ed. D. Seddon, 127–57. 1961. Reprint, London: Frank Cass.

Menand, Louis. 2001. *The metaphysical club: A story of ideas in America.* New York: Farrar, Straus and Giroux.

Mikell, Gwendolyn. 1995. The state, the courts and "value": Caught between matrilineages in Ghana. In *Money matters: Instability, values and social payments in the modern history of West African communities,* ed. J. I. Guyer, 225–44. Portsmouth, N.H.: Heinemann.

Minchinton, Walter E. 1969. *Mercantilism: System or expediency?* Lexington, Mass.: D. C. Heath.

Mirowski, Philip. 1989. *More heat than light. Economics as social physics: Physics as nature's economics.* Cambridge: Cambridge University Press.

———. 1991. Postmodernism and the social theory of value. *Journal of Post Keynesian Economics* 13, 4: 565–82.

Miyazaki, Hirokazi. 2003. The temporalities of the market. *American Anthropologist* 105, 2: 255–65.

Monga, Celestin, and Jean-Claude Tchatchouang. 1996. *Sortir du piège monétaire.* Paris: Economica.

Moore, Sally Falk. 1986. *Social facts and fabrications: "Customary" law on Kilimanjaro, 1880–1980.* Cambridge: Cambridge University Press.

Moraes Farias, P. F. de. 1974. Silent trade: Myth and historical evidence. *History in Africa* 1: 9–24.

Morgan, Lewis Henry. 1977. *Ancient society: Or researches in the lines of human progress from savagery through barbarism to civilization.* Reprint. Chicago: University of Chicago Press.

Muller, Birgit. 1982. Commodities as currencies: The integration of overseas trade into the internal trading structure of the Igbo of S-E Nigeria. M.Phil. dissertation. Department of Social Anthropology, University of Cambridge.

Munn, Nancy. 1986. *The Fame of Gawa: A symbolic study of value transformation in a Massim (Papua New Guinea) society.* Cambridge: Cambridge: Cambridge University Press.

North, Douglass. 1990. *Institutions, institutional change and economic performance.* Cambridge: Cambridge University Press.

Northrup, David. 1978. *Trade without rulers: Pre-colonial economic development in south-eastern Nigeria.* Oxford: Clarendon Press.

Obukhova, Elena. 2002. Living and trusting in the economy of debt: The distribution of newspapers and magazines in Ibadan. In *Money struggles and city life: Devaluation in Ibadan and other urban centers in Southern Nigeria, 1986–*

1996, ed. J. I. Guyer, L. Denzer, and A. Agbaje, 147–72. Portsmouth, N.H.: Heinemann.

Offiong, E. 1949. Manilla as used in the eastern provinces. MSS.Afr.s.1556/7(b). Rhodes House Library, Oxford University.

Ofonagoro, W. I. 1976. The currency revolution in Southern Nigeria, 1880–1948. Occasional Paper No. 14. University of California at Los Angeles African Studies Center.

Okediji, Oladejo. 1999. *Running after riches.* Ibadan: Spectrum Books.

Okonkwo, Una. 2002. Igbo emigrants in Chicago invest at home, 1986–1996: The case of houses. In *Money struggles and city life: Devaluation in Ibadan and other urban centers in Southern Nigeria, 1986–1996,* ed. J. I. Guyer, L. Denzer, and A. Agbaje, 239–55. Portsmouth, N.H.: Heinemann.

Olatunde, Femi. 1993. Money house of deceit. *African Concord* 8, 1: 12–17.

Onugu, Charles Uchenna. 2000. The development role of the community banks in rural Nigeria. *Development in Practice* 10, 1: 102–7.

Oroge, E. Adeniyi. 1985. Iwofa: An historical survey of the Yoruba institution of indenture. *African Economic History* 14: 75–106.

Parry, Jonathan, and Maurice Bloch. 1989. Introduction: Money and the morality of exchange. In *Money and the morality of exchange,* ed. J. Parry and M. Bloch, 1–32. Cambridge: Cambridge University Press.

Passell, Peter. 1992. Fast money. *New York Times Magazine,* Oct. 18, 42–43, 66, 75.

Peel, J. D. Y. 1978. Two cheers for empiricism. *Sociology* 12, 2: 345–59.

——. 1983. *Ijeshas and Nigerians: The incorporation of a Yoruba kingdom, 1890s–1970s.* Cambridge: Cambridge University Press.

——. 1984. Making history: The past in the Ijesha present. *Man* 19: 111–32.

——. 2000. *Religious encounter and the making of the Yoruba.* Bloomington: Indiana University Press.

Peters, Pauline E. 1984. Struggles over water, struggles over meaning: Cattle, water and the state in Botswana. *Africa* 54, 1: 29–49.

Phillips, 'Dotun. 1992. The nominalization of the Nigerian economy. Occasional Paper No. 3. Nigerian Institute of Social and Economic Research, Ibadan.

Pietz, William. 1985. The problem of the fetish. Part 1. *Res* 9: 5–17.

——. 1987. The problem of the fetish. Part 2. *Res* 13: 23–45.

——. 1988. The problem of the fetish. Part 3. *Res* 16: 105–23.

Piot, Charles. 1999. *Remotely global: Village modernity in West Africa.* Chicago: University of Chicago Press.

Poleman, Thomas T. 1961. *The food economies of urban middle Africa.* Stanford: Food Research Institute.

Porter, Theodore M. 1995. *Trust in numbers: The pursuit of objectivity in science and public life.* Princeton, N.J.: Princeton University Press.

Prais, S. J., and H. S. Houthakker. 1955. *The analysis of family budgets.* Cambridge: Cambridge University Press.

Quiggen, A. H. 1949. *A survey of primitive money: The beginnings of currency.* London: Methuen.

Riles, Anneliese. Forthcoming. Introduction to *Documents: Artifacts of modern knowledge,* ed. A. Riles. Durham, N.C.: Duke University Press.

Riley, Bridget. 2002. Making visible. In *Paul Klee: The nature of creation, works 1914–1940*, ed. Robert Kudielka, 15–25. London: Hayward Gallery.

Robbins, Joel. 1994. Equality as a value: Ideology in Dumont, Melanesia and the West. *Social Analysis* 36: 21–70.

Robbins, Joel, and David Akin. 1999. An introduction to Melanesian currencies. In *Money and modernity: State and local currencies in Melanesia*, ed. D. Akin and J. Robbins, 1–40. Pittsburgh, Pa.: University of Pittsburgh Press.

Robinson, Joan. 1964. *Economic philosophy*. New York: Anchor Books.

———. 1971. *Economic heresies: Some old-fashioned questions in economic theory*. New York: Basic Books.

Robiquet, P. 1897. *Discours et opinions de Jules Ferry*. Vol. 5. Paris: Armand Colin.

Rotman, Brian. 1987. *Signifying nothing: The semiotics of zero*. London: MacMillan.

Ruxton, F. H. 1910. Some notes on the Munshi and instructions for political officers. MSS.Afr.s.662(1a). Rhodes House Library, Oxford University.

Sahlins, Marshall. 1976. *Culture and practical reason*. Chicago: University of Chicago Press.

Samarin, William J. 1989. *The black man's burden: African colonial labor on the Congo and Ubangi Rivers, 1889–1900*. Boulder, Colo.: Westview Press.

Sampson, Anthony. 1990. *The Midas touch: Understanding the dynamic new money around us*. New York: Dutton.

Schapiro, Mark. 1997. Doing the wash: Inside a Colombian cartel's money-laundering machine. *Harper's Magazine*, February, 56–59.

Schildkrout, Enid, and Charles Keim. 1990. *African reflections: Art from north-eastern Zaire*. Washington, D.C.: American Museum of Natural History.

Seers, Dudley. 1963. The stages of economic development of a primary producer in the middle of the twentieth century. *Economic Bulletin of Ghana* 7, 4: 57–69.

Sender, John. 1999. Africa's economic performance: Limitations of the current consensus. *Journal of Economic Perspectives* 13, 3: 89–114.

———. 2001. Women's struggle to escape rural poverty in South Africa. Manuscript.

Shaw, Rosalind. 2002. *Memories of the slave trade: Ritual and the historical imagination in Sierra Leone*. Chicago: University of Chicago Press.

Shaw, Thurstan. 1970. *Igbo-Ukwu: An account of archeological discoveries in Eastern Nigeria*. Evanston, Ill.: Northwestern University Press.

Shipton, Parker. 1991. Time and money in the western Sahel: A clash of cultures in Gambian local rural finance. In *Markets in developing countries: Parallel, fragmented and black*, ed. M. Roemer and C. Jones, 113–39, 235–44. Washington, D.C., and San Francisco: ICS Press.

———. 1995. How Gambians save: Culture and economic strategy at an ethnic crossroads. In *Money matters: Instability, values and social payments in the modern history of West African communities*, ed. J. I. Guyer, 245–76. Portsmouth, N.H.: Heinemann.

Smith, Mary. 1965. *Baba of Karo: A woman of the Muslim Hausa*. 1954. Reprint, London: Faber.

Sridar, M. K. C., B. A. Olateju, M. A. Lasisi, and F. N. O. Jaja. 2002. Refuse dumps and waste recyclers in the era of structural adjustment: The environmental crisis and its effects. In *Money struggles and city life: Devaluation in*

Ibadan and other urban centers in Southern Nigeria, 1986–1996, ed. J. I. Guyer, L. Denzer, and A. Agbaje, 173–85. Portsmouth, N.H.: Heinemann.

Stahl, Ann Brower. 2002. Colonial entanglements and the practices of taste: An alternative to logocentric approaches. *American Anthropologist* 104, 3: 827–45.

Steiner, Christopher B. 1985. Another image of Africa: Toward an ethnohistory of European cloth marketed in West Africa, 1873–1960. *Ethnohistory* 32: 91–110.

Stiansen, Endre, and Jane I. Guyer, eds. 1999. *Credit, currencies and culture: African financial institutions in historical perspective.* Uppsala: Nordiska Afrikaninstitutet.

Strathern, Marilyn. 1988. *The gender of the gift: Problems with women and problems with society in Melanesia.* Berkeley: University of California Press.

———. 1992. Qualified value: The perspective of gift exchange. In *Barter, exchange and value: An anthropological approach,* ed. C. Humphrey and S. Hugh-Jones, 169–91. Cambridge: Cambridge University Press.

———. 1999. What is intellectual property after? In *Actor network theory and after,* ed. John Law and John Hassard, 156–80. Oxford: Blackwell.

Strauss, John, and Duncan Thomas. 1996. *Human resources: Empirical modeling of household and family decisions.* Santa Monica, Calif.: Rand Corporation, Labor and Population Program.

Stucki, Barbara. 1995. Managing the social clock: The negotiation of elderhood among rural Asante of Ghana. Ph.D. dissertation. Northwestern University.

Sundstrom, Lars. 1974. *The exchange economy of pre-colonial Africa.* New York: St. Martin's Press.

Swedberg, Richard, ed. 1991. *Joseph A. Schumpeter: The economics and sociology of capitalism.* Princeton, N.J.: Princeton University Press.

———. 1999. *Max Weber: Essays in economic sociology.* Princeton, N.J.: Princeton University Press.

Talbot, P. Amaury. [1923] 1967. *Life in Southern Nigeria: The magic, beliefs and customs of the Ibibio tribe.* Reprint, London: Frank Cass.

———. [1926] 1969. *The peoples of Southern Nigeria.* Vol. 3, *Ethnology.* Reprint, London: Frank Cass.

———. [1932] 1967. *Tribes of the Niger Delta: Their religions and customs.* Reprint, London: Frank Cass.

Talbot, P. Amaury (Mrs.). 1915. *Woman's mysteries of a primitive people: The Ibibios of Southern Nigeria.* London: Cassell and Co.

Tchundjang Pouemi, Joseph. 1980. *Monnaie, servitude et liberté: La répression monétaire de l'Afrique.* Paris: Editions j.a.

Thomas, Nicholas. 1991. *Entangled objects: Exchange, material culture and colonialism in the Pacific.* Cambridge: Harvard University Press.

———. 1992. Politicized values: The cultural dynamics in peripheral exchange. In *Barter, exchange and value: An anthropological approach,* ed. C. Humphrey and S. Hugh-Jones, 121–41. Cambridge: Cambridge University Press.

Thompson, E. P. 1969. Time, work discipline and industrial capitalism. *Past and Present* 38: 56–97.

———. 1978. *The poverty of theory: Or an orrery of errors.* London: Merlin Press.

Trager, Lillian. 1981. Customers and creditors: Variations in economic personalism in a Nigerian marketing system. *Ethnology* 20, 2: 133–46.

———. 2001. *Yoruba hometowns: Community, identity, and development in Nigeria.* Boulder, Colo.: Lynne Reiner.

Turner, N. 1950. Withdrawal of manillas from circulation in Eastern Province, Nigeria. MSS.Afr.s.541. Rhodes House Library, Oxford University.

Udry, Christopher. 1990. Credit markets in Northern Nigeria: Credit as insurance in a rural economy. *World Bank Economic Review* 4, 3.

United African Company (UAC). 1949. The manilla problem. *Statistical and Economic Review,* March, 44–56.

Van Leynseele, P. 1979a. Ecological stability and intensive fish production: The case of the Libinza people of the Middle Ngiri (Zaire). In *Social and ecological systems,* ed. Philip Burnham and Roy Ellen, 167–84. New York: Academic Press.

———. 1979b. Les transformations des systèmes de production et d'échanges de populations ripuaires du Haut-Zaire. *African Economic History* 7: 117–29.

———. 1983. *Les Libinza de la Ngiri: L'anthropologie d'un people des marais du confluent Congo-Ubangi.* Leiden: African Studies Center.

Vansina, Jan. 1973. *The Tio kingdom of the Middle Congo: 1880–1892.* London: Oxford University Press.

———. 1990. *Paths in the rainforests: Toward a history of political tradition in Equatorial Africa.* Madison: University of Wisconsin Press.

Verran, Helen. 2001. *Science and an African logic.* Chicago: University of Chicago Press.

Wan, Mimi. 2001. Secrets of success: Uncertainty, profits and prosperity in the gari economy of Ibadan, 1992–94. *Africa* 71, 2: 225–52.

Webb, James L. A., Jr. 1982. Toward the comparative study of money: A reconsideration of West African currencies and neoclassical economic concepts. *International Journal of African Historical Studies* 18, 2: 455–66.

———. 1999. On currency and credit in the western Sahel, 1700–1850. In *Credit, currencies and culture: African financial institutions in historical perspective,* ed. Endre Stiansen and Jane I. Guyer, 38–55. Uppsala: Nordiska Afrikaninstitutet.

Webster's Encyclopedic Unabridged Dictionary of the English Language. 1994. New York: Gramercy Books.

Zaslavsky, Claudia. 1973. *Africa counts: Number and pattern in African culture.* Boston: Prindle, Weber and Schmidt.

Zeleza, Paul Tiyambe. 1996. *A modern economic history of Africa.* Vol. 1, *The nineteenth century.* Dakar: CODESRIA.

Zelizer, Viviana. 1994. *The social meaning of money: Pin money, paychecks, poor relief and other currencies.* Princeton, N.J.: Princeton University Press.

INDEX

Abacha government: dual exchange rate for the naira, 163; fuel shortages, 102; petrol price, 103

Abraham, R. C., *Dictionary of Modern Yoruba,* 61

abstraction, 19, 24–25

abstract number, 66

accomplishment, individuated, 148

accumulation, 51; of rights in property, 9–10

ackie, 54

Adam, Susanna, 59, 63, 92, 95–96, 101, 161

add-ons, 106, 111, 113

Adebayo, Akanmu G., 59, 64, 95, 120

Adejobi, Oyin, *Articulated Lorry,* 60–61, 64–65

Africa: asymmetry in monetary exchange, 40; Central African currencies, 31–32; conversions in social history, 51; European monetary engagement in, 15–16; exchange institutions, and Western economic theory, 18; imports into markets, 84; indigenous credit institutions in, 160; introduction of documents into transactions, 156; inventive frontiers of knowledge creation, 21; marginalization of from capitalist flows, 25; monetary transactions, 15; multiplicity of forms and meanings of money in history, 11, 14–15; nonequivalent exchange in, 47; numerical scales in history, 53–60; temporal constructions, 159. *See also* Atlantic Africa; Nigeria; West Africa

Àgàtú (onísé), 126

aggregate risk, 137

agricultural expenditure, 126

ajẹju, 104–5

àjọ (savings clubs), 120, 122, 167

Akan: calendar, 161–62; expenditure patterns, 139, 178; kinship, 148; map of, 140; powerful status of women in society, 145–46

Ake, Claude, 7

Akiga, 29, 39

Akin, David, 19

akuda, 66

Alder, Ken, 43

alienation, 19

àlòkù, 87, 91

alternatives, protection of, 94

Amanor, Kojo Sebastian, 147

Amogu, O. O., 72

ancestral status, 71

ancillary payment, 59

anthropology: alienation from definition given to reason, 174; cultural particularism of, 172; and disjunctures, 20; of exchange, 175; of macroeconomic logics, 170

apprenticeship, 121

apprenticeship freedom ceremonies, 125

appropriation, 19

arbitrage, 20, 162; between currency forms, 15; made possible by formalities, 164; speculative, 163

architecture, 80

Ardener, Edwin W., 59–60, 72

Aro, 73; oracle, 77; people, 73; trade diaspora, 81

art, capitalization of, 6, 45

Articulated Lorry (Adejobi), 60–61

"articulation" approach, 170

Asaba, Eze titles, 74

Asante: under colonial rule, 149; differentiation between commercial advance and cash loans, 160; households, 148; system, 54

Asante-Bambara-Niger bend route, 55